TONI MORRISON

Related titles from the same publisher

ALICE WALKER   *Maria Lauret*
TONI MORRISON (New Casebook)   *Linden Peach*
THE STEPMOTHER TONGUE   *John Skinner*
A CRITICAL INTRODUCTION TO
POSTCOLONIAL AND AFRICAN
AMERICAN WOMEN'S WRITING   *Gina Wisker*

Toni Morrison

Linden Peach

TONI MORRISON

Copyright © 2000 by Linden Peach

St. Martin's Press, Scholarly and Reference Division.
175 Fifth Avenue, New York, N.Y. 10010

First published in the United States of America in 2000

This book is printed on paper suitable for recycling and made from fully managed and sustained forest sources.

Printed in Hong Kong

ISBN 0–312–23397–3

Library of Congress Cataloging-in-Publication Data
Peach, Linden, 1951–
Toni Morrison / Linden Peach.
p.   cm.
"Revised version of Toni Morrison (1995), originally published in the Macmillan modern novelist series"–Pref.
Includes bibliographical references and index.
ISBN 0–312–23397–3
1. Morrison, Toni–Criticism and interpretation.   2. Morrison.
Toni–Knowledge–History.   3. Women and literature–United States–History–20th century.   4. Afro-American women in literature.   5. Afro-Americans in literature.
I. Title.

PS3563.O8749 Z827 2000
813'54–dc21   00–023966

For Angela

Contents

Preface and Acknowledgements

This book is a revised version of *Toni Morrison* (1995), originally published in the Macmillan Modern Novelists series. I should like to thank Professor Norman Page, General Editor of that series, for his support and advice on the earlier book and for his kind permission in allowing me to base this study upon it. Indeed, I have retained some of the key principles of the series: this study is aimed at the student and the general reader alike and the approach is primarily critical with an emphasis upon close examination of important texts. However, there is more emphasis upon the critical debates that Morrison's work has generated, upon the development of her fiction over nearly thirty years, and upon the different theoretical frameworks within which her novels may be read. The book charts the increasing emphasis in Morrison's fiction upon specific events located within significant periods in African-American history, and her increasingly searching exploration of the nature of historiography. There is a major focus throughout upon the various genres and verbal narratives that are invoked in the novels and the extent to which Morrison, as an African-American writer, is engaged by the historical perspectives and preconceptions normally associated with them. Readers new to Morrison's work or with some acquaintance with her fiction are guided in a revised and up-dated bibliography to further critical readings and more general debates in African-American scholarship to which Morrison's work can be seen to contribute.

In addition to the support of Margaret Bartley and her colleagues at the publishers, I should like to acknowledge a general debt to my colleagues and students in the Department of English and Drama at Loughborough University for helping me to refine my ideas, and to those in the School of English, Bretton Hall College, University of Leeds, when I worked on the earlier version of this study. Without the support and suggestions of Angela Burton and Vicky Annand the earlier version would not have been completed. I owe Angela, as always, a special debt for her constant advice and encouragement from which this new book has benefited. Special thanks are also due to the staff of the Pilkington Library, Loughborough University, for their speedy and efficient assistance.

1

Biographical and Critical Contexts

I

> Ohio is an interesting and complex state. It has both a
> southern and a northern dimension. The Ohio River has
> historically represented freedom ... The northern part of
> the state had underground railway stations and a history
> of black people escaping into Canada, but the southern
> part of the state is as much Kentucky as there is, complete
> with cross burnings. Ohio is a curious juxtaposition of
> what was ideal in this country and what was base. (Tate,
> 1985, p. 119)

Since about 1970, Euro-American criticism has tended to avoid,
or at the very least be sceptical of, biographical approaches to
literary texts. In fleshing out the name of an author on the cover
of a book, we have learned to be properly cautious; more aware
of our own preconceptions, of how our reading generates the
meaning of a text, and of how works do not have single, totally
conscious or fixed points of origin. While I hope this study of
Toni Morrison's fiction retains a proper scepticism throughout in
these matters, the reader new to African or African-American
literature needs to be aware that in African-American literary
criticism such caution is political. Black literary criticism has been
resistant to the various trends in Euro-American critical practice,
from New Criticism to structuralism, that posit the separation of
the literary text from its author, because reclaiming an identity
and (narrative) voice has been important to the black writer in
countering centuries of dispossession and misrepresentation. At
the very moment when black writers have taken possession of
the voice denied them by imperialism and racialism, they do not
want to be robbed of it again by a European, theoretical sleight of

1

hand. Moreover, for African and African-American writers, the novel has been an important vehicle through which to represent the social context, to expose inequality, racialism and social injustice.

Without exaggerating their importance, I would argue that it is not difficult to find Morrison's place and date of birth in her fiction. She was born Chloe Anthony Wofford, the second of four children, in Lorain, Ohio, in 1931. Both her parents, Ramah (Willis) and George Wofford, came from Southern families. Her maternal grandparents, from Greenville and Birmingham, Alabama, had moved to Lorain via Kentucky where her grandfather worked as a coal miner, while her father had come to Ohio to escape the racial violence of Georgia. As is evident from Morrison's own recollections, Ohio embraced in microcosm the schizophrenic nature of the Union itself in which the free states of the North and the slave states of the South were brought together under one umbrella. Perhaps, in her own perspective on the State lie the origins of two of the major preoccupations of her fiction. First, it reflects the concern in her fiction with the pursuit of individual advancement by black people in a white-determined nation and culture, and whether this is at the expense of their 'blackness', if such a concept is indeed definable. Second, it suggests her interest in the reclamation of 'black solidarity', if again such a thing can really be said to exist, based upon, to use her own word from *Beloved* (1987), 'rememory' of slavery and white America's continual denial of black people.

When Morrison lived there, Lorain was a steel mill town on Lake Erie with a population of approximately 30 000. Workers were drawn to its shipyards and steel mills in the 1920s and many of the migrant workers were blacks attracted there after they lost their lands as sharecroppers in the South. Sharecropping, where a cropper would work for a planter in return for a share of the crop at harvest time, had replaced the old slave plantations, but it was a precarious existence which locked the cropper in a cycle of dependency and despair in contrast to which the industry of the North seemed to offer a bright prospect. For many of these people it was an especially cruel fate when the town was hit by the Depression and only in 1949 did Morrison's own father regain financial stability. Nevertheless, Lorain provided black migrants from the South with a town where apparently class mattered more than race.

Indeed, Doreatha Mbalia (1991), demonstrating the black critic's interest in the social context of literature, traces Morrison's own interest in class to her upbringing in Lorain.

Although there were no black ghettos in Lorain, it was there, according to her own accounts, that Morrison had her first experiences of racism and it would be perverse to discuss the work of a black writer outside the context of these kinds of origins. One such experience, or more likely a combination of such experiences, undoubtedly gave rise to the episode early in *The Bluest Eye* (1970) involving Pecola and a white, immigrant shopkeeper:

> She does not know what keeps his glance suspended. Perhaps because he is grown, or a man, and she is a little girl. But she has seen interest, disgust, even anger in grown male eyes. Yet this vacuum is not new to her. It has an edge; somewhere in the bottom lid is the distaste. (p. 36)

But Morrison's work does not only focus on black experience of white racism. There is a recurring interest in black people who have acquired social status through accommodating themselves to white society and by appropriating white values. Of course, Morrison herself has been very successful as a writer and as a university teacher. Apart from winning the Nobel Prize for Literature (1993), she won the 1988 Pulitzer Prize for fiction with *Beloved* (1987) and the 1978 National Critics' Circle Award for fiction and the American Academy and Institute of Arts and Letters Award for *Song of Solomon* (1977). The novel proved a paperback bestseller with 570 000 copies in print. After the publication of *Tar Baby* (1981), which remained on the *New York Times'* bestseller list for four months, she became the ~~first~~ African-American woman to appear on the cover of *Newsweek*. She has achieved professorial status with the Schweitzer Chair in Humanities at the State University of New York, Albany, and, latterly, the Robert F. Goheen Chair at Princeton University. But, unlike some of her characters, she cannot be accused of emulating white cultural values because she was educated at America's most distinguished black university, Howard University in Washington, where, incidentally, she changed her name to Toni Morrison. In 1949, when she enrolled at the University, Washington was deeply caste-conscious and Morrison recalls in an interview with Nadelson in the *Guardian* in 1987:

2nd [margin annotation]

ZORA NEALE HURSTON on cover of Newsweek in 1943 [handwritten annotation]

Thinking on it now I suppose I was backward, but I never longed for social integration with white people. For a place to pee when shopping, yes, but I was prey to the racism of my early years in Lorain where the only truly interesting people to me were the black people.

Here Morrison may be betraying the influence of her father who believed, as Doreatha Mbalia (1991, p. 102) reveals, that all African people were superior to Europeans because as the victims of white racism they occupied a morally superior position in society. Like Guitar in *Song of Solomon* and Son in *Tar Baby*, he believed that harmony could never exist between the races. His views are voiced by Son in *Tar Baby*, who tells Jadine that black people and white people should work together but not sleep or even eat together.

While Son's viewpoint is one that is explored and debated in a number of the novels, the way in which Morrison writes from a black centre and the way in which white people are at the margins of her work, if they occur at all, are subjects to which she has returned in a number of interviews. For example, in an interview with Claudia Tate, she explains:

> When I view the world, perceive it and write about it, it's the world of black people. It's not that I won't write about white people. I just know that when I'm trying to develop the various themes I write about, the people who best manifest those themes for me are the black people whom I invent. It's not deliberate or calculated or self-consciously black, because I recognize and despise the artificial black writing some writers do. I feel them slumming among black people. (Tate, 1985, p. 118)

The majority of the courses which Morrison followed at Howard University did not explore black history or culture. In an interview with Christopher Bigsby in 1992, she recalls how her suggestion of writing a term paper on black characters in Shakespeare was treated with derision. The apathy which such courses created among a large number of the University's students has been recalled by Mbalia (1991, pp. 105–6) and is recreated in Milkman's attitudes in *Song of Solomon* (1977) that so exasperate Guitar. In the early 1960s, until his note to Hagar which breaks off their 14-year relationship, Milkman's life is one good time after another. In his own words, he is going 'wherever the party is' and is oblivious, as

Melissa Walker (1991) points out, of the Montgomery bus boycott, the violent confrontations over integrated schooling in the South, the sit-ins and freedom rides. In the wake of the Supreme Court order of 1954, the late 1950s and the 1960s saw a rising tide of anti-discrimination boycotts and outbursts of ghetto violence, evidence of a new spirit of anger and defiance, which culminated in the Black Power movement, determined to bring to an end for once and for all black dependency on white power structures.

Morrison graduated from Howard University in 1953 with a BA in English and a minor in Classics; her fiction reflects her know-ledge of literature and classics in addition to her familiarity with African and African-American cultural traditions. But, in many respects, the principal influences on her multifocal fiction are the two authors on whom she concentrated for her MA at Cornell University, William Faulkner and Virginia Woolf. After completing her MA in 1955, Morrison taught at Texas Southern University, Houston, for two years, after which she returned to Howard University in 1957 as a Faculty member. Within a year of doing so, and while an instructor in English, she married a Jamaican architect by whom she had two sons, Harold Ford and Slade Kevin. During her time as a teacher at Howard University she taught two of those who subsequently took a leading role in the emerging black civil rights movement: Stokely Carmichael, founder of the Black Power movement, and Claude Brown. In her interview with Christopher Bigsby, she recalls how Brown asked her to help revise *Manchild in the Promised Land* for five cents a page! However, during her time at the University, she did not take an active role in the civil rights movement herself. One of the reasons for this was the birth of her son in 1961, but another was that she was not a fully committed integrationalist even though she recognised that segregation served the interests of the white racists. A further explanation may have been that, as Elliott Butler-Evans (1989) has pointed out, in the 1960s race rather than gender had become the overriding sign for the oppression of black people so that the political agenda was dominated by black men. Indeed, the absence of a political pres-ence and the suppression of an alternative voice impeded the emer-gence of a black feminist literature. Moreover, the emergent white liberal feminist movement of the 1960s and 1970s failed to address issues related to black women. Nevertheless, a number of the events which were taken up by the civil rights movement obviously affected Morrison deeply and were incorporated in her novels.

Song of Solomon, for example, makes specific reference to the brutal killing of Emmett Louis 'Bobo' Till, a 14-year old, who was flogged, mutilated, lynched, shot in the head, and thrown into the Tallahatchie River with a 70-pound cotton gin fan round his neck for allegedly whistling after a white woman. Secondly, the event which triggers Guitar's search for money is the bombing in church of four little African girls on 15 September 1963, in Birmingham, Alabama.

In the mid-1960s, with a dissolved relationship and two children to support, Morrison left teaching to work in the textbook subsidiary of Random House at Syracuse, New York. Mbalia (1991) is the only scholar to have attached significance to this in terms of the development of her political consciousness. Yet while working here, Morrison edited *The West and the Rest of Us* by the leading African historian Chinweizu, two of the arguments of which are reflected in the novels that followed. *Song of Solomon* and *Tar Baby* both explore on some level how capitalism produces and maintains racism and how, in keeping with Chinweizu's thesis, white power produces white racism whilst white racism in turn serves white power. Moreover, Chinweizu's thesis that some African people have been so brainwashed by European propaganda that self-hatred characterises the African petty bourgeoisie must have encouraged Morrison to pursue her interest in what drove some African-Americans to seek a white American identity.

Morrison began work on her first novel, *The Bluest Eye*, at the age of 30 while teaching at Howard University. It was a long process because she kept revising her ideas and because she was conscious of herself as a black woman entering a field where the high ground was held by whites. Not wanting her employer to know she was publishing with another Press, when the book was eventually published her new identity emerged along with it because she had changed her name and even withheld her photograph from the book jacket. Given the recurring concern in her work with the search for identity and with the significance of names for black people, this is probably one of the most interesting biographical details about her as far as the novels themselves are concerned. It highlights her conviction that black people, at the level of the personal self, have the capacity to 'invent themselves' and, as we shall see, this is a significant trope in most of her novels.

Much of her first novel was written in the evenings while her children were in bed and we can see the influence of her position as a woman bringing up two children alone. It was the first novel to give a black child centre stage; previously, the black child had not only been peripheral but doubly marginalised as a comic figure. The negative portrayal of black children and black people generally is a familiar theme within white fiction which poststructuralist and postcolonial literary criticism have increasingly identified. As a device by which one cultural position has been legitimated over another, it is analogous to the portrayal of the Welsh and Irish in English fiction and popular culture.

Unlike Maya Angelou, Morrison puts very little of her own life overtly into her fiction. However, much of what she read appears to have provided important source material. While Senior Editor at Random House, Morrison brought several black writers, for example, Angela Davis, Toni Cade Bambara and Gayl Jones, to the publication list. The influence of Henry Dumas, whose work she read in the early 1970s and for whom she helped to organise a book party in October 1974, has been identified as particularly important. Mbalia (1991), for example, points out that his work incorporates surrealism, supernaturalism, magic, astrology, myth and science fiction, all elements to be found in a concentrated form in Morrison's *Song of Solomon*. Certainly Morrison borrowed the name of Dumas's racist Arkansas home town, Sweet Home, for the plantation in *Beloved* where she also uses the Dumas name Heyboy (Mbalia, 1991, p. 112).

Song of Solomon, which became A Book-of-the-Month Club Selection, as I said earlier, and won several major awards, proved a turning point for Morrison; it was then that she began to think of herself as a writer rather than an editor who wrote. In 1981, she was elected to the American Academy and Institute of Arts and Letters and became only the second African-American woman to appear on the cover of *Newsweek*. But her international reputation was established when *Beloved* won the Pulitzer Prize in 1988 and reaffirmed two years later when she won the Chianti Ruffino Antico Fattore International Literary Prize. *Beloved* also won the Robert F. Kennedy Award, the Melcher Book Award and the Before Columbus Foundation Award. The contribution that the novel makes to the history of black women was recognised by the Elizabeth Cady Stanton Award from the National Organisation for Women. Between *Song of Solomon* and *Beloved*, apart from *Tar Baby* (1981), Morrison published her first play, based on the brutal murder of Emmett Till which she had previously incorporated

into *Song of Solomon. Dreaming Emmett* was produced by the
Capital Repertory Company in 1986. As Margaret Wilkerson
(1988, p. 185) explains, the play, which uses a dream metaphor, is
concerned with the meanings attached to this lynching, 'at once a
poignant metaphor for the history of black–white relationships
and a profoundly disturbing historical moment in the national
consciousness'. Several features of the play emphasised the
importance of the community in black culture. For example, the
influence of the African dilemma tale – a traditional oral narrative
which puts a dilemma to the community for it to resolve – was
evident in the dialectic which the play established with its audience. Indeed, they were encouraged to enter into a debate with
what was happening on stage when an actor emerged from
among them to challenge Emmett who until this point in the play
had been dreaming only of revenge on his killers. Moreover, the
way in which those on trial appeared in elaborate masks which
they stripped off to reveal further layers of masks recalls African
masked drama, one of the functions of which, as Ladistas Segy
(1976) argues, was rooted in a communal need to participate in a
collective consciousness. In its concern with community, the play
develops and merges two positions which are explored further in
Beloved: that individuals and their family histories are embedded
in their people's history and that the emancipation of black people
can only be realised within the contexts of black communities and
black culture.

Beloved, as I shall discuss in chapter 4, is based upon the true
story of an escaped slave, Margaret Garner, who tried to kill herself
and her children rather than return to slavery. She was not tried for
murder which was hardly considered a crime for a black woman,
but for stealing what was, in effect, her master's property – herself!
Although the story was well known, Morrison undoubtedly drew
on a particular version of it which she published in *The Black Book*, a
compendium of newspaper clippings, anecdotes, songs, personal
genealogies and advertisements chronicling the life of African
people in the United States from slavery to the civil rights movement. In her interview with Christopher Bigsby, Morrison reveals
that her original project was a single work, entitled *Beloved*, which
was to have centred on three events separated from one another by
50 or 60 years. However, the publisher chose to issue the first part
as a novel in its own right, leaving the other two parts to form
further novels. It is now generally accepted that *Jazz* (1992) and

Paradise (1998), which has been published to far less critical acclaim than *Beloved*, constitute the other two parts of the trilogy although some critics have seen it at best as a very loose trilogy while others have not been able to recognise the three novels as a trilogy at all, an issue to which I shall return in chapter 5.

The award of the Nobel Prize to Morrison in October 1993 attracted a certain amount of controversy. Other black writers have won the Nobel Prize – Wole Soyinka, the playwright from Nigeria, and Derek Walcott, the poet from the West Indies – but Toni Morrison is the first African-American to do so. Within this context, the award might be seen as the acknowledgement of a writer from a body of literature which had been neglected for too long. However, at the time the award did not meet with universal approval among black writers and intellectuals. Toni Morrison was seen as representative of a small coterie of black women writers, such as Maya Angelou, Alice Walker and Gloria Naylor, favoured by the white literary and academic establishment. Other black writers, such as Charles Johnson and Stanley Crouch, alleged that it was a triumph of 'political correctness', an endorsement of a writer from a marginalised culture who suited the taste of the dominant culture. No doubt politics play a part in the award of the Nobel Prize, but such speculation is not the concern here. In the media's coverage of Morrison's award, dissent was newsworthy and controversy worth encouraging for the sake of readership as well as debate. The dissent often focused on criticisms which seriously misrepresented Morrison's work. It was argued that she betrayed her origins as a black writer by employing European models. She was not judged a good novelist because her characters were said to have no social context; they were found to be stereotypes, thinly drawn to convey messages that could not be easily understood. Her work was even said not to challenge stereotypes of black people. Such attacks on Morrison's fiction betrayed a profound failure to appreciate how her writing has challenged conventional per-ceptions not only of black culture and black people but of the nature and potential of the novel itself. They also demonstrate an appalling ignorance on the part of some leading writers and acade-mics of the scholarship, much of it by African-American academics, on her work.

In addition to the novels, Morrison has produced an important critical work *Playing in the Dark: Whiteness and the Literary Imagination* (1992), which arose out of the way in which her fiction required her 'to think about how free I can be as an African-American woman writer in my genderized, sexualized, wholly racialized world' (p. 4). The study turns conventional criticism of American literature on its head. Instead of seeing African-Americans as on the margins of the literary canon, the American literary tradition is perceived as centred upon them:

> These speculations have led me to wonder whether the major and championed characteristics of our national literature – individualism, masculinity, social engagement versus historical isolation; acute and ambiguous moral problematics; the thematics of innocence coupled with an obsession with figurations of death and hell – are not in fact responses to a dark, abiding, signing Africanist presence. (p. 5)

Morrison also edited *Race-ing Justice, En-Gendering Power: Essays on Anita Hill, Clarence Thomas, and the Construction of Social Reality* (1992), a discussion of the ramifications of the United States Senate hearings in 1991 on the controversial, if not scandalous, nomination of Clarence Thomas to the Supreme Court, and the accusations of sexual harassment brought by Anita Hill. The essays constitute an important critical document on race, gender, politics and power structures in America as they have developed during Morrison's career as a writer. A further edited work, *Birth of a Nation'hood: Gaze, Script, and Spectacle in the O. J. Simpson Case* (1997) also makes an important contribution to our understanding of how concepts of black identity in America are located in a complex matrix of race politics and institutionalised power structures. Throughout the 1990s, although she has received at times a more mixed critical reception than in the 1980s, her standing has remained extremely high. Two years after the publication of *Jazz*, she won further international prizes – the Rhegium Julii Prize for Literature; the Condorcet medal; the Pearl Buck Award – and prestigious honours – the Condorcet Chair, Paris, and the National Book Foundation Medal for Distinguished Contribution to American Letters.

II

Even a brief account of the biographical context of Morrison's novels is enough to alert us to the dangers of seeing them as purely reactive; for example, as inverting European ways of thinking, as reacting to white racism or subverting Euro-American aesthetic assumptions. This is a point worth pursuing in preparation for the discussion of the novels themselves: first, in relation to one critical approach to African-American writing which Morrison herself has felt strongly enough about to publicly reject; second, in the context of Morrison as a black woman writer; and third, in relation to the Euro-American novel.

The extent to which African-American writing has been marginalised within the paradigms of Euro-American literary criticism has formed the centre of debate among a number of African-American critics. This debate about the relationship of black writing to Euro-American critical practice has focused on whether it should be approached as a separatist or syncretist literature. At one extreme, there has been a tendency to adopt a separatist model of African-American literature, to locate it within a tradition that is African rather than American. The major advantage of this approach has been to lift African-American literature out of its marginalised position within Euro-American critical traditions. Critics, such as Trudier Harris (1991), working with this model have been able to highlight the salient characteristics of African-American literature, for example the way in which it often draws on folklore and myth as indices of an alternative ontology, which generally have not been given sufficient attention by critics using the norms of Euro-American literature as a touchstone for evaluation. Others have stressed the African elements in Morrison's work such as the African concept of 'nommo', the 'magic power of the word to call things into being', in *Beloved* (Handley, 1995).

However, the weakness of the separatist model is that it ignores the syncretist nature of many African-American texts. In other words, African-American writers are often the products of hybrid cultural backgrounds and frequently draw from both their African and European heritage. As Jacqueline de Weever emphasises, 'the Black-American branch produces a literature in which African and African-American traditions are blended. Neither completely African nor completely Euro-American, this new blend is just as firmly American as the novels previously defined as American because this flower can bloom nowhere else' (1991, p. 22). There have been three principal developments: the identification of a tradition of African-American women's writing (as in Barbara Christian, 1985; Susan Willis, 1986; Michael Awkward, 1989; Birch, 1994); the discussion of

Morrison's work in relation to her male black predecessors, James Baldwin, Richard Wright and Ralph Ellison; and explorations of Morrison's work in relation to Virginia Woolf and William Faulkner.

The difficulty of achieving a properly balanced critical approach to African-American writing is exemplified in the application of the 'magic realist' model which has been suggested by Stephen Slemon (1989) as appropriate to postcolonial texts. The term was first coined by Franz Roh in 1925 in relation to postexpressionist art but since the 1940s it has been applied indiscriminately to novels by Latin American writers to emphasise their difference from mainstream culture. More recently, it has been used equally indiscriminately in relation to writers from outside Latin America, including some from the Caribbean, Nigeria and India.

One of the difficulties of this concept is that it has not been rigorously defined, or adequately distinguished from related literary concepts such as fabulation, the fantastic and the uncanny. However, Isabel Allende's definition of 'magic realism' suggests many of the features and concerns of Morrison's novels:

> Magic realism really means allowing a place in literature to the invisible forces that have such a powerful place in life ... dreams, myth, legend, passion, obsession, superstition, religion, the overwhelming power of nature and the supernatural. All these are present in African poetry, Hindu sagas, Arab tales, and used to be present in Western literature up to the Gothic novel and Edgar Allen Poe. Only in the past few decades have they been excluded by white male authors who decided that whatever cannot be controlled doesn't exist. (Lewis, 1993, p. 26)

Indeed, the application of the term 'magic realism' to postcolonial literature generally has helped critics to highlight some of its distinguishing characteristics. Stephen Slemon, drawing on the work of Kroetsch and of Kenyon, argues that the label is especially appropriate to texts written on the margins, as it were, and 'can itself signify resistance to central assimilation by more stable generic systems' (1989, p. 10). In 'magic realism', as Allende's definition suggests, the representational code of realism is locked in a continuous dialectic with that of fantasy. As we shall see in the course of this study, such a dialectic permeates Morrison's texts. But Slemon identifies a further feature which is even more relevant to Morrison's work because it highlights two opposing systems of language: 'codes of recognition', that are inherent in 'inherited language', and what he calls 'imagined codes – perhaps utopian or future-oriented – that characterise a culture's "original relations" with the world' (p. 11).

Morrison's novels frequently return the reader, directly or indirectly, to how inherited Euro-American language organises and structures its culture's relations with the world so as to exclude African-Americans or at best to marginalise them. This is the explicit subject of her first novel, the strengths of which have still not been fully appreciated by critics. But the weakness of 'magic realism' as a point of entry into Morrison's work, even when it is fully defined, as by Allende, is that it can over-emphasise a non-black cultural legacy and lead us to underestimate the cultural paradigms in which she works as an African-American author. In fact, in an interview with Paul Gilroy in 1993, Morrison rejects the label because it denies the cultural origins of her writing: 'Just as long as they don't call me a magic realist, as though I don't have a culture to write out of. As though that culture has no intellect' (Gilroy, 1993, p. 181).

The African-American paradigms within which Morrison works are especially apparent in our second area of focus, Toni Morrison as a black woman writer. Despite being sometimes contradictory on the subject in interview, Morrison writes as a black woman with the experiences of black women in mind. On radio in 1983, while claiming at first to write 'without gender focus', Morrison, backtracking quickly, affirmed: 'I am valuable as a writer because I am a woman, because women, it seems to me, have some special knowledge about certain things' (in McKay, 1988, p. 54). She has advanced this position less diffidently in subsequent interviews, with, for example, Sandi Russell in 1986: 'I write for black women. We are not addressing the men, as some white female writers do. We are not attacking each other, as both black and white men do. Black women writers look at things in an unforgiving/ loving way. They are writing to repossess, re-name, re-own' (in McKay, 1988, p. 46). Indeed, the experiences of repossessing and reclaiming are crucial for black women writers, who start from an especially difficult position which has been summarised by Susheila Nasta:

Whilst, for instance, there are obvious parallels between the experience of women's oppression in previously colonised territories and women's oppression worldwide, there is a danger even in western feminist literary circles (which often have failed to give full critical attention to literary works by black women

writers) of being seduced by easy notions of a 'universal feminism'. The post-colonial woman writer is not only involved in
making herself heard, in changing the architecture of male-
centred ideologies and languages, or in discovering new forms
and language to express her experience, she has also to subvert
and demythologise indigenous male writings and traditions
which seek to label her. (Nasta, 1991, p. xv)

This difficult position has caused some African-American critics to
emphasise how Morrison's novels invert familiar myths and stereotypes. For example, de Weever (1991, p. 134) argues that Morrison
invokes a range of mythical mother figures, such as the nurturing
mother who devours her children, as a reaction to the stereotype of
the black mother. The black mammy is the legendary figure of
sentimental novels and popular films: obedient, obliging, cheerful,
resilient and resourceful. It is an especially damaging stereotype
because it legitimises motherhood as the female function most
commonly associated with black women. As such, the black mother
provides a powerful example of how inherited Euro-American
language organises and shapes our perceptions of black people. Yet
whilst African-American writers must be aware of these stereotypes and how they impinge upon their narratives, they usually
write out of a fully realised sense of the actual lived experiences of
black people which involves more than responding to Euro-
American stereotypes. The Euro-American stereotype, even allowing for the fact that the circumstances and conditions of their lives
have forced black women to function chiefly as mothers, as
de Weever argues (1991, p. 134), ignores many dimensions and
strengths of black women.

At one level, de Weever's (1991, p. 108) characterisation of Eva in
Sula as a figure of death is insightful, providing a fuller mythical
context for the character. The fact that she has lost a leg in an accident, and that she has such projections of sleeping with her son that
she sets him on fire, link her to those mythical figures who have
committed incest and who are either lame or walk with difficulty.
Indeed, it is sometimes the mythical element of, for example, Eva in
Sula and Pilate in *Song of Solomon*, neither of whom, like Eve, has a
navel, which separates these women from the stereotypes of the
black mother. But we must not lose sight of the fact that Eva is
created out of the lived experiences of black women. Eva's sacrifice
of her leg might suggest the price that black people have to pay for

living in a white society, but it is also an indication of her courage, her commitment to her children and her independence of mind – strengths which the Euro-American stereotype denies. It is not surprising that black women writers often do not provide romantic, conventional portrayals of motherhood and that instead of the mammy figure they portray heroines who seek psychic development on their own terms. de Weever points out what she should not have to point out to many women, let alone many African-American women, that 'motherhood is thus not an ideal condition' (1991, p. 157). Her emphasis falls upon how 'the cultural myth of the black mammy, that all-nurturing, all-patient, all-loving, all-accepting woman, is invented to show that she does not exist in reality' (ibid.).

The denouements of many of Morrison's novels favour community, the moral responsibility of individuals to each other, the reclamation of traditional black values and the importance of the ancestor. But as a writer she appears, from the evidence of her texts, to be drawn – almost paradoxically – toward the dramatic potential of enigma, distances, spaces, dislocation, alienation, gaps and ellipses. Although this may be because few writers can resist these sources of drama, it may also be the product of the particular milieu in which Morrison began to write. In the late 1960s and early 1970s, new distances, divisions and debates opened up in African-American writing around the subject of black identity. Two novels published in 1970 in particular – Toni Morrison's *The Bluest Eye* and Alice Walker's *The Third Life Of Grange Copeland* – shifted the focus of African-American fiction. The different address of these novels, despite or rather because of their acknowledgement of conflict and division, reflects the enhanced confidence in black experience as literary material and a wider reassessment of monolithic versions of black identity. Black fiction in the 1970s and 1980s moved away from a homogenised sense of a unified and unifying black community and from overreliance upon the binarism of positive/negative images of black people. It engaged with a pluralistic sense of experience, incorporating the multiple subjectivities that constitute any individual's sense of identity. Issues of ethnicity were explored within a larger hierarchy of articulated differences: racial, gendered, cultural and sexual.

As we shall discuss in more detail in the course of this book, there are strong elements of fantasy, recurring non-realistic structures, in Morrison's novels: for example, Pecola's obsession with blue eyes;

Sula watching her own mother burn to death; Pilate's absence of a navel; Ruth's obsessive breastfeeding of her son and necrophile love for her father; the myth of Solomon's leap; the presence of house number 126; the appearance and dismemberment of Beloved; the concept of rememory. Whilst critics such as de Weever (1991) have drawn attention to the openness of African-American narratives, of which Morrison's use of fantasy is an example, this feature has not been placed in a wider theoretical context. In fact, Mikhail Bakhtin's identification of the inconclusiveness of the novel as a genre in 'Epic and Novel' (see Bakhtin, 1981), that it is always in process of development, can help us to understand how, in the hands of black writers, it has proved such a popular vehicle for non-European subjects and worldviews and has been able to incorporate, as we shall see, the openness of traditional black culture. The way in which the novel, as Bakhtin argues, incorporates other genres in its own peculiar structure, reformulating and reaccentuating them, helps explain how African-American fiction has given a frame and coherence to materials drawn from African, American and European cultural traditions as well as from indigenous oral traditions and folklore.

The works of many African-American writers, and especially the novels of Toni Morrison, do not simply invert Euro-American stereotypes. They give expression to desires, needs and aspirations which are not articulated even by black cultural myths such as that of the black mother. Throughout Morrison's work, there is a recurring concern with black, female-headed households where survival, as one German scholar, Anne Koenen, has pointed out, is dependent upon 'self-inventing' (cit. McKay, 1988, p. 199). Although this process of 'self-inventing' does not always bring success on a personal or social level, Koenen's theory of 'generational degeneration' in Morrison's novels – the farther down the generations of women the weaker their personalities become – is simplistic. It ignores how although the personalities of the daughters are weaker than their mothers' – Hannah is weaker than Eva and Reba is weaker than Pilate – the personalities of the granddaughters are usually very strong. Indeed, their level of 'self-inventing', as we shall discuss later in the chapter on *Sula*, is disturbing because it is so self-obsessed. Morrison's novels argue that black people's emancipation can only be realised within the context of black culture and the black community. Although this always works so as to criticise aspects of the strong granddaughters, Morrison's novels are usually even more critical of women, like Nel in *Sula*, who are role-bound and unable to break out of their oppression.

III

How, as literary critics, we approach the work of an African-American writer – the literary assumptions we bring to it and the critical methodologies we employ – is an important issue in African-American literary criticism. While some critics of African-American literature, whose interpretations of Toni Morrison's fiction we will encounter in the course of this study, have been resistant to certain trends in Euro-American criticism, others have also rejected established methodologies and assumptions in African-American scholarship.

When she was awarded the Nobel Prize in 1993, Toni Morrison was described as one 'who, in novels characterised by visionary force and poetic import, gives life to an essential aspect of American reality' (in the introduction to Morrison, *The Nobel Lecture in Literature*,1994, p. 6). But such is the complex nature of her fiction, and of debates in African-American scholarship, that talk of the 'visionary force and poetic import' of Morrison's work is problematic. While it conveys an important aspect of her work, it eschews the way in which her fiction resists essentialising notions of 'black identity' and 'African-American community', for example, as if they transcend time and history. For Madhu Dubey, this aspect of Morrison's work is a critique of the Black Aesthetic, itself a product of the black nationalist ideology that shaped the cultural context in which black women's fiction of the 1970s was written, published and received. In reversing white culture's negative image of blackness, in which it was associated with ugliness, evil, corruption and death, black nationalism posited a 'definition of blackness as an integral, beautiful and natural value' (Dubey, 1994, p. 28). But, as Dubey argues, in advocating this, the black nationalists proved susceptible to the charge that, however positive the intentions, they were exchanging one essentialist notion of identity for another. But even talk of the non-essentialist aspects of Morrison's work begs a number of questions. Carried to its logical conclusion, Henry Louis Gates, Jr's emphasis upon texts as rhetorical structures, in the quotation below, would suggest that blackness is not a transcendental essence reflected by verbal and visual texts, as black nationalists clearly believed, but a complex sign system produced by and through their figurative language:

> The black literary tradition now demands, for sustenance and for growth, the sorts of reading which it is the especial province of the literary critic to render; and these sorts of reading all share a fundamental concern with the nature and functions of figurative language as manifested in specific texts. No matter to what ends we put our readings, we can never lose sight of the fact that a text is not a fixed 'thing' but a rhetorical structure which functions in response to a complex set of rules. It can never be related satisfactorily to a reality outside itself merely in a one-to-one relation. (Gates, Jr, 1984, p. 5)

Any one of Morrison's novels might be said to provide support for this argument. But if we follow it to its logical conclusion blackness becomes only a fabricated, fictional sign system. At one level, faced with the plethora of negative and muted images of black people in American literature and culture, this is a liberating perspective. But, in a total rejection of the Black Aesthetic notion of an essential, self-present, black subject, we lose what Dubey calls 'a sense of the sheer possibility of blackness' (Dubey, 1994, p. 29).

Despite its rejection of the Black Nationalist Aesthetic, it is hard not to find the sense of the possibility of blackness in Morrison's work of which Dubey writes. Nevertheless, envisaging her work as, in the words of the Swedish Academy's Nobel citation, giving 'life to an essential aspect of American reality' – the use of the word 'essential' is particularly unfortunate here given Morrison's interest in how identities are constructed in historically and socially specific contexts – risks aligning her work with the kind of writing of which Louis Gates, Jr (1984) is highly critical. The Nobel citation might recognise the possibility of blackness in Morrison's fiction but it suggests that we should value African-American writing for its 'sociological' significance. Morrison herself has complained that the work of African-Americans is too often approached from a reductive, sociological perspective, as a resource rather than as a text:

> Critics generally don't associate black people with ideas. They see marginal people; they just see another story about black folks. They regard the whole thing as sociologically interesting perhaps

but very parochial. There's a notion out there in the land that there are human beings one writes about, and then there are black people or Indians or some other marginal group. (Tate, 1985, p. 121)

And her criticism has been echoed by Henry Louis Gates, Jr, himself:

If Euro-Americans have used the creative writing of Afro-Americans primarily as evidence of the blacks' mental or social 'perfectibility' or as a measure of the blacks' 'racial' psychology or sociology, then they have used African literature as evidence of African 'anthropology', of traditional and modern African customs and beliefs. (1984, p. 5)

Indeed, it is because 'of this curious valorization of the social and polemical functions of black literature', that he believes, as in the quotation given earlier, that 'the structure of the black text has been *repressed* and treated as if it were *transparent*'.

It is impossible to get very far in a discussion of Toni Morrison's fiction without acknowledging that it rejects Western humanist assumptions of identity as fixed, unique and coherent, that it provides the reader with critiques of some of the salient black nationalist notions of African-Americanism, and that it cannot be read easily within a framework provided by the traditional realist novel. The circular, multifocal nature of Morrison's novels, blurring the boundaries between fact and fiction, history and fable, and literary and oral cultures hardly needs pointing out. *Beloved* particularly has been approached as a postmodern novel (see, for example, Rafael Pérez-Torres, 1993; Brenda Marshall, 1992). But when postmodernism becomes almost a kind of literary orthodoxy, can postmodern writing still be described as 'daring'? Given the postmodern nature of much fiction written after 1970 – the novels, for example, which constitute the core of contemporary literature modules in universities across the globe and which are often nominated for Anglo- and Euro-American literary prizes – it might seem something of an overstatement to argue, as Jill Matus has, that Morrison's fiction 'reveals a daring and explorative artist whose work now represents a rich testimony to the past and to the special ways in which imaginative literature can speak of that past' (Matus, 1998, p. 153).

Although many writers experiment with form, using shifting perspectives and developing multifocal, often contradictory, narratives, they do not all employ these strategies for the same reasons. The characteristics of Morrison's fiction that might be described as postmodernist are driven by her preoccupations as an African-American writer working out and through particular geographical and temporal locations. As Rafael Pérez-Torres says of *Beloved*, 'while Morrison's text shares narrative affinities with classically postmodern texts, it also suggests a connection between its narrative strategies and the socio-historical realities of Africans in the Americas' (1993, p. 694).

This is not to suggest, of course, as some have incautiously alleged, that multifocal perspectives and the blurring of boundaries between realism and fantasy are unique to African-American and African writing. At one level, one is bound to ask what postmodernism has to do with the African-American writer when postmodernism is all too often associated in white literary criticism with an avant-gardism committed to enigmatic and self-indulgent wordplay. In arguing that '*Beloved* creates an aesthetic identity by playing against and through the cultural field of postmodernism', Pérez-Torres tries to define what he thinks makes postmodernism relevant to Morrison's African-Americanist project: 'It filters the absent or marginalized oral discourse of a pre-capitalist black community through the self-conscious discourse of the contemporary novel' (1993, p. 690). If we substitute Asian for black here, something similar might also be said of Salman Rushdie's *Midnight's Children*. Both draw heavily upon the characteristics of oral as well as postmodern story telling, employing foreshadowing and flashback, digressions and digressions within digressions, and cyclical rather than linear narrative structures. But an important difference between Rushdie's fiction and Morrison's is that Rushdie's is as much pastiche and parody as history. In African-American fiction, as Pérez-Torres (drawing on Louis Gates, Jr's work) points out, 'the linguistic playing, punning, coding, decoding and recoding ... emerges from the pressing necessity for political, social, and economic survival' (1993, p. 694).

What Morrison and Rushdie's novels share that makes it necessary for critics such as Pérez-Torres to qualify them as postmodern texts is that, like much postcolonial literature which displays postmodern characteristics, they reflect a need, as Simon During says, to 'achieve an identity uncontaminated by universalist or

Eurocentric concepts and images' (1987, p. 33). This concept is entertained even more positively by Peter Nicholls who argues that 'the most productive formulation of the post-modern is surely that which regards it not as some new epoch succeeding the modern, but rather (following Lyotard) as a disruptive mode within the modern' (1996, p. 52). But it is Denis Ekpo who perhaps sees the significance of postmodernism more fully for African and African-American writing, suggesting that postmodernism, in providing a reconceptualisation, reconstruction or re-interpretation of African perceptions of the West, might actually offer a route out of 'the Afrocentric ideal of contemporary African cultural and strategic thoughts' (Ekpo, 1995, p. 123).

Pérez-Torres, in distinguishing *Beloved* from what he calls 'multi-cultural novels', also takes the line of argument employed by During further by pointing out that in Morrison's work there is 'no innocence, no aesthetic word play that does not simultaneously trace and erase various structures of political and cultural meaning' (1993, p. 694). There is, then, in Morrison's fiction, if we follow Pérez-Torres's line of argument to its logical conclusion, a strong relationship between the ostensibly disparate realms of form and of politics. In the course of this book, I argue that it is in the ways in which these are integrated that Morrison is an explorative, and often daring, writer.

Although her novels have been written in decades overshadowed by postmodernism and she writes fiction that appears postmodernist, some of the salient principles by which Morrison defines her practice echo the literary academy of an earlier period. In *Playing in the Dark*, she draws a distinction, although she does not use these terms, between 'readerly' and 'writerly' critical practice, the latter capable of embracing, in her view, both 'exploratory' writing and 'exploratory' reading:

> Writing and reading are not all that distinct for a writer. Both exercises require being alert and ready for unaccountable beauty, for the intricateness or simple elegance of the writer's imagination, for the world that imagination evokes. Both require being mindful of the places where imagination sabotages itself, locks its own gates, pollutes its vision. Writing and reading mean being aware of the writer's notions of risk and safety, the serene achievement of, or sweaty fight for, meaning and response-ability. (*Playing in the Dark*, 1992, p. xi)

It is not difficult to see what Morrison describes as the 'sweaty fight' for meaning, through 'places where imagination sabotages itself, locks its own gates, pollutes its vision', in the spiral structure of *Sula*. In *Sula*, as Dubey argues, there is a 'circular movement, back to transform past incidents and to add new layers of meaning, resolving, at the level of narrative structure, the novel's thematic opposition between past and present' (1994, p. 69). But, I would argue that not only *Sula* but all of Morrison's fiction is informed by this kind of circular, backward spiralling movement; that the beginning and closing points of all her novels do not quite overlap; that all her novels frequently deny the reader interpretative access to their major events the first time that they are narrated.

Like the New Critics whose critical methods and ideologies dominated American English Departments in the 1940s and 1950s, Morrison stresses the importance of not divorcing theme from form. But it is equally important to her not to separate form from history. Jill Matus's claim that Morrison's fiction 'represents a rich testimony to the past and to the special ways in which imaginative literature can speak of that past' (1988, p. 153) might be made for numerous writers. Many postmodern and postcolonial writers, even allowing for the complex and contradictory ways in which these labels have been defined, use a variety of techniques to 'speak of the past', many of which are employed by Morrison herself – for example, parallel stories, diverse modes of communication, intertwining the historical with the private and/or the mythical and the 'realistic' with the fantastic. Thus, it is hard to distinguish what is daring and innovative in this dimension of Morrison's work. Yet, because it is in this very area that her primary concerns as an African-American writer are located, the relationship between her works and the specific historical and social contexts with which they are concerned needs and deserves careful explication.

The British critic Steven Connor has argued, in a discussion of English fiction, that the novel is not simply 'passively marked with the imprint of history' but is also 'one of the ways in which history is made and remade'. He does not imply that history is reducible to textuality – another risk behind Louis Gates's argument for the acceptance of black novels as rhetorical structures. Rather he seeks to remind us that 'the processes of writing and reading novels are not fully distinct or finally distinguishable from the forms and processes of conflict, deliberation and evaluation that belong to the social, economic or political realms' (1996, pp. 1–2). Toni Morrison's fiction, written from the premise that the novel can contribute to the way in which history is made and remade, adds another layer to Connor's view of the dialectical relationship between the novel and history. In her work, form itself is envisaged as existing in a dialectical relation to history. In other words, we have to consider not only language and form in history, the staple pursuit of literary histories of the novel, but, as I hope to show in the course of this book, the history in the language and in the form.

The favoured circular movement of Morrison's novels, 'spiralling back to transform past incidents and to add new layers of meaning', in effect readdresses the eviction of black people from historical self-possession and restores black narratives to history. Her work establishes, revisions or affirms relationships between individual and community histories, the larger social and political realms of black history, and the wider global forces of, fundamentally, white history – relationships which, as Morrison suggests in *Playing in the Dark*, have been denied in white American literary histories. It does so in ways that make the language and the mode of writing not merely the mirror or the palimpsest of historical events but agents in the rewriting of particular versions of history.

Her novels engage with a variety of modes of writing, or rather with the history in those modes. The American *Jane and Dick Primer* is an important intertext in *The Bluest Eye*, *Sula* alerts us to the history in the *Bildungsroman*, *Song of Solomon* invokes the history underpinning the American quest novel, and *Jazz* is not only engaged by the history of jazz itself but 'crosses over' with the American novel of the city. But, at this early stage in the book, the argument can perhaps be most clearly illustrated with reference to *Beloved* and its relationship to the slave narrative which by the 1840s was being written to a familiar formula: an initial description by the slave of their plantation origins; the initiation into hardship and suffering; the escape; and the life in the North or Canada. The range and depth of Morrison's familiarity with this mode of writing is clear from her essay 'The Site of Memory' (Zinsser, 1987) in which she cites works as diverse as Olaudah Equiano's *The Interesting Narrative of the Life of Olaudah Equiano or Gustavus Vassa, the African, Written by Himself* (1789), Harriet Jacobs's *Incidents in the History of a Slave Girl: Written by Herself* (1861) and Frederick Douglass's *Narrative of the Life of Frederick Douglas, an American Slave, Written by Himself* (1845). Autobiographical in form and language, slave narratives charted the journey of their authors from bondage to freedom, and from the position of subject in someone else's narrative to that of the subject of their own. Slave narratives were intended, as Morrison argues, to persuade their readers that slaves were 'human beings worthy of God's grace' and to encourage them to press for the abolition of slavery. Although *Beloved* is based on a slave narrative, its purpose is to remind readers of what has been forgotten, and of what was barely depicted in the nineteenth-century narratives for fear of alienating those whose support was needed in abolishing slavery, such as the physical and sexual violence suffered by female slaves. *Beloved* also includes further aspects of slavery which in Morrison's opinion were absent from the slave narratives, the 'internal life' of the slaves and the psychic impact of slavery, even though there were nineteenth-century slave narratives in which the psychic impact of slavery was stressed. Thus, *Beloved* is an engagement not only with the history of slavery but with the slave narrative. Indeed, what emerges most strongly from Morrison's essay, 'The Site of Memory', is her strong sense of the history within the slave narrative as a mode of writing. The first thing they were written to say, she points out, was 'This is my historical life' and the lives were seen as representative of the history and the experiences of the race.

Beloved is not so much a revision of the slave narrative as an engagement with the history in the genre and in its strategic employment of silences, recollections and memoirs. Indeed, these generic features do not simply reflect but are the product of the historical importance attached to slave narratives in the abolitionist campaign in the period leading up to the American Civil War, of the highly sensitive political context in which they were received even by their most sympathetic Northern readers, and of the result of the separation of what Morrison calls the 'internal' and the 'external' life of the slave. There were other features, too, of the slave narrative that reflected its historical origins and conveyed particular cultural perspectives. Morrison herself draws attention to the fact that the formulaic subtitle 'written by himself' or 'herself' was a consequence of, and challenge to, the prohibition against teaching slaves to read and write, while the editorial framework – a white editor insisting that the autobiography was authentic and, often, that little editing was actually needed – was the result of the belief that black people had the minds of young children, incapable of intelligence and literacy, arguments which were frequently invoked in order to justify slavery.

Thus, Morrison's reading of the cultural significance of slave narratives is based on an important recognition that history is as present in what is not said as in what is. But *Beloved* cannot be seen as articulating only what has been occluded. It has an even more complex relationship to black history than that, to the history that is in the slave narrative genre itself and to white as well as to African-American history. With the exception of Cynthia Hamilton (1996), critics have underestimated the extent to which black history is incorporated in the mixed modes of the slave narrative. The slave narrative was after all a hybrid form, evolving from popular traditions of the eighteenth century: Protestant spiritual autobiography, conversion narrative, captivity narrative and travel writing. Significantly, *Beloved* retains many of the salient features of the slave narrative in which black history is embedded – much of the narrative is oblique, there are silences within it, and it is based on recollection and memoirs. The emotional impact of the novel is rooted not simply in the content but, as the New Critics argued of poetry in the 1940s, in the mode of writing in which it is expressed.

This perspective has implications for the way in which black history is envisaged in Morrison's novels generally. A recurring theme in criticism of *Beloved*, *Jazz* and *Paradise* is the return of the repressed (for example, Nicholls, 1996), usually based upon an analogy between the possession of the self by something external to itself and the invasion of the present by the past. At best, the shifts between different historical periods in *Beloved* and *Jazz* have been read in terms not simply of the influence of the past on the present but, as Nicholls says, 'to evoke the traumatic force of a historicity which splits the subject, compelling it to live in different times rather than a secure, metaphysical presence' (1996, p. 58). The concept of the self or the present as standing apart from its history for whatever reasons, including the trauma of a history too painful to bear, is presented in each of Morrison's novels as not only erroneous but as having dangerous implications for individuals, communities and the African-American people generally. However, her fiction frequently emphasises also the history in the body. At its most literal this would include the scars on Sethe's back in *Beloved* and the pockmarks on Dorcas's face in *Jazz*, both important motifs in the respective texts. But the history in the body is analogous to the history in the body (that is, the form) of the texts themselves as well as the history in the present.

One of the reasons why ostensibly it appears plausible to talk of the invasion of the present or the self is that the past can appear to be 'foreign'. The history that is actually in various modes of writing and in the body can be described, in a term from the French philosopher Jacques Derrida, as an 'unfolding of presence'. For it is a past that has never been present and is more the product of construction than recollection. The intertext, as it were, against which these novels is written is not simply the denial of history or of the traumatic force of historicity but the failure to recognise the presence of history, including the most traumatic experiences of history, in the individual body and in particular verbal and non-verbal forms. In *Jazz*, Joe does not simply respond to Dorcas, as some critics have suggested, because subconsciously she reminds him of the mother he has lost. Dorcas literally and metaphorically embodies a history, as does jazz itself, with which both of them are bound up, and, in Joe's response to her, as Angela Burton has pointed out, the boundaries between her body, what her body reminds him of, and the history in her body are blurred (Burton, 1998, p. 177).

Although, as I pointed out earlier, African-American literary criticism has been resistant to certain trends in Euro-American critical theory, Morrison's novels may be profitably read within a Euro-American, New Historicist framework. At first, this might appear to be surprising. For New Criticism which, as I indicated above, dominated the American Academy during the period when Morrison herself was a student of literature, or at least the way in which New Criticism was often interpreted, led to an insistence upon a study of the text divorced from its historical context. Morrison's own work, however, is deeply and obviously 'historical'. For example, *Jazz*, as I will discuss later, is embedded in the migrations of black people from the South to the North which followed the American Civil War and *Beloved* not only describes the psychic and physical abuse suffered by black slaves, especially women, during slavery but pointedly alludes to the atrocities committed on black people during the period of reconstruction. And an increasing number of critics (e.g. Marilyn Sanders Mobley, 1990; Rebecca Ferguson, 1991; Carolyn Rody, 1995) have pursued the interest in Morrison's fiction in the intertwining of history and memory. But, while critics have tended to highlight the connection between Morrison's novels and some of the major specific events of black history – for example, Melissa Walker (1991) historicises *Sula* in relation to the Voting Rights Act, the assassination of Martin

Luther King, the election of Richard Nixon, the escalation of the Vietnam War – the philosophical and theoretical nature of her interest in history has been underemphasised. The fusion of history, 'realism' and verifiable fact with story telling, fantasy and folklore in her work, and the blurring of the boundaries between them, calls into question the nature of historiography itself. Thus, in some ways, a more useful starting point for the discussion of history in her work than even her concern with the occluded facts of black history is the origins of the word history itself. The word 'history', after all, entered the English language from the French 'histoire' (story') and the Greek 'istoria' ('inquiry').

While Morrison may be seen to share concerns with many Euro-American postmodern writers with the so-called 'textuality' of history, her interest in historiography is embedded not in Euro-American literary/philosophical trends but the processes of privilege and occlusion that have marginalised the African-American presence in (white) American history and created distorted black histories, even when written from a black perspective. Any discussion of Morrison's work from a New Historicist perspective must bear this context in mind.

New Historicism is a fairly recent development in critical theory which owed a great deal initially to scholars working in the area of Renaissance Studies. The term is usually used in one of two ways, either as an umbrella term to describe all the recent New Historicist theories about history and literature or to distinguish American 'New Historicists' from the British equivalent, 'cultural materialism'. In introducing New Historicism, Stephen Greenblatt argued that it was 'set apart from both the dominant historical scholarship of the past and the formalist criticism [an umbrella term incorporating Russian Formalism, structuralism and New Criticism] that partially displaced this scholarship in the decades after World War Two' (1982, p. 5). There are two key points here that are obviously pertinent to Morrison's fiction. First, New Historicism displaces traditional historicism; from the New Historicist perspective traditional history since the Enlightenment, and particularly since the impact of eighteenth-century idealism, has been overconcerned with a linear, Eurocentric narrative of human progress and self development. Second, New Historicism counters the kind of literary studies in which the text is assumed to be an ahistorical linguistic structure. While the debates and disagreements among the various New Historicist camps make it difficult to define New

Historicism as a movement, most New Historicist criticism is informed by three principal assumptions that also underpin Morrison's fiction, particularly her interest in the history in form and language themselves: that human behaviour, practice and knowledge are social constructions or inventions; that texts should be read as participating in the construction of human beliefs and ideologies and not simply read against a backdrop to beliefs and ideologies; and that ideological and political interests operate through texts. In uncovering the historical contexts in which literary texts first emerged, New Historicism treats texts as examples of the forms which make power relations in that period visible. In 'The Site of Memory', Morrison uncovers the historical contexts in which slave narratives emerged and reads the narratives themselves as modes of writing in which inter- and intraracial power relations are made manifest.

Doreatha Mbalia (1991) employs historical materialism to explain what she perceives as the uniqueness of the African's oppression, grounded in race and class. However, the word 'context' refers not only to the context in which the text originates but also to the context in which it is read. In this respect, Morrison's fiction lends itself to the interests of 'cultural materialism'. While New Historicism concerns itself primarily with the power relations of past societies, cultural materialism explores literary texts within the context of contemporary power relationships. From a cultural materialist perspective, texts are not only socially produced but socially productive. In other words, a cultural materialist perspective should alert us not only to Morrison's interest in history but to the way in which our view of history can be determined by, for example, the slave narrative or the novel. Throughout this book, New Historicist and cultural materialist perspectives complement each other, for whereas the former reminds us that each era has its own specific conceptual and ideological frameworks, cultural materialism alerts us to the way in which politics and ideologies manipulate texts to serve particular, historically specific interests.

New Historicism is a particularly useful framework within which to discuss Morrison's novels because her interest in story and folklore, despite the plethora of work in this area, still remains undertheorised. Their importance to her fiction cannot be gainsaid. *Beloved*, as we shall see, is indebted to the story of Margaret Garner, a slave who killed her own child rather than have it taken into slavery – or rather to a version of the event published in a newspaper, the *American Baptist* – and *Paradise* is based on a story she heard while on a trip to Brazil in the 1980s about a convent of black nuns who took in abandoned children but who, regarded as an outrage, were murdered by a posse of black men. In New Historicist criticism, there is an especial interest in the relationships among literary and non-literary contemporaneous texts. Literary and non-literary texts, such as the Margaret Garner story, the slave narrative, the story Morrison heard in Brazil, are equally embedded in a network of material practices and as such are constituents of historical discourses that are both inside and outside them. This is especially pertinent to the way in which Morrison's fiction blurs the boundaries between the various texts which it incorporates. *Beloved*, for example, contains a mixture of forms, many themselves associated with slave narratives, such as spiritual narrative, adventure and exemplary biography.

This study of Morrison's novels employs a number of perspectives on language, meaning, narrative and history that are normally placed under the general label of poststructuralist. Although these theories are not as homogeneous as that label might suggest, they do cohere around challenges to the nature of language and to the concept of the individual. Poststructuralist theories of language draw attention to the need for us to question the relationship between language, meaning and what we normally regard as 'social reality' more than we usually do. Language does not merely reflect 'reality', it constructs it. The language that we use to construct what we think is 'reality' contains preconceptions and assumptions that are imposed, sometimes unconsciously, on what we are describing. Language is not a transparent window on to the world; it is more like a piece of stained glass that distorts and colours what we see through it. The fact that language can never be ideologically innocent or neutral is one of the subjects of many of Morrison's novels. But they are also concerned with the way in which language enables certain discourses to circulate and achieve priority over others. The discourses that circulate around, for example, gender and race, and which are often institutionalised in, for example, the family, education and the legal system, pass for truth. But they privilege certain groups such as white Anglo-Saxon males and deny the legitimacy of others such as black working-class females. Poststructuralist theories of discourse and history challenge the way we have tended to think of the individual in literary criticism in liberal humanist terms as a free-thinking, autonomous being by suggesting that we are all the products of discourses that are historically specific. This takes us to the core of much black writing where, although the free-thinking being may still be an ideal, the individual is inevitably perceived as the subject of a political state, susceptible to the forces of control that operate in a given society or social context, and constructed through language or discourse.

In the chapters that follow, discussions of individual works are designed to illuminate important issues in Morrison's work as a whole whilst providing extended treatment of topics and features particular to each book. The next chapter is concerned with two novels that in different ways and for different purposes revision the *Bildungsroman* from a number of African-American perspectives. In the discussion of *The Bluest Eye*, the emphasis falls on the way language is enmeshed with power structures and the dominant social forms that determine 'social reality'. It argues that the success of *The Bluest Eye* lies in the approaches and perspectives it brings to an exploration of the impact of prevailing white ideologies on the black 'community'. *Sula*, too, is not usefully approached through reading habits developed in relation to the realist European novel or the liberal humanist assumptions and historical preconceptions underpinning the traditional *Bildungsroman*. A salient feature of the novel, as of many post-1970 novels, is the way in which it constantly requires the reader to question their own reading of it. The focus, however, is on Sula herself in whom the African-American woman's need to create her own notion of selfhood is complicated by the characteristics she shares with the traditional figure of the African trickster. The novel is seen as invoking not only the *Bildungsroman* or a literary heritage of feminist writing that can be traced to Morrison's MA thesis on Virginia Woolf but the trickster narrative.

Song of Solomon and *Tar Baby* are discussed in terms of the way that they invoke Nathaniel Hawthorne's definition of American romance. But I argue that *Song of Solomon*, especially, may be too easily read as an ironic version of the European romance formula and that such an approach overlooks the importance of black concerns, African myth and Africanist perspectives in the novel. The discussion of *Tar Baby* develops many of the points raised in the discussion of the previous novels or approaches them from a different context. Whilst the novel's debt to the African-American folk tale is apparent from its title, there are dangers in interpreting this too simply or too rigidly. Throughout the discussion, the focus is upon the complex processes by which African-Americans, especially black women, have to negotiate the competing discourses that influence individual and social behaviour.

The way in which any novel consists of a transposition of material from different sources, both literary and non-literary, is the basis of the approach to *Beloved* in chapter 4, in which Morrison is seen as invoking and revisioning a range of genres significant to black history, such as the slave narrative, the spiritual autobiography and the plantation ghost story. One of the most difficult of Morrison's novels because of its subject matter and fragmentary structure, it is also one of the most evocative, moving and cathartic. Chapter 4 demonstrates how a preoccupation with unearthing narratives that have been hidden by or buried within other narratives is integral to the novel and explores the various levels of occlusion within it.

Beloved is seen as the first book in a trilogy that Morrison completed in the 1990s with *Jazz* and *Paradise*. While the trilogy is ostensibly a loose one, the books within it are characterised by a closer focus on specific events, by a profounder concern with historiography, a common interest in obsession, and the way in which each invokes, and crosses over with, narratives that were prevalent at the time in which they are primarily set and from which they reach back into a more remote past. *Jazz* is recognised as significantly influenced by African-American music and the American city novel, but also as invoking, and subverting, in its central sections, the Southern romance formula. Again the experiments with form are seen as determined, like that of the other novels, by aspects of African-American history and experience. *Paradise*, like the other novels in the trilogy, is primarily concerned with a specific event but it contains more principal characters than the others. In part, this is due to the particular verbal narratives that it invokes, revisioning the histories within them from an African-American perspective. But it also invokes a wider range of genres than any of the other novels. This study concludes with a postscript that attempts to take stock of Morrison's achievement to date whilst recognising that, hopefully, there are many works yet to come.

2

The Early Novels: *The Bluest Eye* (1970) and *Sula* (1973)

I

Toni Morrison's engagement with African-American history and with the history that is embedded in particular verbal narratives is more sharply focused and specific in the later novels – *Beloved* (1987), *Jazz* (1992) and *Paradise* (1998) – than in her early work of the 1970s. Nevertheless, the experimental nature of Morrison's first two novels arises, at least in part, from the way in which they are engaged by a range of genres – the *Bildungsroman*, the reading primer, the confessional narrative, the autobiography, the slave narrative – as well as by black nationalism.

Ostensibly *The Bluest Eye* is about a lonely, victimised, black girl, Pecola Breedlove, who is driven insane by her desire to have white skin, blonde hair and blue eyes, and the interplay between her disintegration and a number of black characters who are more fully integrated than herself into white society. But, at the outset of the novel, Morrison adapts the eighteenth- and nineteenth-century convention whereby work by a black American, often slave narratives, carried a preface from a white writer confirming the authenticity of the black authorship. In its preface, which also provides an introduction to some of the chapters, extracts from a Dick–Jane American primer present a standardised, white American family embracing Euro-American views of beauty and happiness. This introduces the major theme of *The Bluest Eye*, based on the discrepancy between white, 'middle-class' American and African-American histories, that the white voice is inappropriate to the contours of African-American life. But in engaging with the assumptions of the white American primer, Morrison's novel unfurls the history in Euro-American standards of beauty and in white America's idealisation of the family from an African-American perspective, highlighting the way in which they come into conflict with the history that is situated, metaphorically and literally, in the black body. And although they appear to be separate histories one is part of the other.

At the end of the novel, Claudia and Frieda overhear snippets of gossip about the Breedloves that summarise the negative social consequences that can arise from the imposition of Euro-American cultural values and ideals on black people: none of them seem 'right', they don't have relatives, and they are ugly. Beauty is as much a political as an aesthetic concept whilst ugliness is not merely a matter of appearance; Andrée McLaughlin points out it is a manifestation in western thinking of an inner ugliness, a spiritual and moral failure, if not an innate evil:

> That which was 'white' (or Anglo, male, Christian, wealthy) was extolled and infused with connotations of benevolence and superiority, while that which was not white (or not Anglo, female, non-Christian, poor) was debased and associated with malevolence and inferiority. (Braxton and McLaughlin, 1990, p. 153)

Claudia herself, as the mature narrator, condemns the American concept of blonde beauty as one of 'the most destructive ideas in the history of human thought' (p. 95). As Jacqueline de Weever points out, the insistence on one standard of beauty contradicts the pluralistic nature of contemporary America where African standards of beauty are frequently adopted by African-Americans, for example, the dashiki, ancient Egyptian long braids and cornrow hairstyles (1991, p. 107). She also surmises that there may have been secret societies in some African countries in the seventeenth and eighteenth centuries concerned to inculcate a confident centre of being in young girls and young women which was then destroyed by slavery.

The first part of this chapter examines how the novel's structure is driven by its exploration of the impact of white ideologies on the black community. The book's particular slant comes from the ironic juxtaposition of the white mythology of the Dick–Jane primer and the lives of African-Americans as part of a larger interplay of differences. In much of her work, especially the early novels, Morrison tends to homogenise 'whiteness', not acknowledging, for example, how the American-Irish have not always been seen as 'white

Americans'. The apparent cultural and moral certainty that informs the traditional white *Bildungsroman* is contrasted with the inner dislocation and search for coherence in the lives of Pecola and her parents. The novel itself is organised into four sequences, each associated with a season and beginning with Claudia's memories of that season. There are seven subsections, introduced by lines taken from the primer extract in the preface, related from the perspective of an omniscient narrator. The lines, reprinted with punctuation and spaces removed, are ostensibly unintelligible so as to emphasise the dislocation between the white Dick–Jane mythology and the norms of black experience. The retrospective nature of Claudia's narrative is an important device in deconstructing a bourgeois black culture in the novel. We come to realise that the voice of Claudia, which becomes fused with that of the omniscient narrator, is that of an older Claudia, living in the North, and that she is tracing the stages that have led to her present maturity of outlook. Thus, on one level, the narrative takes us backwards from the present in the North into the past and the South, whilst, on another level, taking us forward in the events of Pecola's tragedy.

II

The Bluest Eye pursues ironies created by the interplay between two levels of articulation in the narrative. One level of articulation arises from the role of Claudia as survivor and her retrospective account of episodes introduced within the context of a season; the other derives from the black kinswoman who narrates the episodes introduced by extracts from the primer. She is an omniscient narrator who is able to provide access to information which Claudia could not have and is able to involve characters outside of Claudia's immediate range of experience. The ironies arising from these two levels of narration are developed within a wider framework provided by the mismatch between what the primer suggests is the norm and the lived experience of the black families.

In discussing the levels of irony within *The Bluest Eye*, it is important to remember that Toni Morrison's works are not easily approached through reading habits developed in relation to the realist novel where language often gives the impression of 'transparency', in other words that the representation and the represented are the same. In Morrison's novels, language, as the

French critic Roland Barthes recognised, is enmeshed with the power structures and forces underlying what we might call 'social reality': 'And the reason why power is invincible is that the object in which it is carried for all human eternity is language: the language that we speak and write' (Barthes, 1981, p. 459). In Morrison's novels, ideology is not, as envisaged by Marx, an illusion or false consciousness, but, as conceived by the French Marxist theorist, Louis Althusser, the staple of daily living, embodied in language and in social institutions such as the school, the family and the media.

As I pointed out in the previous chapter, the dialectic between inherited codes of representation and imagined codes is one of the features that Morrison's work shares with novels from Latin America classified as 'magic realist'. This dialectic emerges in *The Bluest Eye,* as in subsequent novels, from the realisation of the black culture out of which Morrison is writing and of the distortion of self created by the imposition of white norms on black people. The effect of this imposition is to create a profound sense of fracture. The concept of 'black' in the novel is a construct partly of the characters' own making but mostly social, based on white definitions of blackness that associate it with violence, poverty, dirt and lack of education, whilst Africa is perceived as uncivilised and (negatively) tribal. Black people developed as a social category of low status when Arab trade in African slaves increased, but it was with the European subordination of world peoples as labouring classes that blacks came to form, as Andrée McLaughlin says, part of an oppositional and hierarchical system of cultural constructs that justified a coloniser/colonised power system (Braxton and McLaughlin, 1990, p. 153).

In Morrison's novels, the struggle to define and create a notion of self that is different from the stereotypical expectations of the larger social and symbolic order inevitably involves a process of inner dislocation for the African-American. As in, for example, *Song of Solomon,* this sense of inner disruption is sometimes resolved positively by the intervention of a female or androgynous figure in the central character's life. But this is not true of Morrison's first two novels where Pecola, suffering from a sense of self-loathing and false identity, retreats into schizophrenia after being raped by her father and where Sula withdraws into her grandmother's room to die alone and unfulfilled.

Although *The Bluest Eye* demonstrates Morrison's abiding interest, like that of many novelists, in dislocation, alienation, gaps and ellipses, these features arise out of the distortion of self created by the imposition of Euro-American cultural ideals on black people, including white concepts of beauty. Margaret Wilkerson (1988) has conveniently summarised three of the key characteristics of Morrison's narratives: they are rooted in arresting events (for example, a child having her father's baby, an insurance salesman attempting to fly off a roof, a First World War veteran announcing National Suicide Day, a slave mother killing her own child who later returns to haunt her); personal histories which have been made tangled and complex; and personal lives which skirt the edge of madness. However, whereas Wilkerson argues that the familiar in black folk lore is made strange in the telling, I would argue that in Morrison's work the eccentric (perhaps the ex-centric?) is often made explicable (or centred?). Both the first two novels are retrospective narratives: in *The Bluest Eye*, Claudia tries to understand her own involvement in Pecola's tragedy as the narrative also seeks to explain why a father in the ironically named Breedlove family should impregnate his own daughter; in *Sula*, the people of a black neighbourhood, Medallion, retain and try to understand the implications for themselves and for their community of the apparently bizarre history and behaviour of the equally ironically named Peace family.

The explanation for many of the behaviours in both these novels lies in the impact of prevailing white ideologies and dominant social structures on the black community, the negative consequences of which are inevitable as Claudia, partly in an attempt to abrogate her own responsibility, observes: 'This soil is bad for certain kinds of flowers. Certain seeds it will not nurture, certain fruit it will not bear' (p. 9). As we shall see, the authentic black self is buried so deep in some of the characters that their perceptions of themselves amount to self-hatred. This self-loathing is strongest in those characters who are farthest from their communities; for what they hate most is being different since difference brings abuse and cruelty. The self-hatred is often focused on the body as the most obvious indicator of race; hair and colour, for example, are recurrent concerns.

The black community in *The Bluest Eye* is envisaged as existing like a cell within the larger white body of America, sustained by traditional strengths and values but being weakened by divisions within it. These divisions are the result of an increasingly bourgeois black people, itself a consequence of a complicated process of adjustment and accommodation to white norms. In an interview with Thomas LeClair (1981), Morrison explains: 'The music kept us alive, but it's not enough any more. My people are being devoured.' The structure of *The Bluest Eye* is one of the means by which the novel explores how and why black people are being devoured and is best approached from this perspective. In speaking of African-Americans as being consumed, Morrison is inverting how whites, since earliest colonialist times, represented blacks as bestial. She is ironically adapting how African mythologies about slavery posited the whites as cannibals because blacks taken by them never returned; here perceiving the exploitation of blacks by whites as economic cannibalism. It is a view, though, that ignores how African-Americans have influenced language, dress, manners and culture in America, even in the South.

Not all critics have recognised the success of the novel in deconstructing the impact of white values on African-American people. Valerie Smith complains that *The Bluest Eye* does not 'address hard questions directly' (1987, p. 124); by this she means that it does not undertake to explain, for example, why black Americans aspire to unattainable standards of beauty. Her claims would seem to be borne out by Claudia's preface which is also a conclusion as well as the point from which the novel starts out: 'There's really nothing more to say – except why. But since why is difficult to handle, one must take refuge in how' (p. 3). It is important that this is not the summary of the ostensibly omniscient narrator, but the view of Claudia as an adult trying to come to terms with her own role in Pecola's tragedy. What Claudia says does not suggest, as Smith argues, that the novel will take refuge in 'how'; she issues a warning that what the narrative will uncover by means of explanation may be unpalatable.

The differences between the white and African-American cultures and the sociopolitical contexts of the lives shaped within those cultures are pursued throughout *The Bluest Eye* in the persistent contrasting of the Dick–Jane mythology of the primer with the Breedloves. The chapters which are introduced by lines from the primer extract, sometimes with subtle but significant variations, provide particularly bitter glosses on the bourgeois myth of the ideal family life. Each chapter enlarges on the Breedlove family while the themes are developed further with reference to a range of minor characters.

Black people are visible to whites in *The Bluest Eye* only in so far as they fit the white frame of society. The novel deconstructs this frame literally through dismembering the American Dick–Jane mythology: essential features of their world – house, family cat, mother, father, dog and friend – are separated from each other and their ideological significances probed through their inclusion and recontextualisation as plot elements in the Breedlove narrative. This process of dismemberment is analogous to Claudia's increasing dismemberment of a white doll in an attempt to discover the superiority of white culture:

> I fingered the face, wondering at the single-stroke eyebrows; picked at the pearly teeth stuck like two piano keys between red bowline lips. Traced the turn-up nose, poked the glassy blue eyeballs, twisted the yellow hair. I could not love it. But I could examine it to see what it was that all the world said was lovable.
> (p. 14)

Claudia's destruction of the doll is a complex response that requires us to understand the history in it, of how western culture, as McLaughlin explains, 'inspires hatred toward and among people of African descent, inducing destructive behaviours and an equally adverse disconnection from anything not western' (Braxton and McLaughlin, 1990, p. 170). In removing the various parts of the toy, Claudia dismantles the structure and the history that constitute and sustain it as an emblem of white beauty. Again, this is anticipated in the way in which the mythology of the primer is increasingly dismantled in the preface – the extract is reprinted, first without the punctuation and then with the spacing removed as well until all the letters run into each other. Claudia's obsession with discovering the source of the superiority of white culture leads her initially to torture the white girls whom the doll represents but later to recoil in horror from this violence.

Within the ironic interplay of difference, the text dramatises and explores the consequences of enforced or voluntary abatement to white society, though in a sense no abatement can be entirely voluntary where black people exist in a world defined by the surrounding white society in terms of its blackness. Following Claudia's recollections of Autumn 1940, in which she dismembers the white doll, the first chapter introduced by a primer extract develops the ironic differences between the pretty house of the primer and the abandoned store in which the Breedlove family lives. Here, of course, the differences between the respective family

homes are embedded in differences between the idealised representation of whites in America and the 'real' history of the majority of
African-Americans. The store consists of rooms which have parti-
tions that do not reach the ceiling; there is no bathroom but there is
a toilet bowl which is out of sight though within earshot of the
inhabitants. The ironic inappropriateness of the primer to the
Breedlove family life and history is underscored by the repetition of
the word 'pretty' which occurs only once in the preface and the
way in which the extract breaks off, rather maniacally, with the first
letter of that word.

The stress placed on the word 'pretty' also anticipates the misery
endured by the Breedloves, and especially Pecola, in the following
chapter because they believed they were ugly. That chapter is introduced with a primer extract that talks of family happiness and
which breaks off equally significantly with the first letter of
'happy'. Unlike the ideal, sanitised family of Dick and Jane, the
Breedlove's marriage is quarrelsome and violent, though both
Pauline and Cholly Breedlove need this kind of relationship.
Mrs Breedlove finds zest and passion in her formalised battles
with her husband, whilst he projects on to her a sense of an innate
inferiority arising from the way he has been treated by whites.

Whilst Claudia at this time dismembers the white doll in order to
discover the nature of white superiority, Pecola regularly stares
into her mirror 'trying to discover the secret of the ugliness, the
ugliness that made her ignored or despised at school, by teachers
and classmates alike' (p. 34). The irony here is that the secret is not
to be found within herself, but within the culture that defines her as
ugly. The focus of the novel is on the nature of whiteness: what
Pecola sees in the eyes of the shopkeeper, Mr Yacobowski – 'the
total absence of human recognition – the glazed separateness' –
who as a white Jew should understand prejudice sufficiently to
transcend it.

The world of the primer is very ordered and controlled as the
short, tight sentences suggest, a world in which the 'middle-class',
suburban home stands compartmentalised. Even the verbs are held
in check – there are no adverbs and the sentences do not expand to
embrace or convey the excitement of laughing or smiling or
running; not even the dog's bark appears to interrupt this carefully
constructed and ordered world. Claudia remembers the segregated
Lake Shore Park for being well laid out and ordered, a quality
embodied in the 'clean, white, well-behaved children and parents'

(p. 81). It has an illusory air to it which anticipates the interior of the 'proud' white house where Pauline becomes a servant. There its unreality for black people is conveyed in the details: the pink nighties, the embroidered pillow slips, the blue cornflowers in the top hems of the sheets, the 'fluffy' white towels and the 'cuddly' night clothes.

III

As I suggested at the outset, the exploration of the nature of whiteness in order to expose the negative consequences of a bourgeois black culture gives *The Bluest Eye* a special slant. On one level, Geraldine, who has taken advantage of what little opportunity exists for black women from her background, is an example of a 'middle-class' black woman who has become divorced from her African-American roots:

> They go to land-grant colleges, normal schools, and learn how to do the white man's work with refinement: home economics to prepare his food; teacher education to instruct black children in obedience; music to soothe the weary master and entertain his blunted soul. (p. 64)

On another level, her history suggests that African-American women in her position surrender a deep-rooted passion that whites both envy and fear: 'The dreadful funkiness of passion, the funkiness of nature, the funkiness of the wide range of human emotions' (p. 64). The word 'dreadful' here does not convey the views of the black kinswoman narrator but of the land-grant colleges that inculcate black students in white values.

In placing 'Funk' at the centre of the African-American sensibility, Morrison's text risks confirming a white stereotype of black women. But Geraldine's loss of passion is an indicator of the erosion of her black identity. Her physical being within the cultural frame she has adopted is described in terms of absences. The closest that she comes to experiencing an orgasm is when her napkin slips free of her sanitary belt. In Geraldine's life, the family kitten of the Dick–Jane mythology also becomes the object of displaced emotions. The cat, which she cradles in 'the deeply private areas of her lap', is the only thing to which she can show any kind of warmth.

Geraldine's marriage is described as building a nest; however it seems to consist only of ironed shirts and the phrase 'birthed Louis junior' suggests that parenthood, too, for her is a cold affair. Even the black cat, which with blue eyes seems to signify the ideology to which Geraldine aspires, is as cold as an iceberg. The colours of Geraldine's home, of which we become aware when Junior invites Pecola in to torment her, are those of the primer; there is a red-and-gold Bible and lamps with green-and-gold bases. The word 'pretty' is strategically repeated throughout and the boy himself wears a white shirt and blue trousers.

Pecola disturbs Geraldine because she represents disorder: 'Hair uncombed, dresses falling apart, shoes untied and caked with dirt' (p. 72), while the impact of white standardised concepts of beauty upon young women like Pecola is epitomised in the way in which the blue-eyed, black cat, when thrown at Pecola, claws at her face. Geraldine's final words to Pecola pointedly recall Maureen's to Frieda and Claudia: 'Get out ... You nasty little black bitch. Get out of my house' (p. 72).

The loss of roots and of a sense of community are not uncommon features of, for example, the *Bildungsroman*. But there is a larger, more complex social history in Geraldine's story of which her own personal history is only a part. Instead of passing on ancestral wisdom, the traditional function of the African mother, a role assumed by Pilate in the later novel *Song of Solomon*, Geraldine passes on divisiveness. Ironically, her son, Junior, would like to be accepted by the black boys; he would like to roll in the dirt with them and share their wildness, in effect overthrowing the control and order of the primer. Unable to do so, he takes his frustration out on brown-skinned girls, as black men displace their humiliation by whites on to their wives and children. Significantly, he is also afraid of black girls who are said to hunt in packs. The animal metaphor, suggesting how *he* sees them not how the narrator perceives them, is an index of the extent to which Junior has assumed the derogatory white view of blacks as animals rather than people. The metaphor also implies that there is defence in solidarity and highlights the vulnerability of those who try to go it alone. The image of the dead cat with its blue eyes closed, 'leaving only an empty, black, and helpless face' (p. 71), suggests the cultural vacuum in which blacks who aspire to white norms may eventually find themselves.

The counterpoints to Geraldine in the novel are the three prostitutes: China, Poland and Miss Marie. Not only do they have a sexual autonomy which Geraldine has surrendered but they have economic independence. As such, they are also a counterpoint to other petty bourgeois African-Americans who benefit economically, socially and politically from the exploitation of their own people: the Peal family make money out of racial law suits while the Whitcombs exploit Africans who live in the West Indies.

The novel focuses not only on the intraracial tensions created by the black petty bourgeoisie but on the obsessive nature of their fixation with white values and the lengths to which they sometimes go to deny their blackness. The Whitcombs are so obsessed with not being black, grateful to the decaying British nobleman who gave them their 'whiteness', that they continue to intermarry to maintain it. Louis Junior's hair is deliberately cut short to hide its woolliness, whilst his skin is lotioned to disguise its ashy Africanness. The most ironic example of all, however, is provided by Maureen, the counterpoint to Pecola's humiliation and victimisation. Maureen looks and dresses like Jane, the archetypal Euro-American girl. Whilst Pecola is ignored by her teachers, Maureen is encouraged. Ironically, the lynch rope into which Maureen's hair is said to have been braided reminds us of slavery and oppression, the past on which black solidarity ought to be constructed. Here, a symbol of torture and death has been transformed into an adornment and robbed of its power. This kind of inversion is demonstrated also by the law suits that her parents issue for racism in order to make money, a perverse parody of the real struggle for civil rights.

The inner dislocation that white values create in African-Americans, anticipating Pecola's eventual breakdown at the end of the novel, is embodied most obviously in the case of Pauline Williams. In the movies that provide her with an escape from loneliness and alienation, Pauline encounters and assimilates a value system that classifies her and her family as ugly. The films present her with the white Dick–Jane mythology: 'White men taking such good care of they women, and they all dressed up in big clean houses with the bathtubs right in the same room with the toilet' (p. 95). The line from the primer which introduces this chapter concerns how 'nice' the white mother is and how much she laughs. It is anticipated and contradicted by Claudia's own recollections of Spring in the preceding chapter. Although she doesn't hate her mother for it, her memories of the season are shot through with recollections of the sting left by beatings from thin, green and supple twigs. Green was one of the cheerful colours of the house in the primer extract, but for Claudia, the colour, like the season, brings no cheer; it caused her to miss the 'steady stroke of a strap or the firm but honest slap of a hairbrush' (p. 75). Ironically, it is the way in which the white myths create an inner dislocation within Pauline that causes her to be less than 'nice' to her own daughter. In the white home in which she becomes a servant she finds an order and beauty that causes her to deny her own family and especially her daughter. When Pecola inadvertently enters the white home and frightens the 'little pink-and-yellow girl', Pauline punishes her and comforts the white girl. Pauline has moved with her husband to a community that is more obviously white than the one in which she had lived previously. Her schizophrenia is a product of the subsequent, enforced isolation, exaggerated by the way in which the other black women she meets are amused by her for not straightening her hair, as they have done in imitation of white women, and for retaining the dialect of the South. The novel contrasts not only the isolation of the white, nuclear family with the community of the South – evidenced in the attention Aunt Jimmy receives from her neighbours during her illness and the community gathering at her funeral – but the isolation of the African-American in the North compared with the South.

Even though Pauline's marriage collapses into a cycle of violence and unsatisfying sex, she refuses to leave Cholly for the white woman and a romanticised concept of 'sisterhood'. For Pauline race becomes more important than gender: 'But later on it didn't seem none too bright for a black woman to leave a black man for a white woman' (p. 93). As becomes clear from the monologues that reveal the complexity of her situation, her experience of how white doctors treat white women differently from black women is a crucial factor in her rejection of the white concept of 'sisterhood'. Once again, the point is made that cultural dislocation, as for Geraldine, brings about an emotional and sexual dislocation. The implication that her white employer has married a man with 'a slash in his face instead of a mouth' (p. 94) is that she has never experienced the passion which Pauline used to find with Cholly, encapsulated in the description of orgasm from a woman's point of view:

> I begin to feel those little bits of color floating up into me – deep in me. That streak of green from the june-bug light, the purple

from the berries trickling along my thighs, Mama's lemonade
yellow runs sweet in me. Then I feel like I'm laughing between
my legs, and the laughing gets all mixed up with the colors, and
I'm afraid I'll come and I'm afraid I won't. But I know I will. And
I do. And it be rainbow all inside. And it lasts and lasts and lasts
... (p. 101–2)

IV

The order of the white world, its coherence and moral certainty, is
juxtaposed throughout with the disunity and search for coherence
in the lives of the African-Americans. The chapter which contrasts
the white, mythical mother of the primer with Pauline is followed
by a chapter that takes up the description of the father as big,
strong and protective in the primer extract. This is itself ironic in
the light of the text's subsequent celebration of the inner strength
and fortitude not of black fathers but of black women:

Everybody in the world was in a position to give them orders.
White women said, 'Do this.' White children said, 'Give me that.'
White men said, 'Come here.' Black men said, 'Lay down.' The
only people they need not take orders from were black children
and each other. But they took all of that and recreated it in their
own image [...] They patted biscuits into flaky ovals of innocence
– and shrouded the dead. They plowed all day and came home to
nestle like plums under the limbs of their men. (p. 108)

The chapter, in contrasting Cholly with the strong, protective father
of the primer, begins by fleshing out his past and concludes with
his rape of his own daughter, an incident which can only be understood, if not excused, in the light of this background. Compounding
the irony, the primer extract begins by asking the white father if he
will 'play' with his daughter Jane, a verb which in the Breedlove
episode acquires a much less innocent connotation. There is a
further irony in the way in which Claudia's recollections are of
Frieda relating how her father beat up Mr Henry because he
touched her breasts and of being dragged to the doctor by her
mother in case she had been 'ruined'. Within this account, Cholly is
remembered not for being a strong, protective father but as a
'drunk'.

As Calvin Hernton observes, a salient feature of the black woman's literary heritage is that black women write about the violence and abuse that they have suffered at the hands of black men (Braxton and McLaughlin, 1990, p. 209). This has created problems, however, for black women writers. When they document the violence and rape they have suffered, even as young girls, they are sometimes accused of sowing the seeds of division in what should be perceived, from a black nationalist perspective, as a homogeneous community in the face of white oppression. As Hernton says, 'one of the most galvanizing examples of this is the hostility black men have toward Toni Morrison' (p. 202). This makes it all the more important to understand the complexity of what Morrison is trying to do.

In *The Bluest Eye*, the white father of the primer is invoked as a contrast not only to Cholly but Cholly's own father who abandoned him to his mother. The way in which the novel returns to Cholly's past to contextualise what has happened is a device that Morrison frequently uses in her fiction to suggest that what initially appears to be inexplicably immoral is the result of the unnatural experiences imposed on black people by whites. The opening sentence of this chapter sharply contrasts Cholly's childhood with the way in which Pauline's white charges have been brought up; he was left on a junk heap wrapped in two blankets and an old newspaper. This rejection is compounded by some of his later experiences. His grandmother takes him to her bed for warmth in winter, an act which in the reference to how he could see her wrinkled, sagging breasts seems unnatural, and it is with her that he witnesses violence for the first time when she takes a razor strap to his mother. Here the novel is not only concerned with the way in which Cholly's relationship with his father has been obliterated, but with the way in which white racism and colonialism fractured relationships between mother and child, an increasing and recurring theme in Morrison's work, as we shall see in discussions of her subsequent novels. At the beginning of her final narrated section, the adult Claudia recalls her mother as she was in 1929, so that her newfound appreciation of her black identity and of how Pecola's tragedy involved them all is concomitant with a renewal of her bond with her female ancestral line. After she has been raped by her father, Pecola lies on the kitchen floor trying to connect the pain between her legs with the face of her mother looming over her. The connection is complex, but it is one that the reader as much as

Pecola has to make. We are reminded that Pauline denied her daughter the mother/daughter bonding that, in Morrison's novels, as we shall see in the discussion of *Beloved*, is crucial to black women's self-definition.

Cholly's rape of his daughter is as much rooted in the past as in the present. His young daughter's helpless presence arouses a range of emotions within him, culminating before the rape in a hatred reminiscent of that which years earlier he had transferred to Darlene when the white hunters forced him to 'perform' sexually with her in front of them. Pecola's innocent gesture of scratching the back of her leg with her foot reminds him of the first occasion he was aroused by Pauline. The whole episode is shot through with confusion: between memories of Pauline and the excitement of what is forbidden; between the past with Darlene and the present with Pecola; between desire for Pecola and tenderness for her. When Cholly approaches his daughter he does so crawling on all fours like a child or the animal which whites have made him feel. Nibbling the back of her leg he regresses into the most primal of experiences, while his closed eyes suggest how he is unable to see the full moral implications of what he is doing. Right up until the act of penetration, though, he retains some semblance of moral being, albeit confused, wanting to 'fuck her – tenderly' (p. 128). When he enters and impregnates her, the text makes clear that all moral responsibility and familial dignity have been abandoned: 'His soul seemed to slip down to his guts ...' After he has finished, he stands at the end of the chapter as a pathetic figure made limp, as the sight of Pecola's 'grayish panties' emphasises, as much by the realisation of what he has done as by his ejaculation. Yet he is also a tragic figure broken, as the final references to his hatred make clear, by what white society has done to him and this is reinforced by the way the account of his rape of Pecola brings the incident with Darlene in the woods to mind. When he and Darlene began to make love together, she tickled his ribs and grabbed his ribcage while he dug his fingers into the neck of her dress; his assault on Pecola begins in earnest when he digs his fingers into her waist. The description of how his soul had fallen down to his guts recalls how the flashlight of the white hunters, forcing him to penetrate Darlene, 'wormed its way into his guts' (p. 116) while 'the gigantic thrust' he makes into his daughter reminds us of how with Darlene 'he almost wished he could do it – hard, long, and painfully ...'

The women who gossip about the rape perpetrate the contempt that led to it. The novel comes full circle from its initial questioning of the mode of perception that labels some plants flowers and others weeds. Claudia conjures up an image of Pecola's child that is not ugly, as the gossips suggest, but a counterpoint to the white doll of the beginning and to Pauline's pink-white charges: 'It was in a dark, wet place, its head covered with great O's of wool, the black face holding, like nickels, two clean black eyes, the flared nose, kissing-thick lips, and the living, breathing silk of black skin' (p. 149). Claudia's memory of Pecola's victimisation by so many people anticipates the ironic juxtaposition of the primer excerpt which introduces Pecola's schizophrenia and which focuses on the friend who will play with Jane. Of course, the effect of this is to underscore Pecola's loneliness and lack of friends.

At its publication, *The Bluest Eye*, the first novel to have the experiences of a black child at its centre, would have appeared more innovative than it probably does now to readers familiar with recent postmodern fiction. But even by today's standards, it has retained an experimental air, driven by the perspectives and approaches which it brings to the history and condition of the African-American, at the tense interface between two cultures. One of these perspectives, the way in which language is enmeshed with power structures, pursued throughout the novel by the persistent contrasting of the Dick–Jane mythology of the primer with the Breedlove family, has become a staple subject of postmodern fiction. But, within its ironic interplay of difference, *The Bluest Eye* brings a particular perspective not only to the impact of white ideologies on the black community but to the nature of whiteness and its inappropriateness to determine the contours of African-American history, culture and lived experience.

V

Both *The Bluest Eye* and *Sula* involve an incident in which a gang of bullies is defeated. The difference between the two respective episodes is indicative of the difference between the two novels. In *The Bluest Eye*, the threat posed by the bullies draws Claudia, Frieda, Pecola and Maureen together until Claudia and Frieda become unable to forgive the lighter-skinned Maureen for assuming white standards of physical beauty which they envy. Maureen's subsequent articulation of her contempt for their black skin, in which blackness and ugliness are perceived as synonymous, in turn epitomises the central concern of the novel with how black culture is being destroyed by the impact of white norms upon it, an argument that becomes more complex in Morrison's later novels. In *Sula*, the threat posed by the gang to Sula and Nel brings out Sula's reserves of strength and her unpredictability which help focus the novel's concern with these elements. Sula's response also provides a further example of behaviour in the novel which is explicable in terms of an African rather than an American model of behaviour.

Toni Morrison's second novel, like her first, is written within an innovative but finely crafted narrative framework. As we have seen, *The Bluest Eye* uses an extract from an American primer as its preface and throughout contrasts the white family of the primer with a black family. The novel is divided into four sections narrated by Claudia McTeer looking back on her childhood in which she was involved in the tragic disintegration of a victimised black girl. Within each section there are further subsections narrated by an omniscient narrator and introduced by lines from the primer extract in the preface in order to pursue an ironic interplay of difference throughout. *Sula*, which focuses on the friendship between two black women, is divided into two parts. In the first part, Sula and Nel become childhood friends in a black community and together become involved in the death of a young boy; in part two, Sula returns to the community as an adult after a ten-year absence which is never satisfactorily explained. Each part in a number of ways is an inverse mirror image of the other. Characters introduced and developed in part one are reintroduced in inverse order in the second part and the novel opens and closes with an act of memory. There are ten chapters, each located in a specific year, 1919, 1920, 1921, 1922, 1927, 1937, 1939, 1940, 1941, 1965. Here, the novel invokes the traditional historical novel, reminding us that historical moments acquire significance according to particular narratives in which what has happened is made sense of according to particular cultural perspectives and vested interests. The significant moments in African-American history are different from those in white American history. Moreover, even from a cursory glance at this span of years, it is quite clear that the novel, like *The Bluest Eye*, is fragmentary and elliptical. Indeed, the centre of the novel is literally a blank, a missing decade when the reader knows very little of what happened to Sula. There are other examples of lacunae in the

novel, too, such as the sudden departure of Eva, Sula's grandmother, in 1921, ostensibly leaving all her children with Mrs Suggs
for a day but returning eighteen months later with an amputated
leg for which again no definitive explanation is offered.

VI

The prologue, describing the redevelopment of the black neighbourhood in a small Ohio town by white property interests and the
exploitation of black people by whites, might lead the reader to
expect that this novel, like *The Bluest Eye,* is about black people being
consumed by the surrounding white society. Both novels are concerned with the way in which the geography of an area shapes and is
shaped by its sociospatial politics, but *Sula* places more emphasis on
the ability of the propertied classes to change the geography of an
area in line with their own interests. The prologue to *Sula* points out
that the black neighbourhood is called 'the suburbs now, but when
black people lived there it was called the Bottom' (p. 3). This linguistic shift emphasises how language can be and has been manipulated
by those in authority to maintain their advantage and protect their
positions, a concern developed in all Morrison's work. In the prologue to *Sula,* this issue is developed in the story of the 'good white
farmer' who dupes his freed slave into accepting land in the hills,
'the bottom of heaven'. In adapting the proverbial folk anecdote, a
staple technique of traditional African writing for communicating
ancestral wisdom, Morrison compounds the irony of the prologue
that black people have the higher ground in so far as they hold the
higher moral ground. This moral position is more forcefully delineated in *Sula* than in *The Bluest Eye,* giving the prologue's account of
the black neighbourhood, despite its portrayal of hardship and
poverty, an upbeat confidence that borders on the sentimental:

> just a neighborhood where on quiet days people in valley houses
> could hear singing sometimes, banjos sometimes, and, if a valley
> man happened to have business up in those hills – collecting rent
> or insurance payments – he might see a dark woman in a
> flowered dress doing a bit of cakewalk ... (p. 4)

Against this strong realisation that African-Americans hold the
high moral ground, Morrison develops the prologue's concern with

geopolitical and linguistic boundaries in new but concomitant directions from those followed in her previous novel. They are first developed through the portrayal of Shadrack, a First World War veteran, named after one of the men who survived the fiery furnace in the Old Testament (Daniel 2), who has been driven mad by the horrors of the trenches. *Sula* was written at a time when America was deeply involved in the Vietnam War and casualties seemed higher among African-American than white soldiers. In Shadrack himself there is a history that is often occluded in accounts of the First World War. While in white histories of the war the cessation of hostilities is a cause of celebration, in African-American history it is a reminder of the duplicity in America's attitude toward black people. When America entered the war in April 1917, African-Americans were encouraged to enlist by government propaganda and by the National Association for the Advancement of Coloured People. But they returned to a country where, with four million men demobbed and spiralling inflation, their presence was even more resented. Black men in military uniform found themselves victims of racial violence and lynch mobs. Although they may have been willing to give their lives for America, and many such as the shell-shocked Shadrack and Sula's uncle, Plum, paid a high price, when they returned they still had to travel in segregated railway cars, as Helene observes on her journey to New Orleans.

There are several interrelated perspectives in the narrative's treatment of Shadrack, each of which serves to focus larger themes of the novel. Not only is he struggling to come to terms with what has happened to him but the community is struggling to come to terms with him. The difficulty that the black members of the community have in accepting Shadrack is indicative of their displacement. As Vashti Lewis (Braxton and McLaughlin, 1990, p. 321) points out, in traditional African culture Shadrack would have been treated with awe and respect. In traditional African ontology, it was believed that the spirit of people who lay unconscious for many days left the body and entered the ancestral world (Braxton and McLaughlin, 1990, p. 316). Shadrack focuses the concern of black people to try to place what has happened and is happening to them into their scheme of things. Shadrack's disorientation is resonant of that of African-Americans in twentieth-century America: 'Twenty-two years old, weak, hot, frightened, not daring to acknowledge the fact that he didn't even know who or what he was ... with no past, no language, no tribe, no source, ...' (p. 12). The way in which Shadrack's tin plate is divided – 'reassured that the white, the red and the brown would stay where they were – would not explode or burst forth from their restricted zones' (p. 8) – epitomises the precarious nature of the white geopolitical structures and the western philosophical system of ordering, dividing and classifying in which whites and African-Americans, together with other peoples of colour, are caught up.

Sula invokes histories of the First World War, including war novels and autobiographies, that celebrate heroism and individualism. The focus of the novel is upon the sense of community, positive and negative, that exists behind and transcends the white boundaries that have tried to define and contain it and through which self-centredness, or what the novel calls 'me-ness', sends shock waves. Although Toni Morrison is interested in notions of community, solidarity and ancestry, and the history within them, her novels frequently enter these subjects through examples of dislocation and disunity before moving towards an affirmation of communal values. The deliberateness of this technique is evident from her essay 'City Limits, Village Values: Concepts of the Neighbourhood in Black Fiction' where she argues:

> While individualism and escape from the community was frequently a major theme in Black writing, it should be regarded for what it was: 'A devotion to self-assertion can be a devotion to discovering distinctive ways of expressing community values, social purpose, mutual regard or ... affirming a collective experience'. (Jaye and Watts, 1981, p. 38)

Morrison's assertion of community over individualism here, which is explored from even more complex and contradictory perspectives in *Tar Baby* and the later novels, displays the African roots of her work. For in indigenous African society an individual acting in isolation or heroically outside of the community is not respected: 'When a character defies a village law or shows contempt for its values, it may be seen as a triumph to white readers, while Blacks may see it as an outrage' (ibid.).

The affirmation of community values, social purpose and mutual regard is evident throughout *Sula*; positively in, for example, the way in which the Suggs help Eva, and negatively, towards the end of the novel, in the way in which Sula dies alone and unloved. Her isolation in the novel is underscored by the way in which her mother and grandmother, Hannah and Eva, are absorbed into the community despite their anomalies. Indeed, as Lewis observes, in the African Babangi language, the possible meanings of the name Sula include to alter from a proper condition to a worse one and to fail in spirit (Braxton and McLaughlin, 1990, p. 316). Sula's failure in spirit is emphasised after her death through the preparation of her body by whites instead of by blacks and through Nel's solitary black presence at the internment though members of the black community appear after the whites have left.

In its focus upon the growth to adulthood of two young black women who have a close relationship, *Sula* radically revisions the *Bildungsroman*, and the white, male perspective from which history and society are traditionally presented in it; even by the standards of other daringly experimental women writers Morrison had herself studied, such as Virginia Woolf. Here, as in the previous novel, the behaviour of individuals within the black community is made complex and problematic by the community's unnatural relationship to an engulfing white society. Nel's 'me-ness' develops only after seeing her mother Helene's experience of being black in the larger white society. In describing these experiences, the narrative focuses on Helene as the main protagonist, but also upon the way the child, Nel, interprets and internalises what happens to her mother and how she responds. Eventually, the narrative voice and Nel's perspective become virtually indistinguishable: 'Like a street pup that wags its tail at the very doorjamb of the butcher shop he has been kicked away from only moments before, Helene smiled. Smiled dazzlingly and coquettishly at the salmon-colored face of the conductor' (p. 21).

The name Wright suggests not only conformity to socially accepted values and codes of behaviour but, if we ignore the 'r' instead of the 'w', conformity to white norms. Her mother was the child of a Creole whore and a white man (she is clearly named after Helen of Troy who was the daughter of Leda and of Zeus who disguised himself as a swan and raped her). But she was brought up by her grandmother to deny 'her mother's wild blood' in an environment that drove her 'imagination underground'. Married to Wiley Wright, Helene lived in a house that resembles the one in the Dick–Jane primer: 'a lovely house with a brick porch and real lace curtains at the window' (p. 18). Helene is proud of how far she has climbed socially; unable to find a Catholic Church in Medallion, she has been brought up under a 'multi-colored Virgin Mary', she worships in the most 'conservative' black church she can find. Other blacks – the uniformed black men Nel sees on the train and the figure of Pretty Johnnie whom Eva classes as all white because he has no blood – act as commentaries on Helene.

To a white reader versed in European literature, Sula Peace and Nel Wright may appear as a pair of binary opposites. Sula, ironically named Peace, is the more rebellious and upsets the black community while Nel marries and settles down within it. However, the narrative resists interpretations based on binary oppositions and in doing so suggests that the Western philosophical tradition founded on binary opposites can act as a straitjacket on thought. As Deborah McDowell points out, the novel frequently 'forces us to question our readings, to hold our judgement in check, and to continually revise it' (McKay, 1988, p. 86).

In creating characters who defy received assumptions about how black women should behave, Morrison confronts and challenges a larger history in African-American and white American fiction: a legacy in which black women are either idealised or portrayed negatively. Elleke Boehmer argues that African literature in the past 'has constituted a nationalist and patriarchal preserve' (Nasta, 1991, p. 9). In other words, women are often seen as the idealised bearers of the nation's children, often sons, while 'men have monopolised the field of nationalist identity and self-image'. As Linda Krumholz observes: 'In *Sula*, Morrison both cherishes and criticizes the character Nel, who (ambiguously) embodies the myth of the black woman as a nurturing, self-sacrificing, infinitely strong burden bearer' (1993, p. 554). Some writers, such as Alice Walker, have tried to develop positive self-images for their black women characters by repossessing matriarchal myths, especially the Africa/ Goddess/Mother mythology, but, as Boehmer points out, there is a difficulty here because these matriarchal myths cannot be easily separated from those that support patriarchal authority. Morrison resists subscribing to such unitary icons and develops more dispersed and multifarious concepts of self. As Boehmer, drawing upon Kristeva, observes, 'writing is "transformative", operating through the displacement of what is already signified, bringing forth the not-yet-imagined and the transgressive' (Nasta, 1991, p. 10).

Boehmer's point helps us to develop Anne Koenen's (1985) argument in relation to Morrison's works themselves that in her black, female-headed households women survive by 'self-inventing'

(cit. McKay, 1988, p. 199). The realisation and articulation of the
not-yet-imagined acquires particular importance for many black
women because their quest for identity, as I suggested earlier, often
begins with a negative definition that they must overcome; a
definition compounded, as is demonstrated in *The Bluest Eye*, by the
way in which black men discharge their frustrations on to black
women. In addition, as Isabel Suàrez observes, discussing the work
of the Black British writer Joan Riley, 'to the absence of an authentic
black and female self, we must add the absence of place, of belonging, the absence of an authentic motherland' (Nasta, 1991, p. 229).
Jacqueline de Weever is critical of Morrison's response to this
dilemma, arguing that in Morrison's novels 'it is not the men who
develop a feeling, feminine side, but the women who develop male
attributes' (1991, p. 31). The exception to de Weever's observation,
of course, is Paul D in *Beloved* whom I will discuss in a later
chapter, but she does identify several shared aspects of the way in
which many of Morrison's female characters – such as Sula, Pilate
in *Song of Solomon*, and Jadine in *Tar Baby* – realise the 'not-yet-
imagined': their sense of owning themselves; the way they work
out their own destinies; and the freedom and sense of adventure
they show in seeking to satisfy their own wants, needs and desires
(de Weever, 1991, p. 32). The extent to which Sula is ready to create
her own notion of selfhood is emphasised by the birth imagery
with which she is associated; by the tadpole, for example, which
Shadrack thinks he observes in her birthmark and by the foetal
position in which she dies.

VII

Sula can also be seen as engaging with, and challenging, a particular history of the subject, based on the liberal humanist concept of
the autonomous, self-sufficient and unified self, of which the
Bildungsroman is a product. Unlike the protagonist of the conventional *Bildungsroman*, Sula defies a stable and unified reading.
Although there are moments, as Valerie Smith points out, when the
text seems to validate Sula's way of life (1987, p. 130), the reader
generally struggles, as another critic, Robert Grant, has noted, 'to
"conceive" of such a character whose candour and awareness are
alternately admirable, alienating, humorous and a little frightening'
(McKay, 1988, p. 98). Sula, like Nel, is described in her youth as

having a 'mercury mood' and is 'skittish, frightened and bold – all at the same time' (p. 56). Deborah McDowell has drawn attention to how *Sula* defies the assumption of a self that is knowable, centred and unified and posits instead a view of the self as multiple, fluid and relational (McKay, 1988, p. 81). This is reinforced in the book by the changing nature of Sula's birthmark: to Nel it is a stemmed rose; to Jude, a copper head and a rattlesnake; to Shadrack, a tadpole. Throughout the novel, Sula is associated with water and fluidity even to the extent that some critics have labelled her a water spirit.

Western thought, as the European literary theorist and philosopher Derrida recognised, is characterised by a tendency to construct a hierarchy of values: for example, reason over imagination; mind over body; work over leisure. In *Sula*, this hierarchy, like the traditional binary opposition of good and evil, is resisted by the nature of the novel itself. In *Sula*, Morrison's frequent avoidance of a judgemental narrative voice in favour of a documentary mode, where judgement is implicit rather than explicit, promotes a view of Medallion as a kaleidoscope of different behaviours and viewpoints that are constantly being negotiated. The initial difficulty with Sula and Nel is their failure, if not refusal, to discriminate from the whirlpool of life around them: 'And they had no priorities. They could be distracted from watching a fight with mean razors by the generous smell of hot tar being poured by roadmen two hundred yards away' (p. 55).

Of course, there are values and hierarchies within the community, but these are fluid, as the description of the community's behaviour at Nel Wright's wedding suggests, where 'the church women who frowned on any bodily expression of joy (except when the hand of god commanded it) tapped their feet' and 'even Helene Wright had mellowed with the cane' (p. 79). The background details of Medallion – the razor fights, the doctoring of the punch at Nel's wedding, the women fighting over Ajax – reinforce the volatility of the community, epitomised in the main events of the narrative, which are themselves partly a product of rapid urbanisation in which clear conventions of behaviour have not been developed. The volatile nature of the major characters and their unpredictability are reinforced by the minor characters such as the Deweys who, described as 'mischievous, cunning, private and completely unhousebroken' (pp. 84–5), mirror Sula and Nel who, as youngsters, are described as 'skittish, frightened and bold – all at the same time' and as 'barefoot looking for mischief' (p. 56). Behind this conflict within the community, however, there is a strong impulse toward harmony and balance of which Sula herself makes us aware through her name, Peace, and through the robins – birds traditionally associated with peace – that accompany her return to Medallion.

What is particularly disturbing about Sula, and also Nel to a lesser extent, is that the negotiation across a kaleidoscope of different, potential behaviours occurs, increasingly, at a solipsistic level which is hinted at, again in a documentary style, early in the book: 'In the safe harbor of each other's company they could only afford to abandon the ways of other people and concentrate on their own perception of things' (p. 55). The blanket under which Nel removes the clothes pin from her nose symbolises the solipsism and secrecy into which she is lured by Sula. The voice of authorial judgement intrudes into the documentary at the point where Sula and Nel are described as having substituted detached observation for the active, albeit at times volatile, participation which sustains the community: 'Joined in mutual admiration they watched each day as though it were a movie arranged for their amusement' (p. 55). Not only does the word 'amusement' here undermine the intensity of the emotional and material struggle of most people's lives in Medallion but it contradicts the way in which the constant references to time, to the seasons and to external events in the narrative make clear that nothing is organised for any one particular individual.

At first Sula's solipsistic unpredictability is exciting as well as worrying; as, for example, when she slices off the tip of her finger as a warning to the white bullies. The gesture is disturbing but not simply because it is a desperate act nor because it implies the threat of castration (as does Sula's later nail file and knives fantasy about Ajax). It is unsettling because it appears to be so calculating. The reader is not told what Sula is thinking; only her actions are described and in such careful detail that we suspect they mirror the slow deliberation of her mind.

In the description of Sula and Nel's Freudian peeling of the twig, the author's apparent silence, and the apparent lack of authorial intervention in the documentary, similarly compounds the disturbing silence of the two girls working together and copying each other. Significantly, Nel's copying of Sula in tracing the intricate patterns suggests that Sula's is the more complex of the two psyches. And in the course of the novel, Sula is clearly revealed as the more disturbing and disturbed of the two. The narrative's ambiguity over, for example, why Sula watched her own mother burn to death – whether it was out of a perverse curiosity or because she was struck motionless and speechless through shock – continues to subvert the attachment of unitary meanings to Sula.

In the account of the response of the two girls at Chicken Little's funeral service, where the ceremony designed to bring the community together can only emphasise Sula and Nel's disjunction, the narrative provides explicit insight into Nel's thoughts – 'although she knew she had "done nothing", she felt convicted and hanged right there in the pew' – but not into Sula's psyche. Indeed, the documentary approach at this point draws attention to its failure to provide the same level of insight in Sula's case as in Nel's: 'Sula simply cried. Soundlessly and with no heaving and gasping for breath, she let the tears roll into her mouth and slide down her chin to dot the front of her dress' (p. 65). The disturbance created by the lack of insight into her mind is compounded by the way in which the tears appear to be detached from Sula herself.

But Sula needs to be seen within the context of African literary traditions as much as European ones. The model of the self from African literature is more fluid than those which have been developed in the Hebraic-Christian West. In the African model, individuals are obliged to negotiate constantly different possibilities of behaviour within themselves and this gives a particular significance to the trickster figure in African and African-American writing to which Sula is connected without necessarily being a trickster in the traditional sense herself. And I want to suggest here that *Sula* can be seen as invoking both the *Bildungsroman* and the trickster narrative.

In the European literary tradition, largely under the influence of the binary opposition within European religion, there is often a clear distinction between good and evil characters. However, in much African literature, good and evil coexist within each individual and are subject to an ongoing process of negotiation. This is characteristic of the trickster figure, which Gates, Jr (1988) observes occurs in many black oral narratives from different parts of the world. The trickster, as Paul Radin (1956) points out, is 'the undifferentiated present within every individual', 'the promise of God and man', and is 'he who was before good and evil, denier, affirmer, destroyer and creator' (1956, pp. 168–9).

The trickster, according to Gates, Jr, is normally male and characterised by 'individuality, satire, parody, irony, magic, indeterminacy, open-endedness, ambiguity, sexuality, chance, uncertainty, disruption and reconciliation, betrayal and loyalty, closure and disclosure, encasement and rupture' (1988, p. 6). Although at times he can be like any other citizen or tribal member, he is essentially an amoral being who flouts the most sacred taboos with impunity. The trickster occurs so widely in black literature that there are many variations, but with commonly recurring characteristics: he is always a wanderer, representative of disruption and disorder, sometimes to the point of anarchy, and usually oversexed. As in Sula's case, his outrageous behaviour finally alienates all his fellows and he is left alone as an outcast from society. Such tricksters abound in folk tales: for example, the Medieval French story of Reynard the Fox or the African-American Brer Rabbit, the linchpin of Morrison's novel *Tar Baby*. But similar characters are also found in classical literature, modern European literature, Victorian literature and American literature from the Spanish *picaro*, such as Lazarillo de Tormes, to Patrick McMurphy of Ken Kesey's *One Flew Over the Cuckoo's Nest*.

The most explicit definition of Sula as a trickster comes from Nel: 'Her old friend had come home. Sula. Who had made her laugh, who made her see old things with new eyes ...' (p. 95). Making someone see things differently is one of the key elements of the trickster, but Sula's role is rooted in a decade of which Nel and the reader are never fully informed. Thus, Nel's view that she is witnessing the return of her old friend ironically raises the question to what extent is Sula the same old friend who left. Nel's assessment of Sula as enabling people to 'see old things with new eyes' is given a sinister interpretation by Jude, who reckons she has 'an odd way looking at things', when the black mark over her eye is significantly likened to a rattlesnake (p. 104).

Sula's return is accompanied, as we observed earlier, by a plague of robins, ironically because traditionally they are birds of harmony and unity. But Eva suggests that this may be more of an omen than a coincidence. In the Bible and in African literature, a plague is a visit of judgement on a people. (In traditional African literature, the plague can often only be lifted by a sacrifice on the part of the community itself; after Sula's death Shadrack leads the people in the last National Suicide Day celebration and many of them are killed in the accident at the tunnel.) From the moment of her return, as Eva points out, Sula proves disruptive: 'You ain't been in this house ten seconds and already you started something' (p. 92). Her statement of intention – 'I don't want to make somebody else. I want to make myself' (p. 92) – may seem reasonable given the negative definitions from which black women have to start. But it also expresses an individuality which challenges traditional African regard for community values, hence Eva's immediate angry response. This negative interpretation of Sula's desire to invent herself is reinforced by the way in which Sula turns her buttocks toward Eva, both physically and verbally: 'And I'll split this town in two and everything in it ...' (p. 93).

Paul Radin points out that the trickster figure is 'at one and the same time creator and destroyer ... he possesses no values, moral or social, is at the mercy of his passions and appetites, yet through his actions all values come into being' (1956, p. ix). Sula presents a moral challenge to the community that the community, commensurate with African tradition, must resolve as a community. She destabilises the impulse toward harmony which counters the unpredictability and volatile nature of life in Medallion. Her behaviour on one level may appear to expose the hypocrisy of the community: 'Later, when they saw how she took Jude, then ditched him for others, and heard how he bought a bus ticket to Detroit (where he bought but never mailed birthday cards to his sons), they forgot all about Hannah's easy ways (or their own) and said she was a bitch' (p. 112). But, through the portrayal of Sula, the narrative also exposes a pursuit of individuality similar to the kind which, as with Geraldine in *The Bluest Eye* and Hannah in *Sula*, can lead black people to reject their blackness in favour of assimilation to the norms of the host society.

In part one of the novel, Sula's behaviour, however volatile, is contextualised within the mercurial nature of the community as a whole and of particular individuals. In part two, an older Sula, accomplished and relatively wealthy, is set apart from Medallion. Sula's birthmark which in the beginning of the novel is a stemmed rose, suggesting individual fulfilment and rootedness, eventually becomes ashes, suggesting the potential dissolution not only of herself but of black cultural identity in general: 'She had no center, no speck around which to grow' (p. 119). Ultimately, towards the end of the novel, she is buried by whites. Members of the black community come to the graveyard in a final attempt to deal with her as a community, to integrate her into the community's experience, as the hymn – 'Shall We Gather At The River' – suggests. The question that the hymn poses hangs not only over Sula and her relationship with the community, but over the disrupted community's own prospect of survival.

This is realised in the final chapter of the book which takes the reader forwards, 24 years after Sula's death, to a year just before the one in which the prelude was written for here, unlike in the prelude, the golf course is only a rumour. The chapter begins with an ironic statement – 'Things were so much better in 1965' – which it then deconstructs and undermines. The narrator's voice merges with the observations of Nel in order to lament the passing of community: 'Now there weren't any places left, just separate houses with separate televisions and separate telephones and less and less dropping by' (p. 166). The construction of the language changes as it describes the development; not only is the word 'separate' strategically repeated to stress the new emphasis upon privacy and individuality but the repetition of 'and' gives the impression of a fragmented rather than an integrated space. Two examples of change – the emergence of a new type of prostitute and the tendency to put the old people into residential homes – epitomise not only the loss of community but the extent to which black people are becoming increasingly assimilated into white norms and values. The new prostitutes who operate in diverse economic contexts are 'pale and dull', having lost the 'funkiness' which Morrison, as we saw earlier, identifies with black women; the increasing reliance upon residential homes for the elderly suggests how issues such as old age are no longer seen as 'community' but 'individual' problems. Nel's sorrow at the end of the novel is intense and deep, but there is no community to sing it out as at the funeral of Chicken Little or at the death of Hannah where the women who prepare her body for burial weep for her 'burned hair and wrinkled breasts as though they themselves had been her lovers' (p. 77). Sula's crying for Chicken Little anticipates Nel's weeping for her at the end of the novel for though the tears roll, it is too much an internalised and private a grief 'with no heaving and gasping for breath'.

VIII

There is a further history in African-American fiction that is challenged in *Sula* and that is the history of black, female sexuality. When the second part of the novel provides explicit insight into

Nel's confused and contradictory psyche, the narrative most clearly seems to be presenting a black woman from perspectives which had hitherto not been articulated in African-American writing. Indeed, one of the silences in such literature before 1970 was the sexual experience of black women as perceived by themselves. The reaction of the black men in Medallion to Sula is typical of how black people's sexuality has often been interpreted in literature in terms of male interests and desires. They cannot forgive Sula for having sex with white men even though black men lie with white women. Sula gives expression to her own sexuality in a way in which men have done for generations; she seeks to satisfy herself not others and is willing to have sex without committing herself emotionally to her partners, discarding them as she wishes. This is an aspect of Sula to which Morrison herself has drawn attention in an interview:

> Sula is a masculine character in that sense. She will do the kinds of things normally only men do, that is why she is so strange. She really behaves like a man. She picks up a man, drops a man, the same way a man picks up a woman. And that's her thing. She's masculine in that sense. She's adventuresome, she trusts herself. She's not scared, she really ain't scared. And she is curious and will leave and try anything. (Harper and Stepto, 1979, p. 227)

Sula is subsequently labelled a 'bitch' because her promiscuity threatens the men's prowess and authority. The 'young men fanta-size elaborate torture for her – just to get the saliva back in their mouths when they saw her' (pp. 112–13). Torture, like rape, has nothing to do with sex and everything to do with power, control and domination. To some extent, the narrative's connection of the men's sexuality with their need to be dominant associates black men with those white men who rape black women in their fear of unfettered sexuality.

Significantly, it is when Sula is most promiscuous that she is most obviously labelled as 'other'; her association with the plague of robins is consolidated in community lore and the allegation that she deliberately watched her mother burn to death acquires new credence: 'So they laid broomsticks across their doors at night and sprinkled salt on porch steps' (p. 113). The challenge which she pre-sents is underscored by the different ways in which her birthmark is read by observers; Nel's children see it as a 'scary black thing', which is how Sula herself is increasingly perceived by the community, while Jude sees it as a rattlesnake. The ferocity of their labelling of Sula is an index of their fear of her unfettered sexuality. An increasing tension develops between the community's view of Sula which is alienating and alienated and the narrative's delineation of her sexuality which is increasingly intimate and encompassing. The focus upon her increasing desire to 'assert herself in the act' and the emphasis upon her 'post-coital privateness' give expression to areas of female sexual experience of which her partners are ignorant or to which they are indifferent: 'Whenever she introduced her private thoughts into their rubbings or goings, they hooded their eyes. They taught her nothing but love tricks, shared nothing but worry, gave nothing but money' (p. 121). While it is possible to see the younger black women in Morrison's fiction, such as Sula, Hagar in *Song of Solomon*, Jadine in *Tar Baby*, and Dorcas in *Jazz*, as embracing a possessive and selfish kind of love, it is important to recognise the difficulties that young black women have in negotiating roles imposed by patriarchy and those that they wish to assume for themselves. The relationship between Sula and Ajax acquires significance within this framework. Ajax is not threatened by Sula as other men in the community appear to be. He is attractive to women because he makes them feel important; he listens to them and does not try to patronise or control them. In their lovemaking Sula is able to be, and enjoys being, on top. In the account of the lovemaking between them, the narrative gives expression to the intensity of sexual experience from the woman's point of view and the way in which she tries to control the orgasm so that it is right for her.

Thus, *Sula*, like *The Bluest Eye*, is not usefully approached through perceptions and reading habits derived from the European novel. The titular character in *Sula* is introduced late into the novel and 'killed off' before the end. The novel's centre is literally a blank and there are numerous ellipses and loose ends. In its emphasis on a relationship between two black women, delineated from a woman's perspective, and in the way in which it extends the African-American woman's need to create her own notion of selfhood to her need to have control over her own sexuality, *Sula* breaks new ground. But in both these areas the novel is ambiguous for Sula herself, sharing characteristics with the traditional African trickster, challenges the community and in this point of focalisation causes readers to constantly reinterpret what they read. In particular, there is a kaleidoscopic model of self and behaviour in the novel which confounds attempts to read it in terms of a binary structure or traditional, unified models of self.

3

The 'Romance' Novels:
Song of Solomon (1977) and
Tar Baby (1981)

I

In the Preface to *The House of The Seven Gables* (1851), Nathaniel Hawthorne asserted that 'when a writer calls his work a Romance, it need hardly be observed that he wishes to claim a certain latitude, both as to its fashion and material, which he would not have felt himself entitled to assume had he professed to be writing a Novel'. A definition of romance, therefore, is difficult almost by definition. However, it is clear that for many nineteenth-century American writers the latitude which Hawthorne claimed for romance included working with folklore, myth and ritual; exploring anti-rational structures and levels of meaning; and dramatising the instinctual and the irrational. Quite apart from the Puritan and Calvinistic distrust of mimetic representation in the arts, it was inevitable perhaps that a form of writing which embraced the mythical, the instinctual and the anti-rational would acquire a special place, as Toni Morrison herself has argued, in nineteenth-century American culture. In Morrison's view, romance as 'an exploration of anxiety imported from the shadows of European culture', enabled American writers to confront:

> Americans' fear of being outcast, of failing, of powerlessness; their fear of boundarylessness, of Nature unbridled and crouched for attack; their fear of the absence of so-called civilization; their fear of loneliness, of aggression both external and internal. (*Playing in the Dark*, 1992, p. 37)

As an African-American with a long-standing interest in deconstructing the white frame of reference by which black people have been defined, it is not surprising that in *Song of Solomon* Morrison should appropriate *the* archetype of white American literature: the romance narrative. Or that *Tar Baby* should invoke mythical narratives from Africa and the American South. *Song of Solomon*, which I would like to discuss first, is based around the search of a young black man, Milkman Dead, for his legacy. He has been brought up in a family where his father has shunned his own community whilst striving to become a small businessman respected by white people. His mother has been ostracised by her husband because he believed he had discovered her in a necrophile relationship with her father. Milkman's adolescence and early adulthood are years of irresponsibility and of indifference to the emerging civil rights movement of the time. But his quest for the lost, family gold eventually becomes a search for spiritual values and for the black ancestry in which he had previously shown no interest and which had also been denied by his father. His spiritual mentor in this search and the guardian of the lore he hopes to find is his aunt, Pilate, another member of the family disowned by his father because she is not respectable enough for him.

Song of Solomon is a romance in both the nineteenth-century American sense and, as I shall discuss later, in the European sense. It has features in common with nineteenth-century American romance: it works with myth, folklore and ritual; and it involves anti-rational structures and levels of meaning. But many of the mythical and folklore elements originate in African or African-American ontology. Linda Krumholz has drawn attention, for example, to the influence of two African epics – the Mwindo epic and the Kambili epic on the novel (1993, pp. 563–7). Moreover, it is not concerned with the fears of white America; the fears articulated in the book are those of black America – of the dissolution of 'black' culture and of the erosion of 'black' sensibilities by the pursuit of white American values. Myth, folklore and ritual are seen as the essential means of reclaiming the black cultural heritage in opposition to the white construction of 'blackness'.

White America's construction of 'blackness' is, to a considerable extent, a response to the fears that Morrison herself outlines. As she points out, one of the most important strategies by which white Americans confronted those fears was the transference of 'internal conflicts' to black slaves, 'conveniently bound and violently silenced black bodies':

What rose up out of collective needs to allay internal fears and to rationalize external exploitation was an American Africanism – a fabricated brew of darkness, otherness, alarm, and desire that is uniquely American. (*Playing in the Dark*, p. 38)

The impact of this 'fabricated brew of darkness, otherness, alarm' is well illustrated in one of the most famous white romances of the nineteenth century, *The Adventures of Huckleberry Finn* (1884). Misunderstood quite often as the story of a boy's moral awakening or as a piece of escapist, freedom-of-the-river fantasy, its full complexity has also been missed by those who have seen it as a polemic against slavery or as an indictment of white society. The real subject of the book is European-America's fear of black America and the final part of the novel makes explicit the white fear of losing control. Mrs Hotchkiss's increasingly exaggerated estimate of the number of Negroes involved in freeing Jim is an indicator of this, as is the whites' reaction in wanting to skin every Negro in the place. The warning left on the door of the hut significantly hints at a larger issue than the freeing of one slave: 'Beware. Trouble is Brewing. Keep a sharp lookout'.

In *Song of Solomon*, the way in which white people project such fears onto blacks is evident in Till's murder, a victim of white fears of black sexuality. As I explained in chapter 1, he is alleged to have whistled after a white woman and is accused of sleeping with others. In the novel, the black men who adopt or seek to adopt white, 'middle-class' values do so within a context of entrenched, white power in a society that is frightened of them and that eventually denies them. The novel unfolds against a backdrop of how Not Doctor Street arose as a name for Mains Avenue because the whites refused to sanction the black name of Doctor Street. Moreover, black people tended to refer to Mercy Hospital as Not Mercy Hospital (it was not until 1931 that the first pregnant black woman was allowed to give birth in a ward instead of on the steps) and when a black person, Reba, wins a prize as the half-millionth customer of Sears and Roebuck, it is not publicised (p. 46).

From her reading of nineteenth-century American romance, Morrison argues that the subject 'on the "mind" of the literature of the United States', as texts such as *The Adventures of Huckleberry Finn* demonstrate, was the 'highly problematic construction of the American as a new white man'. Within this context it is ironic, and maybe deliberately so, that in *Song of Solomon* Morrison produces a work that uses American romance conventions to explore the appropriation of white, 'middle-class' American values by African-Americans.

II

Despite its traditional emphasis upon initiation, renunciation, atonement and release through ritual divestment, the experiment with the quest narrative in *Song of Solomon* through Milkman's search for his legacy is determined by its radical content. For example, it is unclear at first that Milkman is the central character. In many respects he is an unlikely hero. For much of the novel, he is uncommitted, unimaginative and draws inaccurate or inappropriate conclusions. But this is a novel that expresses the limitations of holding any one view of anything and suggests that to elevate any one individual to the status of a hero or any one point of view to the level of myth is both reductive and a distortion of 'reality'.

Each voice in the novel appears to provide only its own fragmented version of the truth – the text literally dramatises the gap between telling and what is told. In fact, the way in which the narrative appears to eschew chronological development and linear structure suggests that this fragmentariness is at the heart of the novel's worldview. But through the interplay of different viewpoints, concepts such as community, authority, commitment and individuality, for example, are subjected to scrutiny.

Song of Solomon, like all of Morrison's works, gives priority to ambivalence and discrepancy, eschewing the tendency of Western, Aristotelian philosophical tradition to give credence to single, unified meaning, confident in its modes of ordering and classification. The same story, as Genevieve Fabre argues, is picked up in different places, retold and expanded into further complexity (McKay, 1988, p. 108). For example, Milkman's father, Macon Dead, explains the tension between himself and Milkman's mother, Ruth, to Milkman, alleging that Ruth had an unhealthy fixation for her father and he for her which culminated in Macon finding her in bed with her deceased father, 'naked as a yard dog, kissing him', with his fingers in her mouth (p. 73). But Ruth's own version portrays herself as a lonely person who needed the support of her father: 'It was important for me to be in his presence, among his things, the things he used, had touched. Later it was just important for me to

know that he was in the world' (p. 124). She accuses Macon of
trying to kill Milkman and of killing her father by removing his
medicine. Ruth now appears starved of affection by her father who
was more interested in winning the respect of white people and
acquiring a big house than in loving her as a father should. As a
woman, she is driven to take her dead father as a clandestine lover,
lying at his feet in the cemetery, because her husband has refused
to make love to her in the twenty years they have been married.
Each retelling of a story in the novel, as here, raises new questions
and inevitably generates fresh interpretations.

Song of Solomon is a dialogic novel, a hybrid of multiple motifs
and allusions. Medieval romance motifs are combined, for example,
with biblical references and classical allusions. Black folklore,
realism and the supernatural are woven together and in the Circe
episode realism seems to collapse altogether beneath the weight of
fabulation.

The priority that the novel gives to Milkman's journey should be
placed, then, within the larger, fragmentary nature of the narrative
as a whole. The numerous discourses surrounding his journey have
more importance in the novel than in the traditional romantic
quest, accounting for the fact that it is some way into the novel
before Milkman emerges as the central character. It is not simply a
matter of Milkman's journey dominating the second half of the
novel and the first half of the novel serving to provide a preparation for the hero's quest, as Dorothy Lee (1982) argues. Milkman
emerges as the hero of the narrative at the same time as a hierarchy
of values begins to emerge from the competing discourses of its
first part.

Much of our understanding of Milkman's journey is teleological.
The journey is from the North dominated by urban, white 'middle-
class' values to the black South and it is the latter which reveals the
former fully for what it is. Milkman travels by plane, by bus and
then by foot – emblematic of the way in which he sheds layers of
his former cultural identity. The journey to Circe's home, the house
of the servant who saved Pilate and Macon after their father was
killed and who bears the name of Odysseus' guide to the lower
world, is made difficult as much by his city clothes as by his inepti-
tude. Gradually, he loses his clothes, watch, suitcase and shoes,
symbolising the white cultural values he has absorbed and assimilated at the expense of black values. The loss of the watch is especially significant because Milkman loses the Western concept of

time which is essentially linear as opposed to a traditional African concept of time which is cyclical.

There is an additional element to all of this: the various competing discourses of the first part of the novel are within Milkman himself. His quest resolves the conflicts between North and South, male and female, white and black within his own psyche. In doing so, certain discourses that have been silenced emerge and become dominant in his spiritual-physical makeup.

The white peacock encountered by Milkman and Guitar as they seek to steal Pilate's gold suggests, as Lee (1982) points out, that in order to fly, the black person must reject the imposed white cultural baggage. White peacocks are usually only found in captivity, implying that the white cultural tradition is itself a captivity. Milkman admires the peacock's strut – epitomising how those blacks who imitate whites and assume white cultural values, such as Macon Dead in his Packard car and Ruth's father, acquire a similar kind of social strut. Ironically, Milkman realises that the peacock can fly no better than a chicken. Guitar's response encapsulates the problem:

'Too much tail. All that jewelry weighs it down. Like vanity. Can't nobody fly with all that shit. Wanna fly, you got to give up the shit that weighs you down.' (p. 179)

Hagar learns a similar lesson the hard way in repeating Pecola's mistake in *The Bluest Eye.* She comes to believe that voguish clothing and cosmetics will lift her skyward, but in the rain they literally fall to the streets. Giving up 'the shit that weighs you down', as Guitar puts it, involves considerable personal growth, self-awareness and personal pain. Hagar, like Milkman who was overnourished on breast milk, is a victim of obsessive love; she has not been able to develop sufficient inner strength and resilience. In this respect, the disintegration of her cosmetics in the rain symbolises the fragility of her own personality.

After the hunt in the South, Milkman acquires knowledge of himself, the community and Guitar. The decision to eat the heart of the slain bobcat, as Lee (1982) demonstrates, is redolent of the traditional ritual by which hunters internalised the courage of the prey. The description of the way in which the heart comes from the body 'as easily as yolk slips out of its shell' (p. 282) reminds us of Guitar's point that Milkman is a shell that has to be broken.

This narrative of escape from the Dead household – dead in the spiritual sense as well as in name – is a story of growth reinforced by the interjection of the account of Corinthians, Milkman's sister. In becoming the 'amanuensis' of Michigan's Poet Laureate, Corinthians becomes an ornament within the elegant emptiness of a home where there is no passion. In this respect, Henry Porter's verse, with which he seeks to woo her, is an improvement upon the celebrated poetry. The relationship which Corinthians establishes with him moves from one based on hatred because of the shame she felt, to one in which she becomes a 'grown-up woman'.

III

The ways in which *Song of Solomon* gives more priority to the competing discourses within it than to Milkman's journey as such, which is where Lee (1982) places the emphasis, reflects its African-American concerns. The novel is engaged not only by the conventions of the quest narrative but also by the assumptions embedded in them. The hero of the traditional quest is usually the child of distinguished parents. Milkman's ancestors are distinguished but in non-traditional ways; his own father Macon Dead Jr is a grotesque fairy-tale character whose lust for gold has made him one of the most affluent and most hated black property owners. However, his name underscores the personal, social and spiritual cost of his pursuit of 'white'-defined respectability, even though he sees his accumulation of wealth as an attempt to overcome oppression, prejudice, poverty and the lack of a formal education. It is Guitar who makes explicit the connection between the imposed name, Dead, the appropriation of white values and a more generalised and pervasive white control: 'White men want us dead or quiet – which is the same thing as dead ... . They want us, you know, "universal", human, "no race consciousness"' (p. 222). This is further embodied in the car Macon drives with a winged woman on its bonnet, 'riding backward like flying blind', and the way in which the black community calls the vehicle 'Macon Dead's hearse'. The counterpoint to the figure on the bonnet of the car is the way in which Corinthians spreadeagles herself across Porter's antiquated vehicle; flying to save herself. Significantly, the first trial which Milkman has to undergo in the South in the second half of the novel, a fight in a general store in Shalimar, Virginia, is started because the local people are offended by his money and sense of privilege: 'They looked at his skin and saw it was as black as theirs, but they knew he had the heart of the white men who came to pick them up in the trucks when they needed anonymous, faceless laborers' (p. 266). The importance of this motif within the novel is underscored by Macon's ironic naming of his daughter, First Corinthians, since it was in his First Epistle to the Corinthians that St Paul attacked personal pride, vanity and ambition.

In the traditional European quest narrative, the hero takes revenge on his father and achieves rank and honours. Milkman, in a process which begins when he strikes his father, eventually frees himself from his father's obsessive capitalism and discovers that he is a descendant of Solomon Sugarman, a progenitor of 21 children, renowned for his ability to fly – commemorated in a nursery rhyme and the naming of his launching site, Solomon's Leap. Here, the novel does not simply parody the European quest narrative, it draws on the African concept of the mythological hero and betrays the importance that African culture traditionally attaches to the ancestor. In 'Rootedness: the Ancestor as Foundation', Morrison describes ancestors as 'a sort of timeless people whose relationships to the characters are benevolent, instructive, and protective, and they provide a certain kind of wisdom' (Walder, 1990, p. 330). The title *Song of Solomon* suggests the biblical song of ancestral wisdom and from the beginning the novel is presided over by the figure of Milkman's forefather. Indeed, it has the epigraph: 'The fathers may soar / And the children may know their names'. As Ladistas Segy argues:

> The mythological hero who represented special valor because of his exceptional services to the tribe in the legendary past was regarded as a model, the embodiment of the best of human potentiality. As descendants of this hero, the living through identification with him derived a special tribal pride which was the basis for their ethnocentrism. (Segy, 1976, p. 8)

Song of Solomon is framed by the African-American vernacular tradition of the flying African. The song which Pilate sings to accompany Milkman's birth is a variant of this Gullah folk tale of the ancestor who flew back to Africa to escape the trap of slavery and Milkman's leap at the end of the novel aligns him with Solomon.

The importance of this kind of identification with ancestors in African culture is again stressed by Segy:

> He experienced being part of the mythical past. He was able to identify himself with that which was presented to him as permanent and sacred reality. Because of this identification he was able to step out of his ordinary, egocentred daily life. His individual life was depersonalized, elevated. (1976, p. 8)

However, even this concept of 'sacred reality' represented by the ancestor is open in this particular instance to different lines of interpretation. In abandoning Ryna, Solomon is identified with a number of male characters in the book who abandon women, including Jake Solomon, Macon Dead and Milkman himself. Here, as Jacqueline de Weever points out, the text expounds the potentially dangerous routes out of life, away from the need for commitment and stability, implicit in the Greek myths of Icarus and Daedalus and the folk tales of the flying African (1991, pp. 28–9).

But, in invoking the traditional European quest narrative and black folklore, *Song of Solomon* develops a further history in the latter, the significance of 'naming' to African-Americans. The reclamation of true identity has been crucial to black people who in slavery were named by others. As Guitar explains to Milkman: 'Niggers get their names the way they get everything else – the best way they can' (p. 88). Ironically, a drunken Union army officer working for the Freedman's Bureau put the name of Macon's father's birthplace and the fact that his father was dead in the wrong place on the registration form. The fact that Macon, Jr, has inherited this false name highlights the way in which he is a grotesque distortion of his father. His father's real name was Jake, but his son is more like his biblical namesake, crafty and patriarchal. For Jake, property was not mere property, but the symbol of a bond between the land and the community. The man who appears to Macon, Jr, after his father has been killed by the white Butlers reminds him of his father – indeed he might be the father's ghost. In fact, he is the ghostly distortion of Jake which Macon is to become. The old white man hoarding the gold in the cave to which the apparition takes Macon is an adaptation of a stock situation from the traditional quest, gold being hidden in an ogre's cave. Although it cannot be interpreted solely in this light, the borrowed motif draws attention to itself as a parody of the whiteness which Macon is to assume.

Of course, Milkman's own nickname has ignominious origins; it was given to him by Freddie, the Janitor, because his mother breast-fed him for much longer than normal. It serves to exacerbate the tension between Milkman and his father. Although Macon doesn't understand the origins of the name, he recognises that it sounds 'dirty, intimate, and hot', thereby reminding him of his wife's abnormal fixation for her father and the passion which he denies in himself and in his children. His son's name compounds the shame of his own name:

> Surely, he thought, he and his sister had some ancestor, some lithe young man with onyx skin and legs as straight as cane stalks, who had a name that was real. A name given to him at birth with love and seriousness. A name that was not a joke, nor a disguise, nor a brand name. (pp. 17–18)

In the traditional European quest narrative, there is usually an omen, either during or before pregnancy, against a birth which seems as if it will endanger the father in some way. Before he is born, Milkman is compared to a little bird (p. 9) and he is the first child born in Mercy Hospital. His birth, accompanied by Pilate's Song of Sugarman, is also marked by the insurance salesman's leap from the top of the hospital. But once again it is important not to see the circumstances of Milkman's birth only as an appropriation of a European literary convention. The circumstances around Milkman's birth serve to emphasise key myths. The myth of the flying African is appropriated as is the notion of the sacredness of ancestors. Singing is an essential part of the Gospel church and Pilate's 'powerful contralto' also suggests that the events that are occurring are in some way sacred. Indeed, her song proves to be a significant clue in Milkman's identification of his forefather.

IV

In the European romance narrative, the main geographical element is provided by the lands through which the hero travels on his quest. However, *Song of Solomon* presents us with an ideological geography, as it were. There are three overlapping zones in which people live and which have been created by the white political system. As Guitar tries to explain to Milkman:

'No Geography? Okay, no geography. What about some history in your tea? Or some sociopolitico – No. That's still geography. Goddam, Milk, I do believe my whole life's geography.' (p. 114)

The three zones as portrayed in the novel reinterpret the geography of the USA in terms of a sociopolitical dialectic: a black centre which is also a disenfranchised community, a zone which is a white-dominated sphere, and an intermediate territory which allows for entry into the white zone but to a limited degree only. Indeed, the sociospace occupied by Macon Dead is the overlap between the white and black zones. It is a no-person's land as exemplified in his walk down Fifteenth Street:

> Scattered here and there, his houses stretched up beyond him like squat ghosts with hooded eyes [...] now they did not seem to belong to him at all – in fact he felt as though the houses were in league with one another to make him feel like the outsider, the propertyless, landless wanderer. (p. 27)

By contrast, Milkman's entry to the community occurs in the black heart of the South, at the fight in the general store, started because Milkman is deemed to have black skin but 'the heart of the white men' (p. 266). But the zones in the novel are fluid, of course; political pressures from within can change them as can individual heroes. This is what Guitar, through violence, purports to do even though he operates in the tradition of the trickster and other ambivalent, archetypal figures who, by challenging the hero, push him toward his destination.

The legacy that Macon hopes his son will inherit is the one built by power and property in order to move the sociopolitical boundaries so that the family will one day become integrated with white society. In Europe, social status has been traditionally assessed in terms of land which, passed on through generations, signified power and elitism. White America's puritan heritage gave the nation a sense of election through predestination, an ethic which confirmed the importance of the individual in building the nation's economic prosperity. In America, property and money translated as success through work became an index of a person's spiritual and moral value. In the nation's ideology, wealth was not associated with greed or exploitation but with the exploitation of inner personal resources. Material poverty became an indicator not of a social problem but of individual spiritual poverty. The effect of this ideology on Macon Dead is evident in the way in which he is ashamed of Pilate, fearing that the white men in the bank on whose support he is dependent, and whose respect he seeks, may discover that she is his sister.

We are never told exactly why Robert Smith fails to fly at the beginning of the novel, but we suspect that it is because he is too far removed from his heritage, which is also Macon Dead's failing. For some time, Macon believes that gold will set him free. Milkman repeats this mistake and when he enters the cave to find the gold his father has told him about there is a significant absence of light.

If we overstress the elements of the European romance narrative in this novel, we may overlook the African myths which also determine its structure. Macon Dead, Jr, is a version of a character, Anaanu, from a very old West African folk tale which found its way into America as Brer Rabbit and which is the basis of *Tar Baby* (1981). In one version of the original story, for example, Anaanu is a trickster spider who escapes famine by faking death and at night eats his fill. Macon, like Anaanu, chooses dispossession in order to achieve material gain. Anaanu's pretence of being dead is a form of disguise and Macon, too, in his denial of his sister Pilate and his family adopts a pretence. Both Anaanu and Macon give up their place within the community for personal gain.

Thus, Morrison develops the West African folk tale of Anaanu within a particular American context and within the frame of the Euro-American quest story. The European romantic quest has been readily employed in white American literature to explore ways in which the American dream of spiritual greatness became a dream of material greatness. Whilst this transformation has been treated with considerable bitterness in some white American texts, others that employ the quest motif, such as F. Scott Fitzgerald's *The Great Gatsby*, stop short of condemning the desire for wealth even though they expose the corrupting influence of it in particular examples. Gatsby himself epitomises the American ideal of the self-made man and the capacity in America for people to make their own identities. In becoming Jay Gatsby, James Gatz escapes from his own origins and his naïve quest is linked to Arthurian legendary heroes such as Sir Galahad and Sir Percival and the quest for the Holy Grail. The grail which is Gatsby's quest is a romantic notion of perfect femininity – eventually exposed as false – based on the outward appearance of a corrupt and degenerate system. Gatsby's creation of himself and his quest are compared in the novel to frontier versions of the concept of the self-made man – as a boy, Gatsby made notes on self-improvement on a flyleaf of a copy of *Hopalong Cassidy* and his career begins when he meets Dan Cody, a relic of an earlier America – in order to demonstrate the corruption of the original dream.

In *Song of Solomon*, Morrison combines a number of mythologies so that each acts as a critique of the others. Up to a point, Macon Dead epitomises the white American concept of the self-made man, but, unlike Gatsby, he did not choose his own name. Unlike Gatsby, Macon Dead, Jr, comes to experience a rejecting society and the past which is corrupted in his quest is not a white heritage. In *The Great Gatsby*, the dream can only be achieved by overturning any larger sense of moral responsibility for others. In Morrison's novel, although Macon Dead, too, can only realise his quest by eschewing any moral responsibility for others, he also rejects his black cultural heritage:

> Macon Dead dug in his pocket for his keys, and curled his fingers around them, letting their bunchy solidity calm him. They were the keys to all the doors of his houses (only four true houses; the rest were really shacks), and he fondled them from time to time as he walked down Not Doctor Street to his office. At least he thought of it as his office, had even painted the word OFFICE on the door. But the plate-glass window contradicted him. In peeling gold letters arranged in a semicircle, his business establishment was declared to be Sonny's Shop .... (p. 17)

The fact that his office is situated on Not Doctor Street compounds the irony in this passage because the name is a symbol of black resistance. The name of the previous black occupant of the premises reminds Macon, and the reader, of a history that he can never finally eradicate. The previous name suggests that the shop was at the centre of the community whereas Macon's use of the premises as an office for his property business implies a more overt pursuit of individual wealth and success at the expense of community.

The tension between Macon and Ruth's aspirations for their son is part of a larger discourse within *Song of Solomon* around internal difference in the black community. Macon has little regard for university education and Ruth's aspirations for her son to enter university focus on the status which the medical degree will bring her as well as him, epitomised in the silver-backed brushes engraved with his initials, the abbreviated designation of doctor. The coincidence here again suggests how Milkman, like many black people, is not in control of his own destiny and this is bound up in the fact that he has been unable to choose his own name. The novel suggests on many levels that whereas black people become part of the American 'middle-class' they do not have the same licence as Gatsby, for example, to create their own identities, the ideology on which the American 'middle-class' pursuit of prosperity is founded. Thrown into confusion concerning his identity, Milkman's examination of his face before the mirror, his firm jawline and splendid teeth, remind us significantly of the way in which slaves were examined in the market place and of a history with which black people still have to struggle (p. 69).

V

Milkman's true inheritance, black cultural identity and ancestry, is provided by the women and particularly his aunt, Pilate. Although the epigraph mentions only the male forefathers in the novel and the book is dedicated to 'Daddy', Morrison creates a space in which the women may be recognised and may assume importance. In many respects, the women are outside the soulless, material-oriented, patriarchal world in which the men – Macon Dead and Dr Foster – are locked. Pilate – 'Christ killing Pilate' – has the worst possible name, as Genevieve Fabre points out (McKay, 1988, p. 109). Yet she understands the power of naming; the only name her father wrote hangs in a little box from her ear. She becomes quite literally Milkman's pilot or guiding force. She challenges his indifference and initiates him into the legacy of which black womankind are the guardians, a legacy of traditional wisdom and beliefs. Pilate's lack of a navel associates her with Eve, source of innocence and, paradoxically, of primal knowledge.

Pilate's perfect, soft-boiled eggs symbolise a balance of which Macon and herself seem separated spheres. Whilst Macon appears to follow and exaggerate the side of Jake which wants to own property and which values the status so accrued, Pilate embodies the spiritual and community-oriented part of him. Pilate's own home contrasts significantly with Macon's. Ruth and her daughter make fake roses and the only confirmation Ruth can find of her existence is the ugly spreading watermark left on the dining room table from a bowl which once held fresh flowers. When Lena eventually wakes to what is happening to her, the outburst recalls Guitar's condemnation of how white people want black people quiet and 'dead': 'I was the one who started making artificial roses. ... I loved to do it. It kept me ... quiet. That's why they make those people in the asylum weave baskets and make rag rugs. It keeps them quiet. If they didn't have the baskets they might find out what's really wrong and ... do something. Something terrible' (p. 213). Her hesitation before she can bring herself to say the word 'quiet' underscores its significance for her, and for her whole family, as well as the pain in the realisation. The phrase 'something terrible' is set apart and as such highlights the fear whites have of blacks who rise against their confinement. In the description of the suicidal leap at the outset of the novel, roses occur along with wings and song as specific images, each of which eventually provides this multilayered text with a sense of coherence around the subjects of freedom, spirituality, life-in-death, the value of myth and the role of the ancestor: 'The sight of Mr. Smith and his wide blue wings transfixed them for a few seconds, as did the woman's singing and the roses strewn about ...' (p. 6).

Pilate's house is filled with the smells of nature with which she is associated, of the forest and of blackberries. Of course, her association with nature is another indicator of how she has taken after the positive side of Jake's character, reminding us of the love he had for his peach trees and his ability to make his crops increase and multiply. When Lena turns her anger against Milkman for the way he has ignored them, she draws attention to the dying maple tree (p. 212). Significantly, Morrison herself has pointed out that none of Gatsby's people achieves a fulfilling life in the natural environment, suggesting the importance that she attaches to this aspect of characters such as Pilate (Jaye and Watts, 1981, p. 36).

However, *Song of Solomon* is a complicated novel, not easily reducible to binary opposites. Pilate is a character of whom we can also be critical. Her rootlessness is symbolised by the rocks that she carries, each one signifying somewhere she has been and, like the name she carries in a box and her bag of bones, they symbolise her search for a place of belonging. Some critics have emphasised not her symbolic strengths but her general passivity, and indeed the passivity of most of the female characters, and have seen this as confirming the male bias in the epigraph to the novel.

Nevertheless, it would be wrong to see Pilate, as some critics have, as a totally negative character for such an interpretation would ignore the way in which women like her are the guardians of worthwhile knowledge which the men have yet to acquire. As Nancy Walker (1986) has pointed out, the white romance in America usually embodied a dream of escape that is both peculiarly American and identifiably masculine. Historically, the political and physical experiences of settling and exploring a wilderness have required powers that have commonly been granted to men rather than women. However, in this respect, *Song of Solomon* casts women in a better light than the men: Macon Dead, Ruth's father and Milkman himself are selfish, uncaring people. Macon Dead is ruthless with delinquent tenants, wants to 'own' people and worships wealth. Ruth's father is seen as a 'miracle doctor' by whites, but, obsessed with caste, he does little for African-Americans. Milkman deserts Hagar and most of the men violate family bonds. It is some of the women in the novel who have, or stand a bettter chance of acquiring, the qualities and values necessary for establishing a true sense of community, with respect for the land

VI

At the heart of the reclamation of a non-Western worldview in *Song of Solomon* is a concern with a preconscious mode of awareness encapsulated in myth. Of course, myth may be perceived in mythologising cultures as a means of preserving the wisdom of precedents based on ancestral laws – precedents that often connect ancestral pasts with cosmogonic events. The title of the novel itself reminds us of Solomon's song of ancestral wisdom. But myth may also be preserved as the poetic verbalisation of the unconscious and preconscious. In fact, *Song of Solomon* offers a complex model of the unconscious which is close to the one that Ladistas Segy (1976) claims is characteristic of mythologising cultures. Pilate and Macon would seem to represent the separating out of the two spheres of the unconscious that Segy identifies. Pilate's own sensibility and creative existence give expression to an inner truth derived from her grasp of a supreme reality beyond her everyday existence, a sense of the wholeness of the order of things. She appears motivated by what Segy would call her 'ontological natural self', a psychological self as it exists before the conditioning of the environment. But Macon and Milkman are motivated by a consciousness that has been shaped by the circumstances of their lives and of those of their immediate ancestors. The 'pre-reflective awareness' that Pilate appears to possess has been occluded in them by their assumption of 'white' values, demonstrated by Milkman's repeated failure even to ask the right questions. In the book, reclaiming the black legacy involves reclaiming a mythological and pre-reflective awareness – and all this might appear to a sceptical reader as simply romantic.

Distrust of logical thought and empirical rationalism emerged in America in the 1950s and 1960s, of course, as part of a counter-establishment culture which led many white American writers to experiment with hallucinogenic drugs and philosophies in search of alternatives to Euro-American models of conceptualising the world. Yet this recurring preoccupation among certain American writers of the 1950s and 1960s was underpinned by perceived differences between Western and non-Western worldviews summarised by Segy:

> It is possible to trace present-day Western civilization to Socratic, Platonic, and Aristotelian concepts predicated upon man's intellect, his logical thought processes, which evolved into a pragmatic, scientific, materialistic outlook. The African cultures followed another path similar to the spiritual teachings of the Hebrew prophets, Buddha, Lao Tzu, or Jesus, and produced another way of life based upon man's spiritual needs, a socio-religious, well-ordered, communal (and not individualistic) integrated way of life. (Segy, 1976, p. 17)

Song of Solomon is different in its concern with states of consciousness from the eclecticism of white American literature of the 1950s and 1960s which fused early nineteenth-century European romantic thought with non-Western philosophy. Morrison's novel is concerned with reclaiming and not simply discovering the priorities of a culture founded upon different philosophical and spiritual principles from those of the West. As Gay Wilentz argues, the African values privileged in the novel are exemplified by Pilate who illustrates the role of the African female ancestor in transmitting familial and cultural knowledge; she makes the potion, for example, to improve Macon and Ruth's sex life (1992, p. 86). Indeed, Milkman's acceptance of myth and the supernatural stems from his acceptance that Pilate is without a navel, and it is this openness, though it takes him 20 years to act on it, which separates him, as Wilentz says, from his father.

Song of Solomon has a moral self-confidence that is not to be found in many contemporary white American novels. Christopher Bigsby has gone so far as to see the post-Second World War black writer as the exponent of a liberalism that the modern, white American novel had rejected. This moral self-confidence derives from the belief that there are available truths concealed beneath illusion and falsehood and, as Bigsby claims, this is surely a liberal presumption. But Bigsby fails to locate the source of the narrative's assertion that there are truths to be realised in the reclamation of the priorities of a non-Western culture. His thesis seems to shoehorn the novel into a white liberal tradition to which it simply does not belong:

> And, in terms of black writing, self-perception frequently comes to the protagonist in a visit to the underworld, in a mock death, a dive down into the underground of self and society alike … (Bigsby, 1980, p. 162)

What Bigsby says here is clearly applicable to *Song of Solomon*, but he does not recognise the romance formula in his own survey of black fiction and, more seriously, how the black novel subverts the romance genre. Bigsby discusses the black protagonist in terms of alienation and estrangement that are more appropriate to protagonists in novels by white writers who feel cast adrift on the irrepressible new:

> This is perhaps why so many black novels are set in that past which is part tangible and part mythic; a usable past which can be turned to the purpose of locating a self which had been cut adrift in an American environment it could not define and whose direction it could not deflect. It is a past, too, which must be set against that projected by white historians […] For the black writer, as for the Jew, the past is to be claimed, the implications of an alienated self to be denied, a tradition of moral responsibility to be accepted. (Bigsby, 1980, p. 157)

Despite the good points which are made here, Bigsby's use of 'claim' rather than 'reclaim' is significant. For there is insufficient recognition that we are dealing with more than just a past. The novel is concerned with the mythologising nature of black as opposed to white culture and of the differences between black and white concepts of moral responsibility.

Nevertheless, Bigsby is right to assert that there is something refreshing about the moral strength of African-American fiction after the emphasis of the non-liberal white novel upon 'cosmic conspiracies, fragmented layers of experience whose coherences are contingent, a self which is either a distorting mirror or a transparent membrane offering a pathway to ultimate nirvana ...' (Bigsby, 1980, p. 154). Certainly, *Song of Solomon* does not present the nihilistic vision of many postmodern works that behind every construction of so-called truth lies only another construction. Nor does it abandon the notion that individual projects are worthwhile for the individual and the community simply because all human projects are constructed and inevitably limited, although it does submit them to scrutiny. Macon Dead's project, for example, is obviously very limited. So, too, in a different way is Guitar's involvement with the Seven Days. Guitar, like Milkman, wants Pilate's gold. But, like Milkman before he realises his true legacy, Guitar's project courts death even though the name ironically echoes creation in the Book of Genesis. Arguing for a programme of indiscriminate retaliatory murder of whites in revenge for the murder of blacks, Guitar can love black people in the aggregate, but he cannot love individuals nor give sufficient weight to individual responsibility. Bent on revenge in the name of love, he is divided against himself rather like his father, sawn in two parts at the sawmill.

The concept of individual moral responsibility in this novel is not the same as that to be found in white American liberal novels. The moral vision underpinning the narrative fuses recognition of the black cultural legacy and the reclamation of its priorities including a community-oriented sense of responsibility with a reclamation of a mythological cultural framework. In order to fly, Milkman has to recognise the importance of his cultural legacy and acquire a commitment towards the wider black community. In the early part of the novel, Milkman tries to avoid commitment. Indeed, his name suggests infancy and the egocentricity of a young child from which Milkman has to develop. Overnourished by his mother's milk, he fails to grow until the interjection of Lena's accusation that he has victimised others with his egotism. Within this context, Pilate's explanation as to why she has kept the bag of bones with her makes Milkman ashamed that he has betrayed his mentor who presided over the 'miracle' of his birth. His relationship with Sweet in the South is an indicator of his growth; he is able to enter a reciprocal relationship which culminates in a joyous swim in a spring, symbolising baptism and rebirth.

The black cultural heart of the South is a counterpoint to the North. The superiority of the men in the South is indicated, as Dorothy Lee (1982) has explained, by their names, the names of poets, kings and men of God: Omar, King Walker, Luther, Solomon, Calvin Breakstone. They possess a 'pre-reflection awareness' of the kind embodied by Pilate. Milkman observes incredulously that the men and their hunting dogs speak to each other in:

> ... what was there before language [... .] And if they could talk to animals, and the animals could talk to them, what didn't they know about human beings? Or the earth itself, for that matter. (p. 278)

The importance of belief over fact (the world of science) is evidenced in the sack of bones that Pilate carries. In the end, it does not matter whether the bones are of her husband (as she tells the police) or of a murdered white man (as she believes) or of her father (as Milkman informs her). The bones are a symbol of an obligation to a past event and to a relationship.

Although it appropriates the characteristics of the European romance formula, *Song of Solomon* is a novel that cannot be seen only in those terms. It is a dialogic novel in which the same incident or character is seen from different viewpoints and in which competing discourses are highlighted. Although concepts such as community, commitment, authority and individuality are thereby subjected to scrutiny, a hierarchy of favoured positions emerges in the course of the text which have their origins in African-American culture. Overemphasising how the novel appears to provide an ironic version of the European quest might lead the reader to underestimate how its experiment with the romantic quest form is determined by black concerns, African myth and aspects of an African ontology.

VII

Tar Baby is concerned with the relationship that develops between Jadine, a light-skinned African-American woman raised in the Caribbean by her aunt, Ondine, and her husband, who are the black servants of a retired white factory owner, Valerian Street, and Son, a dark-skinned fugitive on the run for murdering his wife. Brought up and educated at the University of the Sorbonne on the money of her aunt's employer, Jadine's life revolves around New York and Paris where she has become an art historian and a model. Ostensibly, we might think that Jadine is the tar baby of the title. However, the novel is more complex than this and the label seems applicable to different characters at different points in the narrative.

Like Morrison's first novel, *The Bluest Eye*, *Tar Baby* is concerned with what Eleanor Traylor calls 'the carcinogenic disease eating away at the ancestral spirit of the race' (McKay, 1988, p. 146). It, too, focuses upon African-Americans who shun their black identities in favour of the values and norms of white America, for example, Sydney and Ondine and their niece, Jadine. Both servants, as Doreatha Mbalia observes, obviously 'identify more with their employers and their employers' culture than they do with their own people and their own culture' (1991, p. 71), evidenced in the way in which they allow Valerian's wife, Margaret, to call them Kingfish and Beuleh rather than by their real names, and in the way in which Ondine refers to Margaret's kitchen as her own. But there is a larger history to be unfurled here, a history constructed in many Southern romances to which I will return in chapter 5. The origins of their position lie in the Old South which encouraged an alliance between the white upper classes and the slave elite who still sought respect from the white man on the white man's terms long after the American Civil War had ended.

The novel, like *The Bluest Eye*, is as much concerned with the ideological nature of language as with the way in which individual African-Americans have been seduced by white values. This is evident when Sydney proclaims his origins as 'one of those industrious Philadelphian Negroes' to Son, the black fugitive who has entered Valerian's home: 'I am a Phil-a-delphia Negro mentioned in the book of the very same name. My people owned drugstores and taught school while yours were still cutting their faces open so as to be able to tell one of you from the other' (p. 164). Sydney's reiteration of European contempt for African culture, compared with the way in which the woman-in-yellow in the novel proudly bears two upside-down V's scored into each of her cheeks, is an attempt to accord himself more status. It calls into question the meanings attached to the word 'civilised' which is not actually used by Sydney but implied throughout. 'Civilisation' is a concept which cannot be evoked without qualification, especially when differing European and African perspectives are called into play. In fact, Sydney here exploits the potential of language to carry a multiplicity of meanings, both explicit and implicit, from his self-conscious pronunciation of the word 'Phil-a-delphia' to the superiority he attaches to written culture through his pointed emphasis on the word 'book', and his contemptuous reduction of body adornment to cutting the face open. Throughout *Tar Baby*, possession of European prejudices about blacks is an important indicator of the extent to which individuals have lost contact with their roots. Jadine's reflection on the way Son unsettles her is riddled with stereotypical assumptions. She has become so removed from black people that she has come to believe that they are either 'creeps' or possessed of rare sexual energy and dynamism (p. 126).

The narrative structure of *The Bluest Eye*, as we have seen, is focused around the disparity between the different meanings which American English carries for African-Americans compared with white 'middle-class' Americans. The novel explores the extent to which African-Americans are not only caught up in an alien ideology but an alienating language. Henry Louis Gates, Jr (1994) argues that this is a central fact for the black person in America. In order to illustrate the point, he cites the story of Edmund Laforest, a prominent member of the Haitian literary movement, who committed suicide by jumping from a bridge with a Larousse dictionary tied around his neck. Since the ability to use language has traditionally been the litmus test of civilisation, African-Americans have had to establish themselves within European post-Enlightenment civilisation through the language of their oppressors even while drawing on an African ontology or an African mythopeaia. In *Tar Baby*, these twin complexities are further explored within a tripartite focus, connecting meaning, race and difference.

Although *Tar Baby* covers a much shorter period of time than the previous novels – it is set exclusively from autumn 1979 to autumn 1980 – it incorporates a wide range of perspectives through its use of myths, historical allusions and reference to concepts whose meanings have undergone change in different periods and different cultural contexts. In this respect, it utilises a characteristic of language which the early twentieth-century Russian critic Mikhail Bakhtin made the focus of much of his work: that language is not a unified, fixed or stable system, but, as a social and historical process, is always in a state of flux. The initial description of

Valerian's lifestyle indicates the novel's interest in this theme for he reads only the mail, having given up books because 'the language in them had changed so much – stained with rivulets of disorder and meaninglessness' (p. 12). One of the central concerns of *Tar Baby* is the way in which meaning itself is very difficult to pin down, being plural and contested rather than singular and uncontested. Indeed, when Valerian tells his niece to read *The Little Prince*, he emphasises 'pay attention not to what it says, but what it means' (p. 71).

The exact meaning of language is elusive for many reasons, another of which is also fundamental to *Tar Baby*. Meaning, subject to what the French theorist Jacques Derrida identifies as 'the "active", moving discord of different forces', is endlessly deferred because it is always relational, never self-present or self-constituted (1982, p. 18). This phenomenon Derrida labelled *differance*, a word which conflates the senses of difference and deferment. For example, if we consider the word 'family' which recurs in the first novel, we see it has come to represent, or signify, a particular type of group of people related to each other in some way. In the dictionary, the word is said to have a range of possible meanings such as: members of a household; the descendants of a common ancestor; a group of persons or nations united by political or religious ties; a group of allied genera; or a subdivision of an order. These associations are arbitrary; there is nothing in the word, for example, which suggests a household of related people living together. We have learned to associate 'family' and 'household of related people' through custom and convention. But the word is also part of a larger system of language; the signifier 'family' communicates the concept of 'family', or signified of 'family', because it is different from other signifiers such as 'commune'. Thus meaning arises from the interplay of an infinite number of signifiers and as much from what a signifier is *not* as what it is. For this reason, Gideon, one of the black servants, has difficulty explaining the words 'blood bank' and 'eye bank' to his wife, Thérèse. The word 'bank' confuses the issue for her, suggesting that American doctors take organs in order to sell them to rich people. Thérèse is unable to understand the relational nature of language and, indeed, the focus of much of *Tar Baby* is on the ways in which meanings are endlessly deferred, rather like Margaret's son in the novel, always promising to turn up but never finally arriving. Derrida identified what he called 'switch points' in language, linguistic levers which ensure words, again like Margaret's son, never reach their final destinations because they are intercepted, detoured and relayed (1987, p. 78). It is appropriate that a novel by a black writer, especially a black woman writer, should concern itself with the way in which meaning arises from an interplay of signifiers and is endlessly deferred. Homi Bhabha points out that stereotype is not simply a misrepresentation of reality. The colonial subject is denied 'access to the recognition of difference' and to that 'possibility of difference and circulation which would liberate the signifier of *skin/culture* from the fixations of racial typology' (Bhabha, 1994, p. 75). In other words, the skin colour, hair and ultimately race of African-Americans become 'ineradicable signs' of negative difference, unable to break free of this fixity.

VIII

One of the sets of meanings which appear to be endlessly deferred, demonstrating how meaning never stays the same from one context to another, are those clustered around the concept of the tar baby story itself. Craig Werner observes: 'Assuming new meanings as its context shifts ... each new version of the myth influences the con-sciousness of the individuals who, even though they accept the myths that they inherit, gradually assign them new meanings as signs that can be transformed into further myths' (McKay, 1988, pp. 154–5). But before pursuing the implications of how the mean-ings of the tar baby myth have been altered by the various chains of signifiers in which it has become entangled, there is another ques-tion we should ask: why should Morrison draw on myth? Myth is a metaphor for human experience, a means of communicating that experience and of ascertaining its meaning. Jacqueline de Weever sees the reclamation of myth by African-American writers as part of a 'return to myth' among twentieth-century writers generally, especially women writers:

The experiences of black people in the New World, into which they have been forcibly thrust against their will, cannot be told or treated in realistic or naturalistic traditions in which American literature has been cast – the pain of the results of three centuries of oppression is too great to be faced and confronted in a realistic mode. (1991, p. 4)

A particular characteristic of the mythic narrative, then, is that it 'establishes lines to a world that is not only beyond the real world but that, at the same time, transforms it' (ibid., p. 4). *Tar Baby* uses a traditional African myth to project the reader beyond the conventional parameters of the contemporary in order to throw the complexities and tensions of the present into relief. In doing so, the novel inverts and deconstructs a number of prior texts including the West African myth of Anaanu, the trickster spider, to which I referred in the discussion of *Song of Solomon*, and the American vernacular tale of Brer Rabbit. As a fable, the tar baby story is supposed to reveal values, but one of the ironies of the novel is that the values which are unveiled are much more complex than those underpinning the original oral narratives. As a result, *Tar Baby* leads the reader not to a moral resolution, but to more complicated moral dilemmas.

The tar baby myth, originating in Africa as part of a cycle of trickster tales, reappeared in nineteenth-century America, initially as an African-American response to slavery, when it was included by Joel Chandler Harris in his Uncle Remus plantation tales. Despite the different versions of the tale to be found in Africa and nineteenth-century America, the plot elements have changed very little. In the Uncle Remus version, Brer Fox sets the tar baby in the road to catch Brer Rabbit while he watches from the cover of the bushes. Brer Rabbit accuses the tar baby of being 'stuck up' and is determined to 'larn you howter talk ter' specttubble folkes'. Angered by the tar baby's silence, the rabbit strikes him and becomes stuck in the tar. In the version which Son tells, the tar baby is placed in the road by white farmers to entrap Brer Rabbit whom they believe is eating their cabbages. On finding the tar baby, Brer Rabbit is again offended by its apparent arrogance in not responding to his greeting; in the course of their encounter, the rabbit becomes entangled in the tar and completely immobilised. In this version, he is able to escape by manipulating the white farmers' cruelty, convincing them that he dreads being thrown into the briar patch from where he knows he will be able to escape. They cannot resist throwing him in because of their vindictiveness, encapsulating the cruelty of whites generally towards others and specifically towards African-Americans, of which the hostility aroused by the civil rights marches and protests of the 1960s was a reminder, if any were needed.

However, although the basic plot elements have remained more or less the same, as the tale has evolved with each new version in a different context, the tar baby story has acquired fresh meanings. As part of the African trickster cycle, the story is the tale of a scarecrow made out of sticky, gluey rubber to catch the trickster spider, Anaanu, which I associated earlier with Macon Dead in *Song of Solomon*. The scarecrow is constructed by Anaanu's family who are tired of seeing their yams disappear, and it is the apparent haughtiness of the figure which, as in the Brer Rabbit version, arouses Anaanu to anger and results in him becoming entangled with it. As one of the black oral tales of the plantations, Brer Rabbit encapsulates the wit and guile with which black slaves have been able to outwit and survive the cruelty of their white masters. In *Tar Baby*, this strategy is employed by the black servant Gideon. Sydney, adopting the role of the superior black, presumes that Gideon, whom he calls by the name 'Yardman' rather than by his own name, is illiterate. Gideon for his part doesn't contradict him to avoid the extra work that would be given him if Sydney and Ondine knew that he could read. As a character in one of Harris's Uncle Remus tales, however, Brer Rabbit is drained of his guile. The story itself becomes only an example of how white culture identified Negroes with animals, a perspective which helped slave owners reconcile their inhuman treatment of black people with their Christian and democratic principles. Uncle Remus himself, a docile old slave who always wore a benign grin, became the white American stereotype of the acquiescent, faithful Negro slave.

IX

In *Tar Baby*, the various layers of meaning within the original African myth are reclaimed and adapted within a new cluster of significances for America, especially black America, in the late twentieth century. Brer Rabbit clearly re-enters the fable as the trickster figure, this time in the person of Son who, at the beginning of the novel, turns the household of Valerian Street upside down. Yet the text's concern with the way in which meanings are endlessly deferred ensures that Son is never quite reducible to Brer Rabbit even though the last paragraph of the novel makes the identification of the two explicit.

The enigmatic nature of Son is evident from the first and last episodes which frame the narrative. In the prologue to the novel, Son's plunge into the sea suggests not only death by drowning but also rebirth – he is 'yanked' into a wide, empty tunnel and finds himself 'whirling in a vortex'. At the end of the book, he emerges from the sea onto land in a sequence that mirrors the evolution of life; crawling, standing and eventually walking upright. In each episode, Son has a female guide. In the sea in the prologue he is kept afloat by the water spirit, 'like the hand of an insistent woman'. Suspending struggle, he gives in to the current, 'the water-lady cupped him in the palm of her hand', and is guided to the boat, *Sea Bird 11*. As de Weever argues, the water spirit pushes Son into the adventure and by doing so shows her concern for the island and its inhabitants (1991, p. 37). In other words, a supernatural female force enables Son to be born again out of the ocean to transform the lives of two women on the island about whom the ocean goddess would appear to be concerned. At the end of *Tar Baby*, Thérèse offers Son advice on negotiating the rocks and also warns him to keep away from Jadine because 'she has forgotten her ancient properties' (p. 308). Thus, she dissociates Jadine from the women who 'knew their true and ancient properties', to whom the novel is dedicated, whilst associating herself with them. When Thérèse cuts the engine of the boat so that it moves with the tide, we are reminded of how Son had been supported in the prologue by the water spirit. The implication that he has been singled out in some way is reinforced by the lifting mists which suggest the trees on the island are stepping back 'as if to make the way easier for a certain kind of man' (p. 309).

The episode where Margaret Street reports Son to Valerian and Jadine sustains the mystery surrounding him because she is unable to find the right words to describe him; those she does use are misinterpreted or not understood at all. Like the trickster figures, of whom Brer Rabbit is one example, Son has lived on the edges of society. As Melissa Walker observes, the novel 'focuses on individuals who have cut their ties with community, family, and the past' (1991, p. 189). Son is not only a veteran of Vietnam but also a fugitive who, having murdered his wife and her teenage lover, has been on the run for eight years. Changing his name several times, like the trickster figure, Son has assumed different identities among different peoples – William Green, Herbert Robinson, Louis Stover – and, in keeping with the trickster tradition, the reader never learns his true name. The fact that Son is a fugitive introduces another layer of complexity for he has to transform his own life and the lives of others as well. Like the other characters whose equilibrium, as the trickster figure, he disturbs, he has to learn that he cannot run away from his past. He is also more than a trickster figure in that he is, as Mbalia (1991) argues, 'a disciple for African people, a modern-day revolutionary', but one who has to learn that such powerful influences have permeated the African-American psyche that dreams of returning to a traditional African identity in an increasingly capitalist world are naïvely idealistic.

However, Son is also the skeleton in the Streets' closet, literally and metaphorically, for he emerges from a wardrobe in their house. Black, bearded with 'chain-gang hair', he represents the African-American past which Valerian, as a white American capitalist, forgets, with which the black servants Sydney and Ondine have lost contact, and which Jadine eschews. At one level, he quite literally brings a family secret out in the open, the way in which Valerian's wife abused their son, Michael, when he was a small child by burning him with cigarettes. At another level, he brings the larger skeleton of the slave-past out of the closet for both Valerian and white America in general. In reporting Son's presence in the house to the others, the first thing Margaret says is that he is black. Valerian's candy factory uses sugar and cocoa, products of the Caribbean and of the slave system, a fact which Valerian and his black servant, Sydney, choose not to remember. In fact, Valerian epitomises how so many members of the household retreat from the unpleasant facts of the Negro past. His name associates him with a plant whose flowers are used medicinally as a sedative. As Mbalia says of him, he 'is asleep throughout most of his adult life, unconscious or unconcerned by the exploitive manner in which he has accumulated his wealth, ignorant of the physical and psychological abuse of his child by his own wife, unsympathetic to the feelings of his servants, and most important for Morrison and her audience, insensitive to the plight of African people' (Mbalia, 1991, p. 70). Confronted with the image of the woman-in-yellow who spits at her, Jadine, who always averts her eyes from the ugly part of the island, takes a further leaf out of Valerian's book and literally buries her head under the pillow.

X

The complexity of the novel derives from the way in which Jadine and Son are attracted to each other at the same time as each is repelled by the other. They each undergo a process of transformation, initiated by the other; Son's appearance, for example, becomes increasingly European, he sports a borrowed white man's suit, cuts his hair and files his fingernails. The ambiguity in the novel is such that, as in the case of Son, Jadine is difficult to define as a signifier. If Son is ostensibly Brer Rabbit, then, in some respects, Jadine may be seen as a latter-day version of the tar baby itself. As the niece of Valerian's black servants, Sydney and Ondine, she has been educated with Valerian's financial support and is now a Europeanised African, an art history graduate of the Sorbonne in Paris, an expert on Cloisonné, and a cover model for *Elle*. The text develops in Jadine the haughtiness which is misunderstood in the original scarecrow and tar baby stories and which led to Anaanu and Brer Rabbit becoming entrapped. For Mbalia, Jadine 'represents that which is inhuman, built by the European as a trap for other Africans, an artificial lure to tempt them to a Europeanized lifestyle' (1991, p. 75).

But, in the course of the novel, Jadine's association with tar assumes an increasingly wider significance. On revisiting the swamp after her return to the island from New York, her legs burn 'with the memory of tar'. This memory may not only be of a specific incident in her life but a folk memory of how tar was used to mask injuries to the skin of slaves at auction. Yet throughout, Jadine's association with tar is ironic for she is lighter-skinned than this would suggest, significantly called 'Copper Venus'. Ondine's pride that Jadine has replaced a white model on the cover of *Elle* is especially ironic because she doesn't appreciate that Jadine has achieved this as a Europeanised version of black beauty; an irony compounded by the way Ondine stirs milk into the chocolate paste as she gloats over Jadine's triumph. Moreover, at some points in the novel, Jadine appears to be a latter-day Brer Rabbit. Her experience of becoming trapped in the swamp in a substance which 'looks like pitch' is redolent of the experience of Brer Rabbit, for example, as is the way in which she becomes entangled with Son's image in her bedroom mirror: 'She struggled to pull herself away from his image in the mirror and to yank her tongue from the roof of her mouth' (p. 113).

Despite the perceptive points they make, critics such as Mbalia have tended to read the novel as a whole in terms of an oversimplified binary structure. Indeed, one of Jadine's own faults, especially in the first half of the novel, is to see the world as consisting only of binary opposites. Mbalia, for example, maintains: 'What Morrison does in *Tar Baby* is raise the question all Africans must ask themselves: Do I identify with my oppressor or my people?' (1991, p. 68). This leads to some oversimplified interpretations:

> In fact, Jadine has so absorbed the capitalist values of making money and acquiring status that she is ignorant of the traditional African principles that have ensured the survival of African people despite their dehumanized conditions. Unequipped with a sense of humanism, collectivism, and egalitarianism to inform and guide her, she allows her aunt and uncle to wait on her, plays daughter to them instead of being daughter to them, and abandons them to the caprices of Valerian, not knowing what their fate might be. (Mbalia, 1991, p. 75)

Such readings ignore the way in which the novel's concern with the endless deferment of meaning extends to issues of identity. In the novel, identity is both externally multiple and internally fractured. As Derrida argued, all words/signs contain traces of the ones which have preceded them; every sign in a chain of meaning carries these traces in inexhaustible complexity. This is an idea that the novel pursues in relation to identity on a number of different levels. When Son, for example, gets into bed with Jadine in New York, his hands, 'large enough, maybe, to put your whole self into', also carry traces of the occasion when he held and kissed her bare foot, leaving fingerprints in its arch. When Jadine first encounters Son, she has difficulty determining what his hair signifies:

> Here, alone in her bedroom where there were no shadows, only glimmering unrelieved sunlight, his hair looked overpowering – physically overpowering, like bundles of long whips or lashes that could grab her and beat her to jelly. And would. Wild, aggressive, vicious hair that needed to be put in jail. Uncivilised, reform-school hair. Mau Mau, Attica, chain-gang hair. (p. 113)

Similarly, the significance of the woman-in-yellow who spits contemptuously at Jadine eludes her attempts to define it. She almost becomes Jadine's tar baby – she has 'skin like tar against the canary yellow dress' – as Jadine becomes obsessed not so much with the woman as with her own inability 'to fix the feeling that had troubled her' (p. 45).

Despite the parallel concerns with *The Bluest Eye*, *Tar Baby* further complicates and defers the definition of African-American. Son makes the mistake of trying to define African-American identity in terms of an imposed traditional Africanism without recognising that, at one level, it offers little opportunity for growth and intellectual development, especially for black women. Traditional Africa is symbolised for Son by Eloe, but despite its positive qualities – collectivism and egalitarianism – it is a poor, underdeveloped and largely illiterate community. Although New York may be something of a packaged reality, yet another example of a second-hand existence in the novel, as Jadine observes: 'if ever there was a black woman's town, New York was it' (p. 223). Son's estrangement from the blacks of New York is as much an indication of how far removed his ideas of black people are from theirs as it is a comment on the quality of their existence. In fact, the description of New York on Son's arrival, emphasising the fact that all the black girls seem to be crying, all the black men seem to have dumped their blackness and that everyone walks looking straight ahead, casts Son in the mythical role of country mouse. Driven by such a singular perspective, it is less convincing than the account of Jadine's return to the city, enabling her legs to feel longer and her head to feel once more connected to her body. The space which is given in the novel to the cosmopolitan, eclectic nature of New York and Paris is a reminder that traditional boundaries of identity such as place, race, gender and class have become fractured by the flow of people, cultures, information and ideas across geographical frontiers. Eloe is emblematic of the ideal of wholeness, the ideal of the unified personality. But, as de Weever points out, such an ideal is not possible, and especially not for black women (1991, p. 173). In particular, young black women, the postmodern generation, often find themselves establishing identity within the fragmented personality they discover themselves inhabiting; for them life has to be 'lived between the cracks'.

XI

The ambiguous position in which *Tar Baby* leaves Son and Jadine defers the kind of traditional closure that we might expect a novel to reach. Son is running into the rain forest where, according to one version of the myth, naked, blind men – slaves who escaped when the ship carrying them to the island foundered on the rocks – supposedly race horses over the hills, whilst Jadine is left literally in mid-air on an aeroplane to Paris. The book appears to reclaim the open-ended conclusion of the Uncle Remus, Brer Rabbit and Brer Fox version of the tar baby tale. There we are not told the fate of Brer Rabbit; the story ends with him stuck to the tar and Brer Fox rolling on the ground with laughter, threatening to eat him. In response to the young boy to whom he told the story, Remus says inconclusively that 'some say Jedge B'ar come' long en loosed 'im – some say he didn't'. The unresolved nature of the novel's ending might encourage readers to review the narrative, creating their own scenarios of what is going to happen to Son and Jadine, either individually or together. A teleological conclusion to a novel normally makes sense to the reader when the parts that lead up to it are re-examined in hindsight. But the conclusion of this novel possibly serves only to make the reader more aware of how much in the text is deferred, for, as one critic, Craig Werner, has argued, 'the style and texture of *Tar Baby* emphasize multiplicity' (McKay, 1988, p. 156). Whilst Valerian interprets the island as a bastion of European culture, a stay against chaos, Son thinks only of its oppressive racial history, anticipating the concern in *Beloved*, the next novel, with reclaiming repressed and unvoiced narratives.

Parallels within the novel invite the reader to compare similar episodes, but such comparisons often only serve to compound ambiguity and ambivalence of meaning. The swamp-women whom Jadine thinks she sees while pulling herself from the green, tar-like slime have difficulty, like Margaret and Jadine on first seeing Son, interpreting what they are witnessing. At first they mistake Jadine for a runaway child who has been returned to them, but then it appears she might be struggling to escape them. In fact, the swamp-women themselves offer the reader a similar level of difficulty. And they are echoed in the night-women who visit Jadine in a waking dream in Eloe and who include Son's dead mother, Ondine, Thérèse, and Jadine's own mother. They appear to represent traditional black womanhood, if not motherhood, which Jadine denies and from which she is running away. Indeed, there is much evidence to support this interpretation. The fact that Jadine, as the daughter of Sydney's dead sister, is orphaned appears to serve as a symbol of her disconnectedness from her ancestral mothers and it is this discontinuity that some critics believe the woman-in-yellow who spits at Jadine observes in her. Here

Morrison appears to draw upon the African belief that ancestors take an active interest in the welfare of their living descendants, a concept to which I will return in the discussion of *Beloved* in chapter 4. The night-women seem to want to remind Jadine of her moral obligations.

One of the distinctions between Jadine and the woman-in-yellow, who is also one of the night-women, is the difference between their bodies. Jadine has a slim, model's frame but she observes that the woman-in-yellow has 'too much hip, too much bust' (p. 42). Indeed, all the night-women symbolically reveal their child-nurturing breasts to Jadine, whilst the woman-in-yellow offers her three eggs, further emblems of fertility and motherhood. Their action recalls Son's jaundiced suspicions that 'her breast tip [sic] were tiny brass knobs like those ornately carved fixtures screwed into the drawers of Jadine's writing table' (p. 197). Jadine's rejection of the night-women does betray her fear of them: '... they seemed somehow in agreement with each other about her, and were all out to get her, tie her, bind her. Grab the person she had worked hard to become and choke it off with their soft loose tits' (p. 264).

Nevertheless, an interpretation which focuses on Jadine's denial of her black womanhood is here complicated by the fact that Jadine wants for herself roles other than those that black women have traditionally held. Critics, such as Mbalia, have observed Jadine's arrogant failure to acknowledge what black women have achieved even within these (Mbalia, 1991, p. 81). But her reaction to the night-women has to be placed in the context of her full experience of Eloe. Jadine's desire to achieve different roles for herself is reinforced by her recognition that Eloe offers few challenges or opportunities for fulfilment, intellectual or sexual, for black women:

Eloe was rotten and more boring than ever. A burnt-out place. There was no life there. Maybe a past but definitely no future and finally there was no interest. All that Southern small-town country romanticism was a lie, a joke, kept secret by people who could not function elsewhere. (p. 262)

Her frustrations over the place jar with Son's enthusiasm which is emphasised in the repetition of the line: 'Yet he insisted on Eloe'. Ironically, despite Son's association with the female insect that fertilises plants – he pinches Valerian's cyclamen so that it blossoms – he is a woman killer. Werner explains how:

Holding to the folk myth of the white world as a tar baby, Son creates a complementary myth of Eloe as briar patch [...] His myth of safety in the briar patch evades the risk of his relationship with Jadine. By embracing a myth that dehistoricizes Jadine's complex history as a black woman, he increases the possibility of suffering the loss he most fears. (McKay, 1988, p. 164)

It is too simple to conclude, as Mbalia does, that Jadine is a negative character because she has embraced capitalism, as the following quotation from the novel makes clear:

Jadine kissed his hands and he asked her why she left the States in the first place. She said she always thought she had three choices: marry a dope king or a doctor, model, or teach art at Jackson High. In Europe she thought there might be a fourth choice. They told each other everything. Yet he insisted on Eloe. (p. 226)

The text avoids reducing the Jadine/Son and the Jadine/night-women relationships to a singular narrative constructed around pairs of binary opposites in the same way that it confounds any singular interpretation of the swamp-women. As Eleanor Traylor points out:

These women, by allusion, figure the warrior women, the market women, the calabash-carrying women, the queen women, the life-bearing, culture-bearing women of their ancient origins. (McKay, 1988, p. 149)

XII

Despite her obvious faults, Jadine, like Sula, is an independently minded and sexually liberated woman whom the novel, in places, invites us to admire as we are asked at times to favour Sula. Mbalia's criticism that Jadine insults the Eloens by sleeping naked within view of them is rather simplistic (1991, p. 81). Apart from the fact that she finds the heat of her room stifling, Jadine is accustomed to sleeping naked, an index of her liberated sexuality. The night-women make her feel obscene in her nakedness, denying her the liberation she has achieved in Paris and New York, whilst

Soldier expects her to be submissive and accepting of his sexism. His insensitive description of Son's wife as having had 'the best pussy in Florida', the way in which he naturally presumes to ask if Jadine has children, and his assumption that in the relationship between Jadine and Son one of them must be in control reflects the narrow-mindedness of Eloe. Soldier is both disturbed and attracted by Jadine's spirit and independence – 'You a hot one, ain't you' – and the text significantly explores the nature of her sexual independence in her relationship with Son before she arrives in Eloe to encounter the censorship of the night-women:

> Jadine was so ruttish by the time she got to the Hilton, she could barely stand still for the doorman to take her bags, and when she was checked in, and had gotten his room number from information, she did not call him – she took the elevator to his floor and banged on the door. When he opened it, she jumped on him with her legs around his waist crashing him into the purple carpet. (p. 224)

The passage conflates Jadine's assertiveness and her sexual confidence. Like Sula, she is prepared to take the initiative and seeks sexual satisfaction for herself in relationships in contrast to women who suppress their own needs and desires in order to satisfy their men.

If the text suggests that Son's view of Eloe is not to be trusted then Son's view of Jadine must also be open to question, as later in his dream of their life together, and in his view of New York. When Jadine balks because she thinks that Son is about to rape her, he accuses her of embracing the white stereotype of the African: 'Rape? Why you little white girls always think somebody's trying to rape you?' (p. 121). Mbalia sees this as evidence of how Jadine thinks like a European (1991, p. 72). However, Son responds not so much to what she says as to her assertiveness. When she protests at being called white, his response – 'Then why don't you settle down and stop acting like it' – ignores the content and focuses on her behaviour. Jadine is not simply responding to an accusation by a black man that she has betrayed her race, she is reacting to a black man who appears to deny her the right to think for herself. She threatens to kill him for 'pulling that black-woman-white-woman shit' on her and for thinking he can 'get away' with telling her 'what a black woman is or ought to be' (p. 121). Son is incensed by

Jadine not only because she is Europeanised but because she has not accepted the traditional role of a black woman, accusing her of getting where she has purely on the basis of sexual favours. Confessing to Jadine the details of how he killed his wife, Son enjoys her fear and is said to 'bask' in it like 'a cat in steam-pipe heat' (p. 178). He feels both protective and violent towards her; both, in different ways, behaviours that have as much to do with power in relationships as desire. In New York, while waiting to meet again with Jadine, the dreams which Son has of their life together are very traditional. Apparently forgetting her education and career plans, and that he is a fugitive, Son thinks of himself earning the money to keep them while Jadine has their baby. He thinks of the child, significantly, as his son whom he contemplates naming after himself.

Of course, there are criticisms to be made of Jadine as there are of Sula, and the novel also demonstrates her weaknesses. She is hard, as her name suggests, and self-indulgent, seeking only to live in the present, eschewing her obligations to others, and turning her back on her ancestral line. Her commitment to her own individual fulfilment rather than to a sense of solidarity with other black people is evident in the interpretation of the mythic horseriders on the island that she favours; that rather than a hundred ex-slaves there is only one French soldier on a horse. Her surname, Childs, indicates that Jadine is, in different ways, as immature as Son, who is accused by Jadine of thinking 'like a kid' and whose name emphasises that he has failed to wean himself away from Eloe. It is because of these failings that Son and Rosa in Eloe are able to make her feel ashamed, as if what repulses her is inside herself and not in them. But even this is presented in the novel with considerable ambiguity. The account of Rosa's observation of Jadine's nakedness conveys not so much disgust and embarrassment, as Mbalia argues, but interest in Jadine's body itself. The passage takes almost as long to read as Rosa's eyes take to pass down Jadine, recalling how Valerian let his eyes 'travel cautiously' down the full length of Son's body on first seeing him, and thus casting the reader in the role of voyeur:

> Rosa gazed down Jadine's body with a small bowing of her head, and then up again. Her eyes travelled slowly, moving like one of those growing plants Jadine could not see, but whose presence was cracking loud. (p. 254)

The complexity of the relationship between Son and Jadine and the apparent contradictions in their characters were initially under-emphasised by critics. As Elliott Butler-Evans has noted, critics of Morrison's novels, not specifically *Tar Baby*, have tended to inter-pret 'the works as nonproblematic bodies of fiction' and have in-ferred 'univocal meaning' (1989, p. 60). With the exception of Barbara Christian (1985), Butler-Evans argues, they have often focused on the symbolic constructions of a black community, whilst ignoring how the desires of black women are seldom realised there (1989, p. 61). The tensions in Morrison's novels between feminine desires and community needs are often, as in *Tar Baby*, left not so much unnegotiated as in the process of negotiation. Jadine has to resolve for herself the significance of the night-women; she cannot simply reject them. Unable to give up the ambitions that drive her to realise herself, to define herself on her own terms rather than ac-cording to traditional black concepts of womanhood, Jadine comes to see the night-women as reminders of the black female ancestry to which she can turn for support without necessarily re-enacting. As Werner argues, Jadine 'will not simply create a new second-order myth repressing the reality of her past experience' (MacKay, 1988, p. 165). The last sight that we have of her reinforces the impression that she is finding it difficult to retain her single-mindedness. The repetition of the line – 'There is no time for dreaming' – and the self-sacrifice of the soldier ants undermine Jadine's solipsism, indi-cating that she may yet negotiate the conflicting discourses to which she is subject in order to find fulfilment in all aspects of her life. The conclusion of the section suggests this may be the case: 'Still it would be hard. So very hard to forget the man who fucked like a star' (p. 294). Jadine resolves to confront the 'funkiness' that she has denied, together with dreams and notions of death.

The novel not only avoids but challenges the cliché whereby a single-minded woman of independent means capitulates, tamed by a man whose values are made out in the end to be morally superior to hers, and whom it is revealed in hindsight she wanted all along, despite the conflicts, to bring her under his control. That cliché is the product of a particular history of patriarchal-determined, het-erosexual relationships. Although Son sets out to find Jadine, his attitude to Eloe has been changed by her. Significantly, in trying to reclaim for himself what he once found in the women there, he looks at photographs of the night-women of Eloe taken, and there-fore mediated, by Jadine:

Gazing at the photos one by one trying to find in them what it was that used to comfort him so, used to reside with him, in him like royalty in his veins [...] It all looked miserable in the photographs, sad, poor and even poor-spirited. (pp. 296–7)

Although not in any conclusive or simple way, both Jadine and Son have been propelled into a process of some kind of transformation; appropriately, for islands, as de Weever reminds us, are 'places of transformation' in Western culture and they have 'acquired an almost numinous quality' (1991, p. 45). The inconclusiveness of these respective transformations, concomitant with the reclamation of open-ended mythic narratives, highlights the complex process by which black people, especially black women, have to negotiate the competing discourses that determine individual and social behaviour. In *Tar Baby*, the classic concept of the individual with a solid, coherent identity is eschewed for a model of identity that sees the individual as a kaleidoscope of heterogeneous impulses and desires, constructed from multiple forms of interaction with the world as a play of difference that cannot be completely comprehended. While the same may be said of white, postmodern fiction, the way in which individual identity is perceived in *Tar Baby* is not merely the result of literary influence but the product also of the lived experience of African-Americans at the interface of two or more cultures.

4

The Middle Passage:
Beloved (1987)

I

Set initially in 1873, *Beloved*, like Morrison's earlier works, moves from the present to the past, particularly the period 1850–5, and back again. As in her first novel, single events are revisited from different viewpoints in a narrative which employs both first- and third-person perspectives. However, these characteristic techniques of Morrison's work acquire a special edge in this novel which explores how authoritative discourses – for example, historical, biblical, cultural, and political accounts – stifle alternative interpretations, thus serving to silence other voices. *Beloved* can be seen as located at the point of intersection of a range of 'texts' whose importance in American literary history has been played down, ignored or occluded.

Any novel is a transposition of material from different sources – both literary and non-literary. Whilst the French theorist Roland Barthes overstates the case in suggesting that authors can only combine existing texts, he astutely observes how 'bits of codes, formulae, rhythmic models, fragments of social languages, etc. pass into the text and are redistributed within it' (Barthes, 1981, p. 39). His concept of a given text as a point of intersection for a range of different discourses is particularly appropriate to *Beloved* which the reader may feel is the most fragmentary of Morrison's novels. This chapter explores the nature of this fragmentation and its importance to the experience which *Beloved* offers the reader.

In some respects, *Beloved* draws upon the Black Aesthetic discourse of the 1960s in which, as Elliott Butler-Evans points out, narratives as oppositional or alternative texts posited self-reconstruction and redefinition through deconstructing Western assumptions about blackness (1989, p. 26). Unearthing historical perspectives that have been hidden by or buried within other dominant narratives is integral to the structure of *Beloved* in which there are two interrelated levels of occlusion: the distortion of black experience in both white and black historical discourses and the suppressed subconscious. The latter is pursued in the novel at the level of the individual, most obviously Sethe, but also at the level of white America's need to confront what it has done to black people and to itself.

As Henry Louis Gates, Jr, reminds us, 'accused of lacking a formal and collective history, blacks published individual histories which, taken together, were intended to narrate, in segments, the larger yet fragmented history of blacks in Africa, now dispersed throughout a cold New World' (1992, p. 62). By employing this method in *Beloved*, Morrison thought of herself as writing in response to a significant absence. In an interview with Paul Gilroy, she argues: 'Slavery wasn't in the literature at all. Part of that, I think, is, because, on moving from bondage into freedom which has been our goal, we got away from slavery and also from the slaves, there's a difference. We have to re-inhabit those people' (Gilroy, 1993, p. 179).

Beloved invokes black novels written in the 1850s – the decade to which Morrison reaches back in the book – that sought to depict experiences not normally represented by the conventional, fugitive slave narrative. In presenting the protagonist's divided allegiances and internal conflicts, works such as *Narrative of the Life and Adventures of Henry Bibb, an American Slave* (1849), created more complex psychological subjects than the generic slave autobiography. But as a novel of trauma and psychological conflict, *Beloved* is also indebted to another type of narrative closely associated with slavery in nineteenth-century America. At one level, *Beloved* is a romance between Sethe and Paul D, two ex-slaves reunited in post-Civil War America. But, at another level, it is a ghost story. The reunion between Sethe and Paul D is made difficult by the relationships of each of them to Sethe's children, one of whom is a ghost incarnate of the child murdered by Sethe. Both of them are haunted by their pasts and, in different ways and to varying extents, are dehumanised by what they have done or what has been done to them. But the haunting is only one of many for, as Baby Suggs pithily observes, 'Not a house in the country ain't packed to its rafters with some dead Negro's grief' (p. 5).

Since under slavery, as Peter Nicholls has pointed out, the subject is split by a traumatic historicity, 'compelling it to live in different times rather than in a secure, metaphysical present' (1996, p. 58), *Beloved* lends itself to psychoanalytic criticism. One of the most interesting of such readings is provided by Jennifer FitzGerald who, drawing on the psychoanalytic theories of Melanie Klein, argues that Beloved's ambivalent feelings and overdependence on Sethe reflect the major elements of a young child's relationship to the mother identified by Klein: love, hatred, fantasies, anxieties and defences. But FitzGerald also criticises classic psychoanalysis for having isolated psychic experience from the diversities of ethnicity and class. As I have argued elsewhere, her essay takes us beyond the idea of split identity in the self to the way in which *Beloved* dramatises a larger, more powerful sense of schism in the black community as a whole created by the impact upon its needs and desires of a particular historical context (Peach, 1998, pp. 16–18).

It is important to recognise that Morrison does not simply adapt the ghost story in *Beloved*, but engages with the black history underpinning the plantation version of it. As Gladys-Marie Fry has pointed out, ghost stories have a particular significance in African-American slave history. They were employed by whites in the South to limit the movement of slaves, as a less brutal, and often more effective alternative, to physical violence and the patteroller system. The stories that described haunted places, the return of the dead by night and attacks on slaves by supernatural beings, exploited, as Fry argues, the slaves' worst fears. In turn, they were reinforced by activities on the part of the plantation owners that were later adopted by the Ku Klux Klan, donning white sheets in order to pretend to be ghosts and spreading rumours about ghostly happenings. However, the history in the ghost story, often embellished by black folklorists, to which *Beloved* is most obviously indebted is the dependence upon traditional African belief in the spirit world among Africans forcibly transplanted to American soil. In African ontology, through recognition of the importance of ancestors and through ancestor worship, the living and the dead are intimately connected and the ancestors themselves believed to be involved in the affairs of the living.

Beloved also invokes the work of African-American women writers at the end of the nineteenth century, for example, Frances Harper's *Iola Leroy; or Shadows Uplifted* (1892), Anna Julia Cooper's *Voices from the South; By a Black Woman of the South* (1892) and Pauline Hopkins's *Contending Forces: A Romance Illustrative of Negro*

Life North and South (1900). The closing decades of the nineteenth century were intense periods of activity and production for black women, as Hazel Carby (1985) has pointed out. But what has often gone unnoticed is the extent to which their work foreshadows many of the preoccupations of the late twentieth-century, black woman writer, including Toni Morrison in writing *Beloved*. In these works, the founding fathers are very often reassessed in terms of unrestrained patriarchal power; imperialism is envisaged as based on greed and lust; the black body is seen as colonised by white power; and black women are perceived as having been placed by white laws outside the protection of the ideology of womanhood.

II

Of all Morrison's novels, *Beloved* most obviously illustrates Joanne Braxton's assertion that female slave narratives planted the seed of contemporary Black feminist and 'womanist' writing early in the Black literary tradition (Braxton and McLaughlin, 1990, p. 302). But, as I argued in chapter 1, in developing narrative strategies and techniques of the slave narrative in writing *Beloved*, Morrison engages with and develops the history in the slave narrative itself, a history in which occlusion and silence are important dimensions.

It is well documented now that the novel is based on the story of Margaret Garner, a slave who killed her child and attempted to kill herself rather than return to slavery, but what has received less attention is the extent to which the novel is based on a particular version of it. *Beloved* is, in fact, a response not only to the history in slave narratives generally, but the history in Reverend P. S. Bassett's 'A Visit to the Slave Mother Who Killed Her Child', published in the *American Baptist*, 12 February 1856, subsequently included by Morrison herself in *The Black Book* (1974) which she edited while working at Random House. As I indicated in chapter 1, *The Black Book* is a collection of memorabilia representing 300 years of black history, and its scrapbook format, eschewing any kind of linear historiography, is pertinent to *Beloved*, for in both texts Morrison is concerned to take history out of its dominant narratives and get closer to the raw, source material.

The article is not simply an account of what Margaret Garner did, although it begins with the basic details of what happened, but a record of Reverend Bassett's meeting with her. Several features of the account are adapted and used in *Beloved* apart from what Margaret Garner is actually said to have done. His portrait of Margaret Garner seems to have inspired the characterisation of Sethe: she is about 25 years of age, and possesses 'all the passionate tenderness of a mother's love', 'an average amount of kindness', together with 'a vigorous intellect, and much energy of character'. His observation that Margaret Garner's mother-in-law had been a professor of religion for about twenty years was undoubtedly the inspiration behind Baby Suggs, herself the spiritual centre of *Beloved*. The separation of Sethe and Paul D appears to have been inspired by Margaret Garner's mother-in-law's story, as reported by Reverend Bassett, of how her husband was once separated from her for 25 years, during which time she did not see him and did not want him to return to witness her sufferings. But it is the history in Reverend Bassett's account which has most evidently influenced *Beloved*.

The source of the novel's version of how mothers were separated from their children under slavery was probably the mother-in-law's story of how she was the mother of eight children, most of whom had been separated from her. The delineation of the physical violence inflicted on black women slaves in *Beloved* is clearly indebted to Reverend Bassett's report of how Margaret Garner spoke to him 'of her days of suffering, of her nights of unmitigated toil' and of how Margaret Garner's mother-in-law told him that she had been a loyal slave and had never thought to escape until, as she got older and became 'less capable of performing labor, her master became more and more exacting and brutal in his treatment [of her]'. However, a further history that Morrison develops from Reverend Bassett's meeting with Margaret Garner is not in the details that he reports but his reaction to them. Indeed, his response is as important as the story itself for it reflects a history based on misunderstanding and ignorance in how women were treated under slavery. It also betrays traditional, white assumptions about benevolent plantations. Reverend Bassett is shocked by Margaret Garner's story, and by what her mother-in-law tells him. This is not surprising, perhaps, because it was only with the rise of a new militancy in the 1830s that the slave narrative broke out of the pacifist, traditionally Protestant mode in which slaves saw themselves as black versions of Bunyan's Christian. Bassett, it would appear, had always believed that Kentucky slave plantations were more benign than others, a view shared by Mr Garner in *Beloved* when Baby Suggs's son, Halle, eventually manages to buy his mother from slavery. But as Baby Suggs points out, slavery is slavery no matter how the slaves are treated. Moreover, his incredulity at what Margaret Garner has done is based on the way those ignorant of the kind of conditions Margaret Garner had to endure tend to view such crimes. He is insistent upon knowing whether Margaret Garner acted out of 'madness' – whether 'she was not excited almost to madness when she committed the act'. His language here – 'committed the act' – is evasive, avoiding the horrific details of what happened. He is disturbed to find that Margaret Garner's killing of her child was a rational act, that she was as cool then as she was in talking to him. *Beloved* takes up where Reverend Bassett's disbelief leaves off, challenging a particular view of slave history which holds those like Margaret Garner responsible for what they did and not the circumstances in which they found themselves.

The main events of *Beloved* constitute Sethe's slave past which the reader has to construct piecemeal and which Sethe herself tries to avoid: 'As for the rest, she worked hard to remember as close to nothing as was safe' (p. 6). The backbone of the novel is an occluded text buried within the surface narrative which has to be recovered in order to make sense of the whole, as Sethe has to reclaim it also to understand the main events of her life. These events include the death of her mother; her marriage to Halle; a whipping which almost kills her; her escape and refuge in the home of her mother-in-law; her recapture and the infanticide of her child; her period of imprisonment; the subsequent years in 124; her sons – Howard and Buglar – being driven away from there by the ghost of Beloved, the child she killed; and her years in an all-female household where the third member is a ghost-daughter.

When Paul D, a fellow slave, turns up after 18 years and drives out the spirit ghost of Beloved, she returns as a young woman intent on separating Sethe and Paul D in order to claim her mother for herself. But she is more than Sethe's daughter-incarnate; she is also Sethe's personal past and the past of slavery which Sethe has to reclaim. In the second part of the novel, there are three acts of identification – Sethe claims Beloved as her daughter-incarnate, Denver claims Beloved as her sister and Beloved claims Sethe as her mother – emblematic of America's need to identify and confront the narratives of black history; the novel is, after all, dedicated to 'sixty million and more'.

Beloved begins with Sethe remembering some of the above-mentioned events which she would rather forget. But it is clear to the reader, from the very nature of them, that not only can she not forget them but that she needs to remember and confront them. This is obvious in the memory of her dying baby's wound which she herself has inflicted. But there are other suppressed memories, including the way in which she had to have sex with an engraver in order to pay for the word 'Beloved' on the baby's tombstone. The fact that she will not be able to move on until she has come to terms with her past is especially evident from the 'thought pictures' which haunt her of the young men hanging from the trees in the plantation ironically called 'Sweet Home'. Within this context, Paul D's sudden arrival seems predestined: 'As if to punish her further for her terrible memory, sitting on the porch not forty feet away was Paul D, the last of the Sweet Home men' (p. 6). Sethe's account to him of how Baby Suggs died nine years previously sets the tone of much of the novel; '[Her death was] Soft as cream. Being alive was the hard part' (p. 7). Sethe's attempt to come to terms with everything is inevitably painful; she fleetingly remembers words spoken by Amy, the poor white daughter of an unindentured servant who helped her when she escaped from the plantation: 'Anything dead coming back to life hurts' (p. 35). Later in the book, when Amy's nursing of Sethe is described in detail, her words of reassurance appear to be directed at the reader who by this time has read in piecemeal of the horrors of slavery: 'Good for you. More it hurt more better it is. Can't nothing heal without pain, you know. What you wiggling for?' (p. 78). Paul D is as reluctant as Sethe to confront the past. Indeed, in some respects he is more unwilling to do so, believing that he has locked up the past for good in the tobacco tin he carries around his neck:

> It was some time before he could put Alfred, Georgia, Sixo, schoolteacher, Halle, his brothers, Sethe, Mister, the taste of iron, the sight of butter, the smell of hickory, notebook paper, one by one, into the tobacco tin lodged in his chest. By the time he got to 124 nothing in this world could pry it open. (p. 113)

Ironically, the lid is prised open by something supernatural, the ghost of Beloved in the form of a young woman. As she seduces him, he does not hear the flakes of rust fall from the seams and the lid eventually gives. The pain and horror which he has kept sealed for so long is released in his escalating and repetitive cry, 'Red heart', which wakes Denver.

III

Whilst in some respects *Beloved* is a response to Black Aesthetic discourse of the 1960s, as I suggested in chapter 1, the novel pursues possibilities arising out of a range of black literary and cultural traditions, especially the symbols and forms rooted in the experience of black women themselves. Like *The Bluest Eye*, *Beloved*, as a development of the Reverend Bassett's version of the Margaret Garner story, is concerned with the conditions that lead parents to commit acts of violence against their children. In the former novel, as we saw earlier, Cholly Breedlove's rape of his daughter was the result of the guilt and impotence which had been imposed on him by a society in which he was declared worthless. The reasons for Sethe's actions, however, are even more complex than those in Cholly's case, and the horrific event cannot be separated from the slave system which destroyed so many black lives.

Beloved subverts the myth of Southern paternalism in which the slave owners were envisaged as presiding over an extended and subservient family of both black and white. Whilst this narrative was constructed from the South's supposed commitment to family, honour, good manners, culture, and order, the reality had more to do with property and ownership. In self-justification of slavery, the South perpetuated the illusion of a system as stable as its 'Big Houses', in which everyone including master, overseer, house slaves, mammies and field slaves had their place, eschewing the realities of forced labour and servitude, the mundane brutality of plantation life, and the destruction of black families.

Sethe's decision to kill her child rather than have her taken into slavery has to be seen in the context of these conditions. Only a month previously she had endured an almost fatal whipping and suffered the degradation of being chained while the white men sucked her lactating breasts. After a month with Baby Suggs, Sethe's recapture and return to the plantation would have been too much for any one in her position. Her own version of what happened stands in contrast to the other narratives of her child's death in the novel, including the one in the newspaper which Stamp Paid gives to Paul D:

Simple. She just flew. Collected every bit of life she had made, all the parts of her that were precious and fine and beautiful, and carried, pushed, dragged them through the veil, out, away, over there where no one could hurt them. Over there. Outside this place, where they would be safe. And the hummingbird wings beat on. (p. 163)

Morrison clearly sought to base *Beloved* on a wider range of texts than the traditional slave narrative – texts that challenge and revision 'authoritative' versions of slavery. Alternative histories – personal, social, political, racial – embedded in or occluded by official histories determine the structure of the novel. Sethe's murder of her daughter is not only the major traumatic incident at the centre of the narrative but the nodal point where public and private, the visible and the occluded, and white American and African-American histories intersect. Initially, Sethe blames only herself for the murder of her child until her mother-in-law, Baby Suggs, points out to her that the real responsibility lies with white people and the inhumane system that they have imposed upon blacks: 'Those white things have taken all I had or dreamed,' she [Baby Suggs] said, 'and broke my heart strings too. There is no bad luck in the world but whitefolks' (p. 89). In other words, Baby Suggs introduces Sethe to an alternative version of events from the one with which she has lived since killing her child.

Behind Sethe's shouldering of responsibility is a history of the individual as autonomous, free-thinking, self-sufficient and, at all times, individually culpable. But behind Baby Suggs's version there is a different history that insists upon contextualising the behaviour of individuals. Thus, there are conflicting versions, enabling the narrative to explore the implications of these two perspectives of most of the pivotal events in the book. For example, Stamp Paid blames Baby Suggs for abandoning her life as a preacher in 1855; that is for privileging self-interested individualism over the collective needs of the black community. But he comes to see her as a strong woman defeated by whites and by the increasing demands that the women of the community placed upon her.

But in *Beloved*, Morrison also recognises that the history of slavery is much more fractious and complex than many of the slave narratives to which I referred in chapter 1 suggested. Both the periods of slavery and of Reconstruction through which Sethe's life is charted are sites of conflict between shifting perspectives, complex antagonisms and complicated affiliations. For example, Denver, Sethe's 18-year-old daughter with whom she has lived for some years in a house haunted by the ghost of the baby she killed, has a view of white people which her later observations and experiences challenge. Denver has been brought up on Sethe's narrative of how she had been helped by Amy Denver, after whom Denver is named.

This narrative introduces assumptions that subsequently influence Denver, and ideas signified by Amy herself. Amy introduces a subtext of slavery which has often been ignored and which develops Morrison's concern with the capitalist origins of the slave trade. In Amy's own tortured body there is literally and metaphorically a history of the slavery endured by poor, working-class whites, whose treatment at the hands of their masters was not so dissimilar as Sethe discovers from her own. Indeed, as Doreatha Mbalia points out, denied education like the black slaves, Amy speaks in a similar vernacular: 'Be so pretty on me' and 'Mr. Buddy whipped my tail' (1991, p. 95). The introduction of Amy also reminds us that non-European slaves were sought because of their skin colour which prevented them from blending, if they escaped, with the majority population. Similarly, the Cherokee Indians who befriend runaway slaves remind us how the Indians were also taken as slaves and how the death of so many, through for example European disease, was one of the motivating factors behind the introduction of slaves from Africa and the West Indies.

The key significance of the narrative about Amy, however, is the way it leads Denver to draw conclusions that Sethe never intended: she presumes that the majority of white people are like Amy rather than the slave owners. Ostensibly, Amy would seem to challenge Baby Suggs's argument that 'there is no bad luck in the world but whitefolks', as does the way in which Miss Bodwin helps Denver and prepares her for college. But then this affiliation is more complex than initially appears for, as Denver discovers, Miss Bodwin ruthlessly exploits her black servant and in this respect provides the most obvious counterpoint to Denver's view of white people. Moreover, in the statue of a kneeling black boy at Miss Bodwin's back door, bearing the words 'At Yo Service', Denver encounters a visual text which underpins the way in which the majority of whites regarded the black race and, like Miss Bodwin's treatment of her black servant, seems to confirm Baby Suggs's assertion. It is a perspective to which Baby Suggs herself in her sermons in the clearing offers a counterpoint, encouraging pride and self-esteem among the members of her community: 'Love your hands! Love them. Raise them up and kiss them. Touch others with them ... *You* got to love it, *you*' (p. 88). But, of course, this is challenged, in turn, by the behaviour of the women of her community toward her. The neighbours who attend Baby Suggs's feast are the very people who, the following day, are so envious of her position in the community and her comparative affluence that they either remain silent when the suspicious white strangers arrive or actually betray Sethe. In an interview with Paul Gilroy, Morrison explains how she found a 'text' in the Garner story which had not previously been realised:

> It occurred to me that the questions about community and individuality were certainly inherent in that incident as I imagined it. When you are the community, when you are your children, when that is your individuality, there is no division ... Margaret Garner didn't do what Medea did and kill her children because of some guy. It was for me this classic example of a person determined to be responsible. (Gilroy, 1993, p. 177)

The significance of this concern with issues of community can only be understood within the context of the betrayal of Baby Suggs.

In African society moral judgement is invariably a matter for the community to which the individual is answerable. In *Beloved*, the community which initially betrays Sethe significantly comes together at the end of the novel and rescues her from killing Edward Bodwin. Indeed, Paul D's sudden reappearance after 18 years casts him as a representative of the community which judged her for what she had done and which has to be reconvened as the only means by which she can achieve full absolution. They, too, of course, can only achieve absolution for betraying Baby Suggs and Sethe by coming together and rescuing her. Although, at one level, the fragmentary structure of the novel reflects the disunity of recent African-American history and the chaos which slavery created in the lives of black people, at another level, it reflects the deeper structure in the black experience. The way in which the novel moves without warning from the present in which it is initially set to the past, denies the conventional division of the present, past and future into separate units. The black experience is seen as a continuum, as a cycle which returns to the shared suffering that should consolidate the black community. This is the Word to which Hi Man refers and of which Baby Suggs speaks. In a sense, then, the sermon which Baby Suggs preaches in the clearing, which in the novel is itself emblematic of a homogeneous black community, is the really important text which lies buried in this novel. Indeed, *Beloved* is ultimately about the recovery of this lost text.

This is the narrative which Geraldine in *The Bluest Eye* and Jadine in *Tar Baby*, for example, need to reclaim for, pursuing a single-minded version of success based on standardised white definitions of beauty, they deny their black cultural identity through shame and self-hatred. Geraldine, especially, epitomises the kind of self-interest which, in *Beloved*, divides the black community and causes its members to betray Baby Suggs. None of the narratives in *Beloved*, however, can be read independently of another, as the image of the quilt suggests. The integration of the different narratives within the novel is one of the keys to the healing process which it commends. This is evident from Paul D's return to Sethe at the end of the book; he sits rocking beside Sethe, a movement signifying healing and giving comfort, his eyes falling on the quilt which, like the novel, is more than the sum of its parts. The characters who achieve release in the novel do so through reclaiming or claiming narratives beyond those in which they have been locked.

Within this more complex and pluralised history of slavery, the meeting place – in *Beloved*, the clearing – assumes a special significance. Religious meetings provided a much-needed opportunity for African-Americans to come together since plantation practices prevented them from having meetings, relationships or even speaking together. As Lomax argues:

> By listening and fervently responding to the pure poetry of the Negro preacher, the Negro masses got a sense of history and moral philosophy. There is something incredibly informative about sitting Sunday after Sunday and year in, year out, listening to a minister trace out the history of the Jews from the day God spit out the seven seas to the time John the Revelator closed the Bible and said all truth had been revealed. Even those of us who couldn't read came to think of history as a moving, changing thing; we were never allowed to doubt that man as a created thing had purpose and that we, to be sure, were a part of that purpose. (Lomax, 1962, p. 47)

Baby Suggs, like other preachers, gave the slave community, as Lomax suggests, a context in which it could place itself and which could act as a refuge and source of strength. Of course, as I have suggested, this did encourage some slaves to see themselves as black versions of Christian from *The Pilgrim's Progress* and adopt a rather passive attitude toward their lot. *Beloved* takes issue with this, however, suggesting that in the apparent acceptance of white-man's law many slave communities, through for example their own mocking humour which many white plantation owners did not understand, were less compliant and passive than appeared. Moreover, Morrison recognises that in matriarchs like Baby Suggs there is a further history that has been played down or ignored. She is an example of what Joanne Braxton identifies as the outraged female ancestor, angry at the abuse of her people and feeling keenly every wrong done to them (Braxton and McLaughlin, 1990, p. 302).

Beloved, then, not only reclaims a number of occluded narratives around slavery but suggests that the history in the slave narrative is based on a number of 'texts' within nineteenth-century African-American culture. One of the most significant of these was the North itself described by Paul D: 'Free North. Magical North. Welcoming, benevolent North' (p. 112). Once again, however, there is a degree of irony here for the North was not always welcoming and not as supportive or effective as it could have been even in its intervention in the South. The final tableau of the novel in which Sethe attacks the white abolitionist Edward Bodwin, Miss Bodwin's brother, with an ice pick is especially ironic in this respect. She mis-takes Bodwin, who has come to 124 to give Denver a ride to work, for a slave catcher. Although literally false, Sethe's assumption is emblematic, at another level, of black history after the Civil War, as Walker argues (1991, p. 43). When Stamp Paid pulls a red ribbon from the river connected to a piece of a young black girl's scalp, he recovers another narrative, as it were – the way in which emancipa-tion brought not freedom but the widespread slaughter of former slaves. If death did not catch them, there was little by way of opportunity for the ex-slaves. When the Federal troops were with-drawn in 1877, the blacks were left materially, socially, education-ally and politically impoverished. Of the threequarters of them who remained in the Southern states, the majority were in agriculture, locked into a semi-feudal system of tenancy or sharecropping which replaced the slave plantations. The impotence of many of the white liberals to deliver the promise of emancipation is illustrated in the way in which Edward Bodwin constructs a text of his own past as an abolitionist – 'Nothing since was as stimulating as the old days of letters, petitions, meetings, debates, recruitment, quarrels, rescue and downright sedition' (p. 260) – serving to underscore the paucity of his present which is epitomised in the image of a man searching for toy soldiers and a watch he had long ago buried in the yard of 124.

Generally speaking, however, the myth of the North, mediated by African-American story-telling traditions and the lived experience of the plantations, provided an important inspirational fantasy. While I do not wish to suggest that the North as envisaged by African-Americans was entirely an imagined country, the myth was more real than the reality. Seen often in biblical terms as the Promised Land, the 'textuality' of the North underscores the importance of the Bible as a text in the histories embedded in or occluded by the slave narrative. In *Beloved*, the words which Sethe uses to claim Beloved – 'Beloved she mine' – and which Beloved uses to claim Sethe – 'I am Beloved and she is mine' – have their source in *The Song of Solomon* which had inspired the title and, in part, the concern with ancestral wisdom in her earlier novel. But, the epigraph of *Beloved* reminds us that its title comes from a part of Paul's epistle to the Romans in which he, in turn, is quoting Hosea in the Old Testament. One of Hosea's three children was called 'not beloved', a representative of the Israelites who had been temporarily rejected as punishment for their own betrayal. After a period of retribution, God reclaims the lost people:

> I will call them my people,
> which were not my people;
> and her beloved,
> which was not beloved.

On the plantations religious instruction was intended as a form of social control. The Bible, read from a particular historicised, cultural perspective, was one of the means by which colonial authorities tried to inculcate Western values and introduce European or Anglo-European notions of culture to Africa. Indeed, its apparent dualism – 'Black Satan' and 'the snow-white Lamb of God' – appeared not only to justify slavery, but to confirm a particular version of its history. However, the Bible, like all texts, is not just one text but a multilayered narrative. Interpreted from a black perspective, it is a different work from the one used by whites to justify slavery, providing images appropriate to the African-American condition and black history: delivery of the Righteous, retribution of the Wicked, Judgement Day, Zion, the Promised Land. Through its delineation of the history of the Jewish nation, the Bible expounded the trials and miseries of slavery. It offered slaves a source of communal strength through notions of faith, grace and the Holy Spirit, and even a means of achieving healing.

In discussing the biblical sources of the title of *Beloved*, critics such as Melissa Walker (1991) have failed to pursue the implication that African-American writers have gone to a different text, a different Bible, from whites. Yet, as I have tried to show, it is a thesis that actually highlights a major concern in the novel with reclaiming occluded or absent texts. Indeed, it is the absent text around the word 'beloved' that highlights the political message of the book. The source of the word 'beloved' is not only in Romans but in the words spoken by the preacher over Beloved's grave. Sethe, who bought the name for her daughter's gravestone with ten minutes of stand-up sex with the stone engraver, would have liked to have had the other word – 'Dearly' – which the preacher spoke over her dead child. As Walker points out, there were other words too: 'we are gathered here together ...' These words clearly and obviously draw attention to the main subject of the novel, the reclamation of a sense of community and solidarity in the face of fragmentation and isolation.

The behaviour of the whites, too, is anchored in texts which we need to recall if we are to understand slavery. Schoolteacher, for example, who makes a study of Sethe, is a student of the discourses around the pseudo science of hierarchies expounded by scientists such as Herbert Spencer and Francis Galton. White intellectuals came to rely upon colonial anthropology and vulgar interpretations of Darwinism to give coherence and respectability to popularly held racist myths. As Barbara Christian points out, schoolteacher's equivalents, plantation managers with interests in contemporary anthropological theories, did write treatises on slaves based on scientific observation of them and measurement of various parts of their bodies (Braxton and McLaughlin, 1990, p. 338).

One of the most damning weapons of white, colonial power structures was the representation and stigmatising of Africans and African-Americans as beasts. This is a stereotype which *Beloved* specifically inverts whilst exposing it as the product of white cultural hegemony and a particular historical narrative of black people:

White people believed that whatever the manners, under every dark skin was a jungle. Swift unnavigable waters, swinging screaming baboons, sleeping snakes, red gums ready for their sweet white blood [...] But it wasn't the jungle blacks brought with them to this place from the other (livable) place. It was the jungle whitefolks planted in them. And it grew. It spread. In, through and after life, it spread, until it invaded the whites who had made it. Touched them every one. Changed and altered them. Made them bloody, silly, worse than even they wanted to be, so scared were they of the jungle they had made. The screaming baboon lived under their own white skin; the red gums were their own. (pp. 198–9)

The passage begins with an account of how whites have seen blacks that subtly exposes the history in their views. These perspectives are rooted in the discovery and exploitation of foreign peoples; the inability to appreciate the otherness of other cultures; and the fear of so-called alien cultures which in turn led whites to construct a notion of blackness that said more about their concept of whiteness than the other races. Then the passage inverts these narratives. The constructions imposed by whites on black people are said to have impacted on themselves, and in the potted narrative that follows we see how white ethnocentricity contains the seeds of its own destruction.

1V

As I suggested at the outset, Sethe's healing and rebirth can only begin when she has knowledge and understanding of the absent narratives in her own history. The novel hinges upon what is called 'rememory', the basic concept of which is that memories have a physical existence beyond the minds of the individuals in whom they originate; it is possible to bump into and inhabit another person's memory. Paul D is associated with rememory throughout the novel. At the beginning of the book, he brings Sethe 'rememories' of what happened to her husband, Halle, and explanations as to why he did not come to console Sethe. Sethe literally learns to inhabit and take for herself these 'rememories' which are Paul's. In doing so, she begins to piece things together and Sethe's experience in this respect mirrors the experience of the reader in tackling the intricately woven structure of the novel. At the end of the novel, for example, just before Paul D returns to reclaim Sethe from death, he is haunted by something he does not understand, something on the edge of consciousness. Suddenly, he realises that it is a memory of Baby Suggs dying, although the memory is not his own because she died nine years earlier, in his absence. Such shifts between different narrative levels and challenges to ideas of causality are techniques used by Morrison to represent a sense of community in the novel. One of the concluding images, to which I drew attention earlier, is of Paul beside Sethe's bed, rocking and staring at the patchwork quilt. The novel itself is like a quilt and it is important to remember that the quilt, a feminine art form, was used to map the ancestry of a family as each successive generation added to it.

The concept of rememory and the notion of a repossessed ancestry are inextricably woven together. The privileging of memory by African-American writers is a political as well as an aesthetic project. Morrison recognises that in slave autobiography there is a history which the very existence of the slave narratives challenges – a history in which African-Americans are portrayed as not having a memory. As Henry Louis Gates, Jr, points out, the white lie that black people did not have a memory was encouraged as part of the myth that black people and American Indians had lower mental capacities than other races: 'metaphors of the "childlike" nature of the slaves, of the masked, puppetlike "personality" of the black, all share this assumption about the absence of memory' (1992, p. 61). Typical of this viewpoint is the way in which a novelist, Mary Langdon, writing in 1855, described blacks as 'mere children ... You seldom hear them say much about anything that's past, if they only get enough to eat and drink at the present moment' (cit. Gates, Jr, 1992, p. 62). But in fact the connection between rememory and the reclamation of ancestry, racial pride and self-esteem is much deeper than even Gates, Jr, suggests.

The idea of rememory, as defined in *Beloved*, even though Morrison may have obtained it from the work of Virginia Woolf, is appropriate to a dispossessed people. Since slavery destroyed not only whole communities but entire families, banning their religions, stopping their music and eradicating their cultures, the only way in which an individual could acquire any sense of their ancestral line was to possess and piece together the stories and memories of others, to literally acquire for themselves the texts of which they had been deprived. The full significance and the extent of the fracture which slavery created for black people can only be appreciated in the light of the African concept of ancestry. In African cosmology, as I suggested earlier, ancestors are important because they provided access to the spirits who, as Morrison makes clear in her essay on the subject, intruded for the benefit of social cohesiveness into people's lives. Obliterating black slaves' contact with their ancestors thus also destroyed their contact with the spirits. Through its powerful figurative language, the novel impresses the enormity of this fracture on the reader. The fragmentary nature of the novel means that even if readers succeed in putting together the events of Sethe's life since 1855, it will not necessarily allow them to achieve a grasp of the whole text. The gaps and enigmas that remain suggest that the enormous sense of displacement and fracture for millions of Africans is not something that can be 'passed on' in both senses of the phrase.

So, in *Beloved*, in engaging with the history in the plantation ghost story, as I maintained earlier, Morrison counters the ignorance in those of white origin of the role of the ancestor in African-American ontology. The sense of fracture which is at the heart of the book – together with a concomitant sense of healing – is maintained, if not actually initiated, by the slippage of the signifier 'Beloved' – the 'ghost' – throughout the novel. At one level, Beloved subverts the notion of the outraged mother figure as an outraged ghost-daughter intent upon claiming the mother who killed her for herself alone, but she eludes precise definition. Initially, she appears to be the spirit ghost of the murdered baby, commensurate with the concept of the revenging 'undead' with which plantation ghost stories sought to intimidate the slaves. But no sooner has the reader acquired this view of her than she reappears, or seems to reappear, in the form of a young woman. Eventually, she appears to represent not a single child but the pain and anguish of the 60 million blacks who have died. It is in relation to this role that the chaos and disunity of the many sections of the novel in which Beloved appears make sense. Passages are left unpunctuated and Beloved herself uses words out of order while omitting words important to the sense altogether: for example, 'Where your diamonds?'; 'Tell me your diamonds' (p. 58). She frequently gets concepts wrong: 'Your woman she never fix up your hair?' As Sethe's puzzled reaction suggests – 'My woman? You mean my mother?' – Beloved here has got hold of the wrong 'text' (p. 60). The incoherence and chaos of the sections involving

Beloved, which at one point become poetry, are manifestations of the disunity and isolation that she represents.

As a character, then, Beloved is commensurate with the fantastical in African literature which is usually traceable to concrete, social and historical events. But, in moving from one plane of reference to another, she literally destabilises the novel which itself also moves with an equally destabilising effect from one narrative plane to another. This fluid movement from and between different modes of writing – slave narrative, folklore, myth, ghost story, autobiography, confession, romance, historical 'realism' – is central to the novel because just as Morrison's creative use of the Bible in the epigraph exemplifies how African-American writers find an 'African' text in the white man's religious book, *Beloved* reminds us of other texts inside the plantation ghost story and the slave narrative which have come down to us through white male or black male chroniclers.

V

It is no coincidence that the two main healers in the novel, Baby Suggs and Amy, are women and that Paul D, one of the most sympathetically portrayed black men in Morrison's work, is associated with the feminine. In this respect, Morrison once again seems to invoke the work of late nineteenth-century, black women writers. As Hazel Carby (1985) has pointed out, the most significant absence in texts by nineteenth-century, black women is the black father (1985, p. 276). According to Carby, this confirms the denial of patriarchal power to black men. But writers, such as Pauline Hopkins, used this space, like Morrison in the late twentieth century, to explore the possibilities of alternative black male figures – in peer relationships or as partners and lovers – within a female-oriented narrative.

In *Beloved*, Morrison presents us with a black woman's version of slavery as a counterpoint to a narrative that has until now been told primarily from a male point of view. This is made clear when Stamp Paid visits 124 and hears, indecipherable to him, 'the thoughts of the women of 124, unspeakable thoughts, unspoken' (p. 199). The black centre of the novel, associated with the spiritual and with healing, expounds the pain, humiliation and violence endured and, in many cases, transcended by generations of black women.

One of the most powerful texts in the book in this respect is the pattern made by the scars on Sethe's back. Her own reading of them, since she has never actually seen them, is virtually a 'remem-ory' of Amy's reading of them:

> 'Whitegirl. That's what she called it. I've never seen it and never will. But that's what she said it looked like. A chokecherry tree. Trunk, branches, and even leaves. Tiny little chokecherry leaves.' (p. 16)

Characteristically of *Beloved*, there are different 'texts' on Sethe's back depending upon how the scars are read. Amy's reading imaginatively transforms the pain and humiliation of slavery. Later Sethe does the same in remembering the hanging of the Sweet Home boys: 'Boys hanging from the most beautiful sycamores in the world. It shamed her – remembering the wonderful soughing trees rather than the boys' (p. 6). When Sethe and Paul D make love un-successfully because they are both carrying too much personal baggage, symbolised by the clothes which they do not entirely remove, Paul sees the scars differently from Amy and Sethe, indeed, differently from when they began to make love; now they become only 'a revolting clump of scars' (p. 21). His inability to reclaim Amy's text signifies the distance he and Sethe have yet to travel.

Sethe and Paul D's lovemaking and the issues involved are revisited obliquely later in the text in the account of the two turtles mating. The male turtle mounts the female from behind, reminding us of how Paul approached Sethe at the stove. The female has to stretch out her neck to touch the male's face, risking everything like Sethe coming out from her protective shell of forgetting in making love with Paul. The shells of the turtles clash as the pasts which Sethe and Paul bring with them and with which they have to come to terms also conflict. The apparently trivial incident of the two turtles becomes a visual text which acts as a commentary upon a key event in the book. Lest we fail to give this seemingly unimpor-tant occurrence due consideration the text refers us back to it when Beloved, apparently bent on revenge against Sethe in the vein of the plantation ghost story, seduces Paul D with her back to him, hoisting her skirts and turning her head 'over her shoulder the way the turtles had' (p. 116). At this point in the novel, the description of the landscape, read emblematically, provides a further narrative and the context for Beloved's death which she and others have to understand. The account of the seasons – 'Each one enters like a prima donna, convinced its performance is the reason the world has people in it' (p. 116) – reminds us of the white ethnocentricity which underpinned much of the African slave trade although slavery in Africa did not begin with the European. Autumn has 'bottles of blood and gold', encapsulating the motivation, the greed and the consequences of slavery, whilst Paul D hears the end of slavery, the end of white supremacy: 'the voices of a dying landscape were insistent and loud' (p. 116).

The reader is given an insight into the caring nature of Paul D when his first thought on hearing of Baby Suggs's death is: 'Was it hard? I hope she didn't die hard' (p. 7). At the end of the novel, Sethe, wondering whether Paul will bathe her, recalls:

> She looks at him. The peachstone skin, the crease between his ready, waiting eyes and sees it – the thing in him, the blessedness, that has made him the kind of man who can walk in a house and make the women cry. (p. 272)

These lines are a repetition of the omniscient narrator's description of Paul D when he first visits and makes love with Sethe:

> Not even trying, he had become the kind of man who could walk into a house and make the women cry. Because with him, in his presence, they could. There was something blessed in his manner. Women saw him and wanted to weep – to tell him that their chest hurt and their knees did too. Strong women and wise saw him and told him things they only told each other: that way past the Change of Life, desire in them had suddenly become enormous, greedy, more savage than when they were fifteen, and that it embarrassed them and made them sad; that secretly they longed to die – to be quit of it – that sleep was more precious to them than any waking day. Young girls sidled up to him to confess or describe how well-dressed the visitations were that had followed them straight from their dreams. (p. 17)

When sitting and rocking at the end of the novel, Paul recalls Amy who rocked Sethe's pain as she lay beside her, recalling how her own mother sang as she rocked.

The account of how Paul has a special affinity with women is a glimpse into a further text rooted in the interior life of black women. In piecing together the structure of the novel, we weave this text together as well; a text so inextricably a part of the book as to give its language its particular charge. This is evident, for example, in Sethe's account of her own mother to Beloved:

> I didn't see her but a few times out in the fields and once when she was working indigo. By the time I woke up in the morning, she was in line. If the moon was bright they worked by its light. Sunday she slept like a stick. She must of nursed me two or three weeks – that's the way the others did. Then she went back in rice and I sucked from another woman whose job it was. So to answer you, no. I reckon not. She never fixed my hair nor nothing. She didn't even sleep in the same cabin most nights I remember. Too far from the line-up, I guess. (pp. 60–1)

For the women to be forced to work by the light of the traditional symbol of the female underlines the brutalisation of their identity as women. The use of the verb 'sucked' emphasises how the white man's system has reduced black women to breeding stock – as does the stealing of Sethe's milk. Coupled with the noun 'job', it also re-inforces the denial of the closest of emotional bonds, that between mother and child, and how slavery exploits post-natal rejection by turning the separation of mother and child into a systemised form of breeding. 'Line' and 'line-up' emphasise the factory-like nature of the system while betraying its role in supporting a capitalist, in-dustrial society. The inclusion of the word 'stick' is effective not only in completing the consonance but in emphasising the life-denying nature of the whole process. A stick, like a slave, has been broken off from its life source and is thereby dry and dead. Paul D eventually comes to realise that in listening to Sethe he has made the mistake of hearing a traditional narrative – 'This here Sethe talked about love like any other woman; talked about baby clothes like any other woman ...' – whilst in fact she 'talked about safety with a handsaw' and 'didn't know where the world stopped and she began' (p. 164).

The novel takes us, as Christian says, into the chaotic space of mother-love and mother-pain in which a mother kills her child in order to save it (Braxton and McLaughlin, 1990, pp. 338–9). Writing in this space which is occluded in the traditional slave narrative, Morrison employs the new context to develop a subject touched upon in *Sula* where Eva kills Plum, who has returned from the First

World War a narcotics addict, because she cannot stand to see him suffer any longer. *Beloved* pushes at the very boundaries of this chaotic space. When Sethe tells Paul D about how they stole her milk, the horror of what happened is such that it causes him to handle the pouch containing the tobacco tin, fearing it will bring forth everything that he believes he has sealed away. Her account brings to the fore, uncompromisingly, the bond between mother and child which slavery destroyed:

> All I knew was I had to get my milk to my baby girl. Nobody was going to nurse her like me. Nobody was going to get it to her fast enough, or take it away when she had enough and didn't know it. (p. 16)

The song which Amy sings to ease Sethe's pain conflates mother-love with mother-pain; combining tenderness with vicarious suffering. The memory of the song and of the way in which her mother used to sing to her highlights the absence of her mother. Yet it is her remembered presence which enables Amy to bond with and heal Sethe, saving her and her child from certain death. The narrative we have at this point in the novel is the one which Denver relates to Beloved, fleshing out scraps of information which she had gleaned from her mother. The narrative, which is Sethe's story, brings Denver and Beloved together, as Amy's recollection of her mother unites her and Sethe.

The denial and obliteration of motherhood and mothering in slavery, Morrison's novel argues, distorts the whole notion of womanhood for black women. In *Beloved*, it is reclaimed, as best as it can be, by rescuing the mother–child bond from the chaotic space in which it was forced to exist. As Barbara Christian argues, it is through their reflections on this precarious role that the female slaves in *Beloved* are able to try to understand themselves as women and the concept often proves crucial to the survival of what is otherwise, in psychoanalytic terms, a split subject (Braxton and McLaughlin, 1990, p. 338–9).

Although set in the nineteenth century, *Beloved* has numerous implications for both black and white cultural identity in the twentieth century: the need for contemporary America to reclaim the full narrative of slavery, especially the suffering of black women; the need for white America to understand how slavery was justified as an intellectual and scientific project that failed to recognise the human cost; and the need for all potentially dominant cultures to appreciate that the brutality and racialism of slavery has extended far beyond the emancipation of slaves in the nineteenth century into contemporary America.

Morrison herself saw the African-American novel as a healing art form:

> For a long time, the art form that was healing for Black people was music. That music is no longer exclusively ours; we don't have exclusive rights to it. Other people sing it and play it; it is the mode of contemporary music everywhere. So another form has to take that place, and it seems to me that the novel is needed by African-Americans in a way that it was not needed before ... .
> (Evans, 1984, p. 340)

Healing is at the centre of *Beloved* and is centred on Sethe as Amy, Baby Suggs and, finally, Paul D contribute to her healing process. Baby Suggs's message is also one of healing, through learning to value oneself and to join with others in a supportive sense of community. Almost the final thing Paul D remembers in the novel is Sixo describing Thirty-Mile Woman: 'She is a friend of my mind. She gather me, man. The pieces I am, she gather them and give them back to me in all the right order' (pp. 272–3). But the novel does not exorcise the enormity of the fracture which slavery and white racialism have created – although it concludes on a note of healing, there is no definitive sense of closure. At the most basic level of the story, we do not know how completely Sethe will be healed or whether she and Paul D have been sufficiently successful in exorcising their respective pasts to be able to make a life together. Their particular narrative ends with Sethe's incredulity – 'Me? – Me?' – while the novel concludes with a pain and loneliness that's 'an inside kind – wrapped tight like skin [...] No rocking can hold it down' (p. 274).

5

The 1990s: *Jazz* (1992) and *Paradise* (1998)

The text of this book was set in Electra, a typeface designed by W. A. Dwiggins (1880–1956). This face cannot be classified as either modern or old style. It is not based on any historical model, nor does it echo any particular period or style. It avoids the extreme contrasts between thick and thin elements that mark most modern faces, and it attempts to give a feeling of fluidity, power, and speed. ('A Note on the Type', *Paradise*, 1998)

I

If *Beloved*, *Jazz* and *Paradise* really constitute a trilogy, then, ostensibly, by conventional standards it is a loose trilogy. I say 'ostensibly' because, although Morrison is by no means the first writer to produce an unconventional trilogy, the absence of the usual overt continuities, or even obviously inverted structures, encourages us to look deeper for what these novels have in common. All three novels share the concern of the earlier texts with African-American history, with personal and collective memory and with the nature of historiography. But the latter is much more pronounced in the trilogy; each novel is more clearly focused on a particular period in black history from which it then weaves its way to and fro further into the past, for each of the texts is preoccupied with what in *Paradise* is called 'tracery'. Moreover, all three novels are centred on a traumatic event, of which details and background information are released in piecemeal fashion, out of their chronological sequence, in different voices and through different perspectives. In all three novels, in different contexts and at different levels, there is an abiding concern with obsession.

The two novels written in the 1990s, completing the trilogy which Morrison envisaged in the previous decade, again employ techniques that are normally associated in Euro-American literary criticism with postmodernism. Despite the implication in 'A Note on the Type', both *Jazz* and *Paradise* echo specific periods, styles and historical models. But neither novel is confined to any one of these, and, in blurring the boundaries between particular styles and historical models, each is something of a hybrid. In both texts, what are normally labelled postmodern techniques are employed, as in *Beloved*, to exploit the narrative possibilities of modes of writing and/or expression that were prevalent at the time in which the novel is primarily set, even though all three novels reach further back in time than their original setting. *Jazz*, which is located initially in Harlem in the 1920s, employs a combination of techniques to be found in jazz, oral narratives and postmodernist writing to develop the literary possibilities of that musical form but also of other modes, particularly the American city novel. *Paradise*, initially set in the period 1970–6, is particularly rooted in utopian/dystopian fiction that was popular in the 1960s and 1970s but also echoes at times the family or dynasty novel and the open-road genre. Again, however, both novels develop not only features of these other modes of writing and communication but the history in these forms. And in doing so, they invoke a variety of histories, and a variety of ways of conceptualising those histories. In her introduction to *Race-ing Justice and En-gendering Power* (1992), Morrison highlights not only the need for perspective, context and analyses in historiography but for a focus 'on the history routinely ignored or played down or unknown' (p. xi). But she is particularly interested, as is clear from *Playing in the Dark: Whiteness and the Literary Imagination* (1992), in what is ignored, played down or unknown in the history embodied in some of the major genres of American literature, including those that have been inherited from Europe. Many of the characteristics of American literature, she argues – individualism, masculinism, historical isolation versus social engagement, an obsession with innocence and configurations of hell and death – are a response to an, often obliquely acknowledged, Africanist presence.

While numerous critics, not surprisingly, have drawn attention to the influence of jazz on the structure of Morrison's novel, to which I shall return in a moment, Morrison herself, in an interview with Salman Rushdie, has linked *Jazz* to 'the Great American City

Novel' (Rushdie, 1992). But such has been the attention given to the obvious links between the novel and jazz music that the way in which the novel relates to this literary form has been overlooked. However, as *Beloved* develops the history in the form of the slave narrative, *Jazz* develops the history in the American city novel. The American city novel was, initially, a product of the most important aspect of nineteenth-century American social history – the transition, particularly in the North, from a rural to an industrial and urban economy. But, from an African-American perspective, as *Jazz* emphasises, a more significant transition was the movement from a slavocracy to industrialism. Essentially a narrative contrasting the innocence of country and small-town life with the destructive experience of the city, the city novel is often embedded in a more complex history than critics have tended to suggest. For example, an important focus in the city novel is the power relationships at work in a city at any particular time, determining who has access to particular city spaces, who has the greater freedom of movement, who it is initiates movement, who dominates particular spaces, who engages in what kinds of pastimes, and who exercises, and who is subject to, control. Again, these are issues that are raised in the introduction to *Race-ing Justice and En-gendering Power* (1992); the debates over the candidacy for the Supreme Court, Morrison argues, have subsumed not only matters of 'racial justice and racial address' but 'the problematics of governing women's bodies, the alterations of work space into (sexually) domesticated space' (pp. xix–xx).

In invoking the American city novel, as Morrison admitted the novel does in her interview with Salman Rushdie, *Jazz* defamiliarises the history in that genre from an African-American perspective. In this respect, her work may be linked to earlier black novels such as Carl van Vechten's *Nigger Heaven* (1926) and Claude McKay's *Home to Harlem* (1928). But there are other, more contemporary, feminist writers who employ the city novel in different ways and from a variety of fresh perspectives, such as Gloria Naylor's *The Women of Brewster Place* (1980), Alix Kates Schulman's *On the Stroll* (1981), Phyllis Burke's *Atomic Candy* (1989), and Andrea Dworkin's *Ice and Fire* (1986). Each of these engages with the complex history(ies) that are either explicitly or implicitly embedded in the city novel.

Generally speaking, city novels depict histories that are fragmented and fractious. But they also epitomise, as Pauline Palmer has pointed out, 'the contradictions of aspiration and disillusion which modern life involves' (1994, p. 322). *Jazz*, taking up this generic feature of the city novel from a black perspective, casts it in different light. The novel is set, primarily, in Harlem during 'The Harlem Renaissance', in 1926, midway through a decade when the United States was in the throes of 'The Jazz Age' or 'The Roaring Twenties'. Perhaps emphasising that Morrison's engagement is as much with the history in the genre of the city novel as with Harlem itself, Harlem is unusually anonymised in the text as the 'City'; a device which not only embodies the dreams and possibilities with which African-Americans invested the city but highlights its authoritative nature.

White histories of the 1920s tend to see its creative and cultural ferment as a response to the Armistice of 1919. But the period had a different significance for African-Americans and it is this, rather than the post-war euphoria which was essentially part of white history, that Morrison tries to recover in *Jazz*. In this respect, the focus of interest is the same as in the early novels; the black communities which exist behind and which transcend the boundaries drawn up by the whites to define and contain them. At one level, Harlem's significance derives from black migration, itself a response to the 'want and violence' (p. 33) of reconstruction, one of the narratives in black history which, as I argued in the previous chapter, is reclaimed in *Beloved*. A fundamental and irreversible shift took place during the half century after the Civil War; initially the Southern cities drew large numbers of ex-slaves from their hinterlands, but the segregation, the violence and the poverty drove hundreds of thousands of African-Americans northwards. But if this narrative had to be reclaimed for the African-American novel, it was already preserved in the blues which articulated for generations of black people the aspirations, difficulties and frustrations of their transition not only from slavery but from a rural to an urban lifestyle.

The city generally assumed legendary significance in African-American mythology through stories told, for example, by porters and waiters working on Pullman trains or through letters sent from friends and relatives. But, in *Jazz*, as in *Beloved*, priority is given to the 'internal', the psychic dimensions of migration. These included discontinuity, aspiration and disillusion, themselves salient features of the presentation of history in the city novel. But Morrison revisions them in terms of black history. In the Northern cities, African-Americans had the opportunity to make decisions, including whom to love, denied them in the South. Although they rarely enjoyed the unbridled liberties of the mythology, they could enjoy higher wages, though never as high as the stories which circulated in the South would have them believe. Indeed, aspiration and disillusion, which Pauline Palmer sees as epitomising modern life and identifies as a generic feature of the city novel, is given a specifically African-American interpretation in *Jazz* in Joe and Violet's early experiences. While Violet works as an unlicensed, freelance hairdresser, Joe initially works shoe-leather and then rolls tobacco, cleans fish at night and toilets by day, waits tables, takes hotel work and eventually becomes a sample-case man selling beauty products. But as well as embracing in its very form the aspiration and disillusion of modern life, the city novel epitomises the complex and multilayered nature of its social geography which is also highlighted, but from an African-American perspective, in *Jazz*. When Joe and Violet move from 140th Street to a bigger place on Lennox Avenue, they face intraracial hostility from lighter skinned blacks who try to keep them out.

Nevertheless, whatever the discrepancies between the dream and the reality, there were significant new-found freedoms and excitements in the city. And in *Jazz*, Morrison retains the sense of excitement and aspiration which is part of the form of the city novel and, after all, a crucial aspect of migration itself. But once again, it is an expression in the novel of black, rather than white, history. The language used in the South to describe the cities of the North actually took on the same biblical connotations – The Promised Land, Canaan – as during the period of slavery. Indeed, Harlem's own legendary status is encapsulated in *Jazz* in the narrator's initial description of it, related from the point of view of the incoming migrants who are said to fall in love with it unequivocally and 'forever'. The description in fact echoes accounts of Harlem at the time from writers such as Langston Hughes, who wrote on his arrival:

> I can never put on paper the thrill of the underground ride to Harlem ... At every station I kept watching for the sign; 135th Street ... I went up the steps and out into the bright September sunlight. Harlem! I stood there, dropped my bags, took a deep breath and felt happy again. (1986, p. 81)

For Hughes, Harlem is a place where he can breathe again and rediscover himself. At one point the City in Morrison's novel has no air, only 'breath'. In *Jazz*, the City allows people to be themselves; 'their stronger, riskier selves' (p. 33).

The city as a subject was approached more tentatively in *Tar Baby* where, as we have seen, Jadine's enthusiasm for the opportunities that it provided for black women stands in contradistinction to Son's initial impressions of New York. Son's view of the city is redolent of those voices of the 1920s disillusioned with metropolitan life; like writers such as T. S. Eliot, Son stresses a social and moral malaise. But Son provides a specifically black slant: the men are accused of having eschewed their black identity and the women are said to be crying beneath their plum lipstick. *Jazz*, however, like black writing on Harlem in the 1920s, stresses the way in which the city allows black people to be 'more like themselves'. Whilst Son in *Tar Baby* searches in vain for elderly black people and black children on the streets of New York, Harlem in the 1920s is a different kind of place packed with black children, young girls, men, mothers and 'barfly women'. In this respect, *Jazz* betrays the influence of earlier African-American novels, such as Herbert Simmons's *Man Walking on Eggshells*, well known for the way in which its literary photography details the culture and lifestyle of black youth in St Louis in the 1940s and 1950s and makes a 'character' of the city itself.

But there are further works that intersect with Morrison's revisioning of the city novel in *Jazz*. In the previous chapter, I argued that *Beloved* was not only a development of the history in the Margaret Garner story but of the history in a particular version of it which Morrison included in *The Black Book* (1974). *Jazz*, up to a point, is similarly a development of the history in one of the photographs, and the accompanying texts, in *The Harlem Book of the Dead* (Billops, Van Der Zee and Dodson, 1978). Morrison, who wrote a foreword to this book, must have read the description of the photograph by the photographer, James Van Der Zee:

> She was the one I think was shot by her sweetheart at a party with a noiseless gun. She complained of being sick at the party and friends said, 'Well, why don't you lay down?' and they taken her in the room and laid her down. After they undressed her and loosened her clothes, they saw the blood on her dress. They asked her about it and she said, 'I'll tell you tomorrow, yes, I'll tell you tomorrow.' She was just trying to give him a chance to get away. For the picture I placed the flowers on her chest. (p. 84)

Generally speaking, critics have seen *Jazz* as fleshing out this story, as *Beloved* does the Margaret Garner story, which, of course, is true. But in these events there is a social as well as a personal history, with which Morrison's novel engages. It is a history that invokes the city novel; for it is a history of aspiration, disillusion, discovery and loss. And in doing so, it reveals the spaces, and the absences, in which *Jazz* as an African-American novel is written.

Morrison must have read not only Van Der Zee's text but the accompanying poem by Owen Dodson, in which the girl – as Felice says of Dorcas – is concealing the true nature of her injury and giving herself, and not just her lover, a chance to get away. Morrison's novel constructs the personal history which has led to a young girl in Harlem doing this. But, once again, her personal history invokes, and becomes blurred with, a larger history of Harlem in the 1920s that is not only in the city novel but jazz itself:

> They lean over me, and say:
> 'Who deathed you who,
> who, who, who, who ...
> I whisper: 'Tell you presently ...
> Shortly ... this evening ...
> Tomorrow ...'
> Tomorrow is here
> And you out there safe.
> I'm in here, Tootsie. (p. 52)

II

Although *Jazz* is indebted to the aesthetics of African-American music, Morrison admitted in an interview that the title might not be right for the novel, believing jazz itself to be more in the background of the book as image and metaphor (Bigsby, 1992). Despite her reservations, the influence of jazz, where the melody is introduced and then subsequently unravelled and embellished, is clear from the outset where the essence of the story is unfurled within the first ten lines and then subsequently retold from different viewpoints. Nearly every critic who has written on the jazz influence on Morrison's work has pointed out how in jazz musicians play against each other, each establishing their own sound in the ensemble which is sometimes developed in long, improvised pieces. In the novel, various characters relate their versions of what has happened, imitating the improvised, collective nature of jazz performance. The text, divided into unnumbered, unequal sections separated by blank pages, is structured as jazz itself, through repetition, embellishment, amplification, variation, and solo displays. Even by the standards of Morrison's previous novels, there is an overt improvised quality to the book in its use of time and ellipses, as well as in the way the narrator frequently hands over to different voices. The light, airy music of ragtime, to which jazz is partly indebted, was an attempt to capture the mood of the decade which the novel in places also tries to recreate in its prose style. But there was a heavier, melancholy strain to the 1920s and to jazz itself which we also find as a counterpoint to the optimism in Morrison's novel.

Eusebio Rodrigues has argued that 'more than just a story of three individuals [Joe, Violet and Joe's lover, Dorcas], the novel, a continuation of *Beloved*, jazzifies the history of a people' (1993, p. 742). I would suggest, however, that the novel is not concerned with 'jazzifying' the history of African-Americans but with the history that is in jazz itself. Indeed, Morrison has suggested as much in her description of the novel as 'a jazz gesture' which draws on what jazz says about the people of the time and about the sensual way in which people related to one another (Bigsby, 1992). Urban black music embraced the complexity of human relationships and the stresses placed on them, often with anger and frustration but sometimes with melting sentimentality, and both these emotions are played off against each other in Morrison's novel. While the image of women projected in the films of the time, which were essentially white, is light-hearted, unconventional and daring, in song, where there was a more obvious black presence, it was more melancholic, even tragic. Indeed, the jazz records of the period and the plot of the novel are directly linked in that it is Duke Ellington's 'Trombone Blues' that Dorcas goes to fetch, leaving her baby sister unattended.

As Arnold Shaw points out, there were numerous songs of unrequited love and of loss. Despair and resignation were keynotes of popular torch songs such as 'I'd Rather Be Blue over You (Than Be Happy with Somebody Else)', 'I Cried for You (Now It's Your Turn to Cry over Me)', and 'Day by Day You're Going to Miss Me' (1987, p. 78). The novel highlights the same concerns of the period as the music: loneliness, the changeability of feelings, emotional insecurity in personal relationships, and the anguish of failure. In doing so, it draws on the personalised nature of jazz lyrics which enabled singers and songwriters, such as the one featured in the novel, to break new ground in exploring emotional situations. Taking its cue from jazz, the novel alternates between external description and internal longings such as Violet's longing for Golden Gray and to be white herself; her desire to have a baby, which becomes 'heavier than sex: a panting, unmanageable craving' (p. 108); the kind of loss suffered by Violet and also articulated in the novel by Alice; and the jealous thirst for vengeance experienced by a number of the novel's characters. Indeed, it is the sensuality, the unpredictability and the dissonance of African-American life during the Jazz Age which the novel probes and develops.

I have already suggested, in drawing attention to Morrison's own linking of *Jazz* with 'the Great American City Novel', that jazz provides only one of many contributory strands to this text. Cautioned by Morrison's own scepticism about the appropriateness of the title, we should resist trying to discover a singular source for her aesthetics, especially given the development of her experimental, multifocal narratives over more than two decades. *Jazz*, like *The Bluest Eye* and *Song of Solomon*, moves backwards and forwards in time. Like *Song of Solomon*, it takes us on a reverse journey from the one which many black Americans undertook after the Civil War; the novel in retracing the past lives of Joe, Violet and their families takes the reader from the North to the South, from the city to the country, and from the twentieth to the nineteenth century. Indeed, the impact of the previous century is more significant in *Jazz* than in *Song of Solomon*, underscoring the importance upon it of *Beloved*. In an interview (Bigsby, 1992), Morrison argues that *Beloved* was 'necessary' to the writing of *Jazz*: 'I would not have understood what the later period was without knowing what it reacted against'. For Morrison, '*Jazz* is about the release of love' and she believes: 'It wouldn't have had the force it did, had I not realised the threat which love posed during slavery and reconstruction.'

III

From Cholly's rape of Pecola in *The Bluest Eye* and Eva's rumoured amputation of her leg on a railway line in *Sula*, Morrison's texts have involved and have often revolved around a series of unpredictable, even ostensibly inexplicable, events. *Jazz* opens with an incident anchored in the kind of subjectivism which in her novels is never totally socialised. But Violet's interruption of Dorcas's funeral service is only one of the acts for which she is well known; others include the occasion when she suddenly sat down in the street. Such incidents, to which I will return later, challenge the routinised behaviours of others by which everyday reality is maintained. When the funeral episode is revisited later in the novel, the emphasis is placed upon the ushers who have to eschew the respect for their elders with which they have been brought up in order to remove her. Indeed, as the two hairdressers who observe Joe with Dorcas in the Mexico club point out, it is only his wife's 'craziness', not her lack of skill, that has prevented her from becoming licensed like themselves.

It is not only Violet's eccentric behaviour – ex-centric in the sense that it is marginal to the centred patterns of social behaviour – which serves to focus the unpredictable in this novel. Although we learn later in the novel that Dorcas reminds him of his mother who abandoned him, Joe's falling in love with Dorcas is initially unexpected and his murder of her, although we can later surmise that it is because he did not want to be abandoned a second time, is initially inexplicable. The reason for this is that in the first full-length description of his character, Joe is reminiscent of Paul D in *Beloved.* Like Paul D, he is a man whom women trust, in whom they confide and with whom they establish something of the rapport usually reserved for other women. But, in *Jazz,* the level of interest in the unpredictable is enhanced by the unreliability of the narrator whose identity is uncertain and whose grasp on the narrative is finally lost: 'The fact that the narrator of the book doesn't always know what happened is part of that conflict between imposed knowledge, fate, and a dissonance, an uncertainty, which is what makes life so original' (Bigsby, 1992). From one of the narrator's first asides – 'Maybe she [Violet] thought she could solve the mystery of love that way. Good luck and let me know' (p. 5) – we are made aware that she is a destabilising element in the narrative. Whilst overtly directing the reader's response, for example, in the description of Dorcas's aunt as hardheaded and sly, she admits she is not the best judge of character; she has lived too long in her own mind, she hasn't mixed with people enough and she needs to get out more.

An inevitable dimension of the city novel's generic pattern of aspiration and disillusion is a concern with the unpredictability of migration and modern urban life. This is in turn often linked, as in *Jazz*, to the violence and criminality of the city with which jazz, of course, originating in the red-light district of Storyville, was itself associated. Lawlessness was the flipside of life in the city in the 1920s – the narrator in *Jazz* alludes to ordinary people taking the law into their own hands. Indeed, the first crime novel by an African-American writer was set in Harlem, Rudolph Fisher's *The Conjure Man Dies: A Mystery Tale of Dark Harlem*. The decade appeared wild and disorderly because, as Malcolm Bradbury observes, it was an era of new manners, of self-conscious fashions and of the exploration of new tastes (Bradbury and Palmer, 1971, p. 12). Nevertheless, the social space of Morrison's novel, where the instability of the urban meets the unpredictability of jazz, is especially volatile and Dorcas's association of the war with partying during the Jazz Age encapsulates the uncertainty and unpredictability of people's lives in the 1920s: 'In war or at a party everyone is wily, intriguing; goals are set and altered; alliances rearranged. Partners and rivals devastated; new pairings triumphant' (p. 191). Indeed, as Eusebio Rodrigues has pointed out, despite the impact of her earlier experiences upon her, 'the story of Dorcas reveals the tremendous impact the City makes on the young and defenceless. It deludes them into believing that they are free to do what they want and get away with it' (1993, p. 747).

Yet here the city novel is again developed from an African-American perspective. For Dorcas's behaviour is the product not only of the wildness of the city but of a wildness that is in her body, literally and figuratively – the horse's hooves that spook Wild into running blind into a tree are the hoofmarks that appear on Dorcas's face, reminding Joe of his mother. In fact, at her death, when she is asked the name of the killer, Dorcas seems to become Wild refusing to disclose the name of her son. Here, Morrison, as an African-American writer, revisions the motifs of continuity and discontinuity in the city novel. For the displacement of communication and collectivism by individualism and self-centredness had a greater significance for black migrants from rural America than for many whites; African-Americans, faced with the racial violence that they thought they had left behind, found that they had lost the collectivity that in the South had enabled them to cope with it. Indeed, Doreatha Mbalia argues that 'the message in the novel is that African people are connected by their history and their culture' (1993, p. 632). In fact, all the female characters benefit when they displace self-interestedness for community – Alice returns to Springfield, no longer afraid of sexuality; Felice grows into a confident, black woman; Joe and Violet come together again; and Golden Gray discovers a humanity previously denied him by his cultural upbringing.

The interconnection of the geographical and the political in Morrison's fiction means that its delineation of social spaces lends itself to analysis within the framework of what is now called 'new' or 'postmodern' geography. In postmodern geography, long-held positivist notions of space as static and autonomous have been displaced by a new-found emphasis on space as the product of wider sociopolitical processes and discourses (Soja, 1989; Keith and Pile, 1993). This provides an especially useful approach to *Jazz* where African-American music in the 1920s, developed by both black and white musicians, was building a space which shaped and was shaped by people's behaviour and which, in turn, was influenced by this particular musical discourse. In this respect, an important analogy is provided in the novel by the marchers in July 1917 who are 'moving slowly into the space the drums were building for them' (p. 53). Many of the characters in *Jazz* similarly occupy a space which jazz is constructing for them, a space in which morality, lifestyles, familial patterns and religions are being renegotiated.

In the novel, it is Alice who specifically identifies the role of jazz in shaping the social space into which people are being drawn:

> It was the music. The dirty, get-on-down music the women sang and the men played and both danced to, close and shameless or apart and wild [...] It made you do unwise, disorderly things. Just hearing it was like violating the law. (p. 58)

But Alice, whose attitudes to men and sexuality have been affected by her husband's affair, misinterprets what is happening. It is not that the music is responsible for disorderly things but that the disorderly things are part of the history in the music itself. There are two dimensions to what is expressed in the music. First, there is anger at the violence that blacks in the North experienced at the hands of whites – as in the example of what happened to Alice's brother-in-law – perhaps fearful of an ever increasing African-American presence as men returned from the War and families continued to migrate from the South. Second, the music conveys emotional/spiritual longing and hunger, themselves products of a history in which black people had been forced to deny their emotional, spiritual and physical needs.

The narrator, enthusiastic about Harlem and excited by its people, becomes increasingly aware of, and interested in, how the new-found self-consciousness of the Jazz Age is linked to lawlessness as an integral feature of life in the decade. Even the gangsters at one point are said to be aware that they are 'being watched for excitement' (p. 7). The 'hoodlums' as they were more affectionately known, were idealised by the public despite the blood on their hands. Prohibition was such an unpopular law in the United States that the agents who tried to enforce it found themselves cast as the real villains of the 1920s while the bootleggers, the speakeasy owners, the rum-runners and the hijackers became, as the narrator in the novel suggests, hoodlums 'handing out goodies'. In the first image that we have of the City, its buildings are being cut in half by daylight as if by a razor, a metaphor that keeps Violet's attempt to slash the face of Dorcas's corpse to the fore whilst anticipating the generalised violence of the metropolis. But here, it is difficult, if not impossible, to distinguish between the 'looking faces' of the inhabitants and those carved by the stonemasons. According to the narrator, survival depends upon being streetwise, a key element of which is learning to 'watch everything and everyone and try to figure out their plans, their reasonings, long before they do' (p. 8). This dimension of life in the city in the 1920s becomes a salient feature of the structure of *Jazz* where not only are different voices and interpretations of events played against each other as in a jazz performance but where one person appears to be constantly watching, while in turn being constantly observed by, others.

IV

Although the Harlem of the Harlem Renaissance – the city of intellectuals such as W. E. Du Bois, E. Franklin Frazier, Langston Hughes and Zora Neale Hurston – barely enters the novel, like the racial violence, the segregation and the marches of the 1920s to which the novel frequently alludes, it is an important part of the background. But if these elements cannot be ignored, neither can the wider world of the 1920s which, although not everyone had equal access to it, impacted on the lives of young, social black aspirants. Whilst not benefiting much themselves from it, it is no coincidence, as Jill Matus has pointed out, that Joe and Violet both work at the unlicensed margins of the beauty business since the cosmetics and hair-straightening heiress A'leila Walker was an important presence in Harlem at this time (Matus, 1998, p. 132). But while it was in the manufacture of cosmetics that Negro women first achieved spectacular success, this aspect of black cultural history is integrated with several themes in *Jazz*. Hair straightening and skin-lightening creams were part of a process for some black women of denying not only their black identity but black history and not only black history but the history that was in their bodies. Here Morrison revisits the motif of the commodification of the body that she first mooted in *The Bluest Eye*. For in both novels, the reader is alerted to the history in the concept of black beauty that is based on cosmetics, a history that embraces the way African-Americans have had to live in a culture dominated by white standards of beauty, in which Caucasian features such as straight, light hair and blue eyes are positively iconicised while Negroid features are associated with ugliness and a lack of morality. Violet, influenced by the stories she has been told by True Belle about Golden Gray, longs to be white. But within this cultural context, the history in, as opposed to simply of, black appearance also embraces the way in which skin colour becomes a feature of quite complex inter- and intraracial prejudices. It is a history in which light skin is shunned by some darker skinned African-Americans, as evidence of some kind of betrayal of black identity, but conversely welcomed by others as signifying some kind of racial and social advancement. Moreover, while white society finds some black skins an anathema, aspects of white society, associating black skin with a primitive animality, eroticise lighter African-American skin, as Jadine's success as a model in *Tar Baby* illustrates.

In *Jazz*, interest in cosmetics and skin-lightening creams among black women in the Jazz Age is part of the book's development of the aspiration/disillusion pattern of the city novel within a specific 1920s context. For the 1920s redefined the social aspirations of many African-Americans, including those whose perceived goals were clearly beyond their reach. The Jazz Age was the decade which saw the motion picture industry come into its own and by 1926 there were over 20 000 cinemas in America. But the perceived influence of the movies in *Jazz* is different from in *The Bluest Eye* where the emphasis is on its representation of white, middle-class American values and standards of beauty. In *Jazz*, the stress falls on the preoccupation with visual images in a culture where visual impact is given priority over other sensual impressions. Nevertheless, *Jazz* returns to subjects raised in Morrison's first novel, the loss of sensuality and the separation of the 'internal' and the 'external'.

Despite the pretence of 'realism', the cinema is the most 'imaginary' of art forms in which representation is quite often far removed from the recording of an authentic experience. Set primarily in what was the decade of cinema, it is not surprising, then, that the distance between image and reality is a key motif in *Jazz*. Dorcas, for example, is accused by the narrator of regarding everything as if it were a picture show, evidenced in her obliviousness to the fact that Joe is a married man, much older than herself and very restricted in the amount of time he can spend with her. The difference between the image that she has of them as a couple and the reality of their relationship is especially obvious when she raises with Joe the possibility of them eloping for a while together. But there are other characters, too, who occupy spaces as imaginary as the image on the cinema screen. For example, Joe associates Dorcas with a piece of sweet candy and Violet, in her longing for a baby, takes dolls to bed. And when Golden Gray arrives at his father's home with Wild, whom he has decided to help, he behaves according to how he has been brought up: taking care of his horse, his trunk and, only then, Wild. For he has been conditioned to think of Africans as possessions, inferior to his horse and his personal belongings.

The split which theorists such as Kristeva and Lacan have identified between the 'I' who speaks and the 'I' who is spoken becomes increasingly pronounced in the novel. What worries Felice about the time when she and Dorcas made up love scenes and described them to each other is the picture which she had of herself doing it. Violet perceives each of the public events in which she behaves eccentrically as 'scenes'; she sees herself doing them as if she were someone else. Both the 'scenes' described in the novel involve a violation of conventions attached to observation. Violet, in attacking Dorcas's face, violates the custom of 'viewing' the corpse whilst in stealing the baby she reneges on the trust implicit in being asked to 'watch' a child for its mother. Dorcas as a teenager is distracted from watching over her baby sister, with tragic consequences.

As I suggested at the end of the previous section, watching, being watched and looking in mirrors are, in fact, salient motifs in the novel: Violet's birdcages have mirrors where the birds can watch themselves; Dorcas practises in front of the mirror to tell Joe that she wishes to end their relationship; and Joe needs a mirror to see the pictures which Dorcas has drawn on his body with lipstick. Barbara Rigney (1991) maintains, in a discussion of Hagar in *Song of Solomon*, that mirrors are dangerous objects in Morrison's fiction because of the images that they reflect, usually conveying white standards of beauty or the illusion of a unified self. Both these dimensions are evident in *Jazz*. Dorcas and Felice come to realise that whilst mirrors reflect back to women their fascination with their own image, it is a fascination dominated, as Rosalind Coward maintains, with discontent; every woman's mirror image is disturbed by the critical glance of the cultural ideal (1985, p. 80). The reflection of a unified sense of self is especially pertinent to *Jazz* for this is a novel where the visual image reflects an apparently authoritative sense of 'reality' that the individual is otherwise unable to muster. After killing Dorcas, Joe panics when the visual memories of her begin to fade as if without them there is nothing.

But in *Jazz*, mirrors also mark a transition from one social reality to another where what is reflected represents a greater regression from social norms. One of the indicators of this dislocation is the way in which the 'inner' and the 'outer' become increasingly separated, leaving the 'external' to become increasingly identified as the self, and, in turn, associated with the illusion of a unified self. Eventually, in the inverse of his experience of remembering Dorcas, Joe, discovering that he is only able to recall a visual narrative of his life with Violet, is unable to reclaim how he felt with her.

The separation of the 'external' from the 'inner' sense of self pervades the representation of the Jazz Age in the novel and, also, presents a particularly perverse development of the discontinuity that is a generic trope of the city novel. In addition to having become distanced from previous experience through life in the city, the black migrants now find themselves alienated from their former sense of self in which the inner, the spiritual and the emotional, and the outer were perceived as interrelated. So, in Harlem in the 1920s, Dorcas seems to live apart from her body as if it is something that is only 'worn' by the real self. Indeed, one night at the age of 16, she is said to have 'stood in her body' whilst she and Felice come to 'know that a badly dressed body is nobody at all' (p. 65). The knowledge referred to here is not a universal truth, if indeed any do exist, but a tuning into the culture of the decade. Morrison's pun on 'nobody' emphasises the extent to which people in the Jazz Age, as represented in the novel, are judged on external appearance. The brothers who attract attention at the party which Dorcas and Felice attend know this, they have smiles that are said to function like light bulbs. It is a ruthless subculture to which they belong and to which Dorcas is attracted; especially for women who, as objects of the male gaze, are judged by men on the basis of the visual impression they make. Dorcas, 'the peppermint girl with the bad skin' (p. 69), finds herself 'acknowledged, appraised and dismissed in the time it takes for a needle to find its opening groove'. As Coward points out, 'the ability to scrutinise is premised on power' (1985, p. 75). Women's inability to return such a critical look is a sign of subordination, often averting the eyes rather than risking, as Coward says, male attention turning into aggression. One of the scenarios played out before the narrator in her early description of the City involves a meeting between a man and a woman. Although we, like the narrator, know nothing about them, it is clear that we are watching a display in power relationships. All the actions confirm that the power lies with the man: he silences the woman's earnest conversation (we do not know what it is about) by touching her lips; he is able to tilt her head which causes her to relax and to loosen her grip on her purse; and he places his hands on the wall so that she is below them. As readers we have no knowledge of what is being said; it is like watching a silent movie. But the body language would seem to suggest that a woman is judged attractive to the male when she conforms to his expectations of her behaviour, particularly sexual behaviour.

Surveillance of the space created by the African-American music and of the streets is converted in the subculture of the 1920s into the pleasure of being watched; at a party, a mere touch is enough to lift one's spirit to the ceiling 'where it floats for a bit looking down with pleasure on the dressed-up nakedness below' (p. 188). But this pleasure in being watched is both a reflection of the preoccupation of the age with the visual and part of the emancipatory spirit of the decade. As Shaw points out, the Nineteenth Constitutional Amendment, passed on 28 August 1920, which gave women the right to vote, significantly affected the mood and mores of the 1920s (Shaw, 1987, p. 12). It helped turn the 1920s into a radical decade as far as behaviour and consciousness were concerned; characterised by an emancipated sexual mores, an increasingly accelerated and tense pace of life and an enormous shift in the moral focus.

Jazz and the blues articulated a cultural and political struggle over sexual relations directed at reclaiming women's sexuality and their bodies from the objectification of female sexuality within a patriarchal order. But jazz and the blues were only partly responsible for creating the culture of the 1920s. The films of the time also appeared to celebrate the new woman and the new morality, although they often ended with the 'flappers' and 'It' girls marrying into middle-class respectability. They carried titles such as *Forbidden Fruit, Flapper Wives, Weekend Wives, Bedroom and Bath, Madness of Youth, Children of Divorce, Modern Maidens,* and *Dancing Mothers.* Advertisements for them spoke of 'Brilliant men, beautiful jazz babies, champagne baths, midnight revels, petting parties in the purple dawn, all ending in one terrific smashing climax that makes you gasp' (Bradbury and Palmer, 1971, p. 51). *Jazz* is located firmly in black Harlem, however, and the wider, essentially white world of the 'flappers', which was the focus of work by white writers such as F. Scott Fitzgerald, only enters the novel indirectly. Yet, as we shall see, it is to this kind of morality that the narrator's own attempt at an improvised piece on love is intended as a counterpoint.

Dorcas herself epitomises the interconnection between the recalcitrant nature of the decade and its music; how social and sexual boundaries were being challenged; and the increased emphasis upon the importance of being in the social gaze. She never allows herself, nor is ever allowed, to come into her own existence because those who are drawn to her eventually reject her or are rejected by her. Her men friends are generally frightened off, not only because she encourages them to break the law but because she gives them the impression that there is no inner consistency to her. For her everything seems to be a kaleidoscope of actions and reactions with little beyond; everything appears to be like 'a picture show'. It is significant that she has to practise her leaving speech to Joe in a mirror because in her world nothing is stable enough or meaningful enough to permit vital linguistic communication to begin. Although there is quite a lot of social and sexual contact, there is no intersubjectivity; she comes to enjoy occupying the gaze of others. When she is with Acton at the party in which she is killed, for example, she touches him not for her own pleasure but because she knows that other girls in the room are watching her enviously. He appears to have a magnetic power over others as if he fills a gap in their lives. But the emotional space in which Dorcas finds herself is confusing, located between the demands of Acton and the undemanding gaze of Joe. In setting their contradictory expectations and views of her in opposition to each other, Dorcas imitates the structural nature of jazz.

Having become increasingly an object of other people's gazes, it is appropriate that Dorcas becomes a spectator at her own death. One of the first things she notices is that heads are turning to watch her fall while the superficiality of constantly occupying spaces constructed by the gaze of others is betrayed by Acton's response to her; he is more concerned about the blood on his jacket and shirt than the fact that she has been shot. As the recurring mirror images throughout the novel suggest, surface is more important than substance. Dorcas eventually occupies, if only she would realise it, a world given over to surfaces, outlines and veils. Indeed, Dorcas herself is less worried by the prospect of death than by missing something important which she senses is about to happen.

The recurring motifs of watching and being watched, to which I drew attention above, are central to the novel's pursuit of an obsession with external appearances. Whilst Colonel Wordsworth Gray's rage at the fact that his daughter is pregnant by a black boy expresses itself in a violent slap, the repulsion in the look which her mother gives her has the greater and more lasting impact. As throughout Morrison's work, the body is the visible representation of the identity by which black people are victimised. When Vera Louise and her black maid, True Belle, bath her son, he is conscious of, but does not understand, the looks that pass between them as they examine the backs of his hands and his hair. At another level, Violet's longing for a child, which is described as a 'deep-dreaming' in which she is drowning, finds expression in obsessively staring at infants and toy displays at Christmas. But it is Dorcas who is the object of the key fixations with which the novel is concerned. Joe's and Violet's obsessions with her are united yet distinguished one from another in their shared fixation with her photograph staring from their mantelpiece. In describing Joe's behaviour after he has killed Dorcas, how he thinks about her all the time and how he cannot work or sleep, Violet is really describing in so many words her own preoccupation with the young woman. Violet's obsession with Dorcas is realised in her search to discover everything she can about her, but Joe's obsession reaches its climax in his journey to kill her. As intensely as Dorcas appears to stare out of the photograph at Violet, Violet studies the detail of

Dorcas's gaze, even noticing that her split ends need trimming. Each of them sees different things in Dorcas's gaze: whilst for Joe, who sees the face of his mother who abandoned him, her face exudes calm and generosity, for Violet her stare is haughty and greedy.

The women included in the initial description of the City in *Jazz* are located in the space between the visible objectification of women within the male gaze and the reclamation of their bodies and their sexuality as sites of their own subjectivity:

> The woman who churned a man's blood as she leaned all alone on a fence by a country road might not expect even to catch his eye in the City. But if she is clipping quickly down the big-city street in heels, swinging her purse, or sitting on a stoop with a cool beer in her hand, dangling her shoe from the toes of her foot, the man, reacting to her posture, to soft skin on stone, the weight of the building stressing the delicate, dangling shoe, is captured. And he'd think it was the woman he wanted, and not some combination of curved stone, and a swinging, high-heeled shoe moving in and out of sunlight. (p. 34)

Here the reader's attention is drawn to what mediates these images. The socially constructed space which the women have come to occupy according to recognised patterns of behaviour is emphasised more than the women themselves. For the women remain anonymous types rather than individuals. But what is also depicted is the man's status as spectator, his relation to the body images which serve as a means of articulating identity and difference, and even of challenging boundaries. As often in the visually dominated culture of the twentieth century, images of women reflect the obsessive distancing of them.

Individual gestures are signs that acquire meaning from the subculture which they signify. The verb 'clipping' emphasises the woman's self-confident sexuality and the way she walks so as to centre herself in the male gaze, reinforcing the high heels themselves as one of Western culture's most potent sexual symbols. Her swinging purse signifies a daring abandonment which calls attention to herself and to what women in a city with a great deal of crime might otherwise wish to conceal. At the centre of a socially constructed space she is able to create an identity, albeit with a masculinised bias, that signifies devil-may-care self-confidence. A woman drinking beer in public in the 1920s signified the subversion of traditional notions of femininity and conventional modes of behaviour; a recalcitrance which epitomised the Jazz Age itself. Again the high-heeled shoe is significant; in itself suggesting sexuality, but swinging from the woman's foot conveying a sense of unfettered, sexual confidence which the man who is cast as a voyeur finds – and is meant to find – seductive.

Arnold Shaw attributes many of the changes in what was socially acceptable behaviour for women to the Nineteenth Constitutional Amendment including 'women smoking in public, bobbing their hair (to look more like men), seductively raising the hem of their skirts, rolling their stockings to expose bare knees, and flaunting their sexuality' (Shaw, 1987, p. 12). But all this was encouraged, as he observes, by the music of the decade and although his description is of white rather than black women, the relaxation of social conventions in the way in which women dressed and behaved, as Morrison recognises, had an impact upon black women, too. Alice's memories in *Jazz* of how her parents brought her up is indirectly an assessment of how far conventions had changed in the 1920s and how what was happening in white New York was impacting also on Harlem. Alice's upbringing is also intended as an explanation for the repressive attitudes which she passed on to Dorcas and may be one of the reasons, notwithstanding the impact of the fire upon her, why Dorcas turned out as she did.

In effect, Alice provides a commentary on the repression which the 1920s removed for women. She remembers being instructed that there was a 'womanish' way to sit, with legs crossed, being warned about slumping at table and being told firmly about 'switching' when she walked. As soon as her breasts developed they were 'bound and resented' while her legs were always hidden; her parents frowned when they could not lower the hems any further. In the style of jazz composition, Alice's memories embellish the narrator's description of the women discussed above and act as a counterpoint to them. However, the contrast is not simply a matter of changing fashions. The women who clip down steps in high heels swinging their purses and who drink beer in public exude a new-found confidence and pride in themselves and their sexuality. As a counterpoint to Joe's observations toward the end of the novel on the easy availability of some of the women, Alice respects women who have not surrendered to male expectations, especially those who protect themselves with violence.

Alice's memory of the Swedish tailor for whom she worked telling her of the black woman who slashed his face from ear to mouth and her memories of other men with facial injuries articulate the depth of the change that was taking place. For behind these stories of men getting their comeuppance there are untold narratives of sexual harassment, of black women being fondled in kitchens, called names and even being punched in the face by police. Once again in the style of jazz composition, Alice revisits an earlier statement by the narrator, embellishing it and approaching it from a different angle. Her ruminations on the folded blades which some black women carried, their packets of lye and the shards of glass which they taped to their hands provide a commentary on the narrator's earlier insistence on the need to be streetwise, to watch people and try to figure out what they are going to do before they know themselves.

At their most obsessive, both Joe and Violet confirm the narrator's observation early in the novel that if you do not know when to love and when to quit you end up being controlled by a force outside yourself. The extent to which Joe is in the grip of his obsession when he sets out to murder Dorcas is conveyed in the way his consciousness appears to collapse in retreat from the seeming unreality around him. Fearful of being rejected a second time, in his mind the figures of Dorcas and Wild are elided. As he journeys with his gun into the City to find her, he is driven at a deep level by a primitive instinct which emerges while his moral being lapses into amnesia. Obviously something is gained by this return to a primitive, instinctual being, to the time when he was taught to hunt by Hunters Hunter, but the narrative emphasises what is lost. His speechless, physical contact with the other passengers in the railway carriage, such as the woman who returns the bag in which his gun is concealed, is emblematic of the way he is regressing from the world around him. Increasingly, he moves unconsciously in the space between his past and his present and the different levels which compose social reality. Thus, the fact that he thinks of himself hunting not Dorcas but the mother who abandoned him determines how he interprets the women around him. His observation, as mediated by the narrator, of the girls who 'clack' down the stairs from the train, and his noticing their red lips and their stockinged legs that appear to 'whisper' to each other, betray his deep suspicion of women. The City women whom we discussed above, acquiring meaning from the subculture in which they are based, are now in Joe's eyes agents in their own prostitution. Up to a point, the make-up and stockings are signs of the power which they have accrued in reclaiming their bodies and their sexuality as parts of their own subjectivity. But to Joe these are signs of their fickleness and their readiness to abandon those who love them.

In the style of jazz composition, the novel concludes with the narrator attempting an improvised piece on the quality of mature love which acts as a counterpoint to the relationship between Joe and Dorcas. Dorcas, as we have said, emphasised the body as something to be seen, trying to persuade Joe at one point that they could sit together at round tables with lamps on them. But the final improvisation on love recommends that the body is 'the vehicle' not 'the point' of love; whereas Dorcas stresses the visual, the narrator here emphasises touch. Indeed, the concluding sections of the novel subvert all the earlier insistence on watching and being watched: 'They are under the covers because they don't have to look at themselves any more; there is no stud's eye, no chippie glance to undo them' (p. 228). The 'whispers' between long-time lovers under the covers contrast with, and are a commentary upon, Dorcas's aspiration that she and Joe will be able to spend their time touching each other intimately in secret beneath the tablecloths. Whereas many of the characters in the novel are concerned with looking out into the various gazes upon them, these older lovers are perceived as being turned inwards towards each other.

In the final page of the novel, the narrator, like Wild herself in some respects, reveals herself as someone who has only experienced the kind of secret affairs promoted in the music, the films and the jazz culture of the time. But, as Doreatha Mbalia has pointed out, by the end of the story, the narrator is 'qualitatively different because she has learned from her mistakes' (1993, p. 638). She envies the way in which legitimate lovers are able to express their feelings in public by touching each other across a table and straightening or brushing each other's clothes. Her own improvisation on love celebrates monogamy and faithfulness; a counterpoint to the so-called new morality of the Jazz Age. Conversely, much of the novel – the difficulties, anguish and frustrations of love in the 1920s – acts as a counterpoint to this final piece – as we would expect in a jazz composition.

V

As I suggested above, discontinuity is a salient motif in many city novels, arising from the radical difference between life in the city and the small town or rural area that has been left behind. But meandering between the city and the country, between Harlem and Vesper, Virginia, *Jazz* complicates this aspect of the genre. The history in jazz and the African-American music that the black migrants from the South bring with them to the North complements the novel's critique of the history which Morrison finds in the city novel. Displacing nostalgia in the face of discontinuity, to which the city novel is, implicitly or explicitly, prone, country images in *Jazz*, as Eusebio Rodrigues has pointed out, 'when used for city life, become charged with irony' (1993, p. 747). But, at another level, the discontinuity between life in the city and in the rural South from which the black migrants came is analogous to the discontinuity they experienced in being transported from Africa to America. In both cases, the former life exists for subsequent generations only in the form of traces, as Joe's name itself indicates. Within this context, the fact that Joe has only scraps of information about his mother – a scrap of a song or a trace of her presence left behind in the wood – which sometimes he has not even heard or seen for himself is analogous to the fragmented knowledge that the slaves had of their African homelands.

The history in black music, as I indicated at the outset, is not only the history of the migration but of the period before migration. Following the way in which *Beloved* articulates what has been absent in histories of slavery and Reconstruction, *Jazz* revisions the history of the rural South in which Joe and Violet have their origins. In reaching back to the South of the 1870s, *Jazz* takes the reader on a reverse journey from that undertaken by its key protagonists. However, not only is the style of the novel different in the chapters that reach back to the nineteenth century from those depicting life in 1920s Harlem but the reader is presented with a semi-mystical, almost fabulistic Southern landscape. These stylistic differences, together with the spatio-temporal shift, underscore the impression that these Southern chapters, reflecting perhaps the arbitrariness and unpredictability of jazz, are part of a digression from the main story lines. So much so, in fact, that a number of critics, such as Angela Burton (1988), have responded to the challenge, arguing that they are carefully integrated with the main themes, and have maintained that they not only develop the salient motifs but may actually be crucial to understanding what is at the heart of the novel.

As Morrison's depiction of life on the slave plantations for black women in *Beloved* is an engagement with the history in pre-Civil War slave narrative, her engagement with the South during the period of Reconstruction is posited on the history in Southern romance narratives. However, this has not been generally noticed by critics even though the style, the mythical nature and the content of the chapters depicting life in the South clearly parody the Southern romance narrative. The Southern romance narrative itself is, in fact, appropriate to the concern in *Jazz* with black history. Not because the South is as obviously crucial to African-American history as the African-American is to the history of the South but because the romance wrote up the history of the South, and of African-Americans, in a particular kind of narrative. Moreover, it is possible that Morrison is once again invoking work written by black women in the latter part of the nineteenth century, especially the work of Anna Julia Cooper. In Cooper's *Voices from the South; By a Black Woman of the South* (1892), for example, the Southern narrative is seen as the key to understanding the unwritten history of the United States. It is deemed responsible for the dominance of Southern influence, its ideals and ideas, themselves evident in the way patriarchal power established and sustained gendered and racialised social formations.

While the Southern romance did not invent the South – the cotton gin and the slavery plantations that it made possible were largely responsible for that – it transformed a rural, largely illiterate, region into a mythologised geographical and racial entity capable of engendering profound emotion. Although the historical novel did not originate in America with the publication of Sir Walter Scott's Waverley novels – Virginians had written novels concerned with historical events before the appearance of Scott's work – it was due to his influence that the historical romance became a major genre in America and especially in the South, through the work of, for example, William Gilmore Simms (1806–70) and John Kennedy (1795–1870). The genre came to mediate relationships between the physical landscape of the South and artistic practice, enabling the clash of philosophical, moral, social and cultural values to be reconciled in a Romantic vision of the past, of tradition and of genteelism.

The Southern chapters in *Jazz* present the reader, somewhat mischievously, with some of the stock themes – miscegenation, the abandoned child, concealed paternity, the adoration of the 'white' child – of the Southern romance; the geography that the romance narratives mythologised; and some of the stock characters: True Belle, the old black mammy figure; Golden Gray, the illegitimate son who is the product of miscegenation; the savage, wild female associated with the mystical landscape; and the wealthy young daughter of a powerful white landowner who has a sexual relationship with a black man. The parody echoes, though, the way in which some of these themes were ridiculed in the work of nineteenth-century African-American women writers. Anna Julia Cooper's *Voices from the South*, for example, parodies, as in this part of *Jazz*, the South's preoccupation with 'blood', inheritance and heritage in the search for aristocratic lineage and proof of biological, racial superiority. And there are other parallels between this central section of *Jazz* and the work of nineteenth-century black women novelists and intellectuals. As Hazel Carby points out, some of them argued, on the evidence of the white press, that, despite the miscegenation laws, white women, like Morrison's Vera Louise, encouraged black male/white female relationships. Frequently in their work, mixed race figures, as in this section of *Jazz*, are seen historically, symbolic of particular social relations and practices, and are employed to express the relation between races prevailing at a particular time (Carby, 1985, p. 274).

If *Beloved* is concerned to reclaim what had been occluded in slave narratives, *Jazz* rescues aspects of African-American history distorted in the Southern romance from stereotype and formulaic story telling. To this end, Morrison employs a mysterious, unreliable narrator, a variety of voices, irony and innuendo. Much of the narrative is oblique, or appears so initially, and there are a number of loose ends. We never know, for example, what happens to Wild, it is only hinted that she may have been killed in the canefield burnings, nor what happens to Golden Gray other than that he gives up his mission to avenge himself on his father after discovering his true, black paternity. The Southern romance formula is undermined primarily, however, by intertwining the realistic nature of Joe and Violet's story with the folklorish, generic elements of Golden Gray's story. On his way to his father, he encounters Wild and, disappearing into the dark wood, he assists at the birth of Joe along with Hunters Hunter. Hunter, who as a boy had a relationship with Vera Louise Gray, the white daughter of a rich landowner, becomes a father figure to Joe, teaching him to hunt. Joe and Violet's more down-to-earth story stands in sharp contradistinction, despite the interconnections between the two stories, to these folklorist, almost mythical, features. Violet's story is one of dispossession and its psychic impact upon individuals. Her father is absent when he is needed most, her mother commits suicide and the family is rescued by True Belle, Violet's grandmother, who in the Golden Gray story is the stereotypical black mammy but in the Violet story is the benevolent black ancestor. Indeed, the more down-to-earth narrative of Violet and Joe encourages us to see some of the stock characters and motifs of the Golden Gray story differently. As Doreatha Mbalia argues, 'Wild in *Jazz*, signifies defiance, rebelliousness, aggressiveness, selfishness, and silence – all caused by class exploitation and race and/or gender oppression' (1993, p. 625). The novel, in fact, encourages us to consider the reasons for Wild's behaviour, as *Beloved* encourages us to think about the extenuating circumstances that drove Sethe/Margaret Garner to commit infanticide, and the conditions that black women from before Sethe's mother's generation to Violet's generation have had to endure. Thus, ultimately, the Southern romance is undermined by what it occludes or at best sanitises, such as segregation, the brutal eviction of African-Americans from the land, and the exploitation of black labour. In 1901, Joe and Violet are evicted from land that they thought they owned; Joe is almost burned to death in the 1917 summer riots in New York; Dorcas's father is pulled from a bus and stomped to death while her mother is burned to death; and Dorcas herself, as an eight-year-old orphan, is rescued by her aunt from the riots in East St Louis. The context of Violet's life – her mother's suicide, falling in love with a half-white boy she has never even seen – helps to explain the unpredictability in her character, to which I drew attention earlier. After all, there are traces of Wild in her, as in Joe; traces of Wild's defiance and aggressiveness.

Jazz, then, is a novel which is not so much about the music but the lives of the people during the decade which the music helped to create. Although jazz obviously influenced the structure and style of the novel, it would be rather limiting not to see the book in the way in which we have approached all of Morrison's novels in this study. Like her other works, *Jazz* is concerned with aspects of African-American history and experience which had not previously been fully articulated. Its experiments with form and language are a development of the history to be found in jazz music itself, but also of the history, together with its occlusions, distortions and 'absent presences', to be found in the 'Great American City Novel' and in the Southern romance narrative.

VI

Paradise focuses on an ostensibly isolated and self-sufficient black town, although, as we might expect in a novel by Toni Morrison, that position is revealed as more complex as the novel proceeds and frequently circles back upon itself. As in the other two novels in this trilogy, as I pointed out at the beginning of this chapter, a major traumatic event is at the heart of the narrative – in this case the raid that the men of Ruby lead on an adjacent, ostensibly separatist, female community, the Convent, occupying what was formerly an embezzler's decadent mansion.

Separatist movements, particularly cults in which women celebrated female rituals and sought to (re)claim the pastoral, were an important motif in post-1950s science fiction and American 'last days', futuristic narratives. Indeed, Reverend Pulliam and Pastor Cary in *Paradise* actually try to turn what began happening in other places during the war into an apocalyptic narrative: 'Evil Times, said Reverend Pulliam from New Zion's pulpit. Last Days, said Pastor Cary at Holy Redeemer' (p. 102). Separatist ideas, however, have been developed differently in African-American science fiction from white American science fiction. Octavia E. Butler's *Mind of My Mind* (1977) for example, develops the idea of the ghetto as a separate community. Set in the near future in a suburb of Los Angeles, the inhabitants face problems conventionally associated with the American city ghetto such as drug addiction, prostitution, racialism and child abuse. Samuel R. Delany's *Dhalgren* (1975; rev. 1977) similarly seems to have the traditional image of the American ghetto in mind. Again it is set in the near future where a decayed and violent city is located adjacent to other cities at the outer edge of the 'normal' world. However, one of the most innovative revisions of the notion of a separatist community from an African-American perspective is Octavia Butler's *Kindred* (1979) in which a woman living in present day California is snatched away to an antebellum Maryland plantation where she experiences the powerlessness of being a black female slave.

Of course, separatist or cult writing has a long history in the United States, reaching back to the late eighteenth and early nineteenth centuries in communities established by groups from Europe seeking religious freedom such as the Shakers (1780) or the Rapp's colonies at Harmony, New Harmony and Economy (1804–1905) and to the native-born communities of the mid-nineteenth century such as those established by the Transcendentalists at Fruitlands (1843–4) or Brook Farm (1840–1) and by the Oneidan Perfectionists (1848–80). There is, of course, an equally long history of female separatist communities that the Convent in *Paradise* invokes. The Shaker communities, founded by Mother Ann Lee, offered women autonomy, an equal voice in their management and separate and independent living quarters. Generally speaking, their practices were more joyous than in the patriarchal sects.

In contrast to much post-1950s separatist writing, the presence of the Convent as a female 'collective' is embodied in the structure of *Paradise* itself – each chapter of which bears the name of a woman from the town or from the Convent. In each chapter, the movement between characters and the focalised narrative call into question not only the source of any given idea but the construction of 'reality' itself. The sense of a female collectivity which emerges from the chapters – blurring the boundaries between the Convent and the town, and between race, age and ideology – extends and interrogates the initial impression that we have of the Convent as a separate community from Ruby. This is evident, for example, when Dovey consults other women – her sister (and sister-in-law), Mable Fleetwood, Anna Flood and other women in the Club – over the argument generated by the motto on the Oven (p. 83). Moreover, the novel explores the extent to which there is a female collectivity, however heterogeneous, not only adjacent to but within Ruby itself. In the work of many black women writers, including Morrison herself, Alice Walker and Gloria Naylor, older women such as mothers and aunts are often the most independent characters with a strong sense of their own completeness. But part of the history in the bodies of black women – for example, in how they carry themselves, how they position themselves in relation to others and even in how they dress – as *Paradise* recognises, is the history of how they have been inscribed as 'Woman'; and the 'collectivity' of women in the novel is based on this.

But, of course, *Paradise* is more than a version of the separatist genre. As an African-American writer, Morrison invokes the history in American separatist literature, while employing some of its salient themes and motifs to engage with the black nationalist movements of the 1960s and 1970s and the Black Aesthetic. In doing so, she dramatises the conflicts not only among the various black schools of thought – 'integrationalists', 'separatists' and 'pan-Africanists' – but within them. The history in these debates was one of frustration that what was enshrined in the Civil Rights Acts of 1957 and in the Supreme Court Rulings of 1956–9 was not immediately realised and of anger at the hardship and oppression which continued to be endured by African-Americans, particularly in the South. The 1960s saw mass protests in Birmingham, Selma, Alabama; marches on Washington; Freedom Rides designed to test the segregation that African-Americans routinely encountered in their daily life; interracial attempts to educate and register voters in Mississippi; and the Selma-to-Montgomery march of 1965. It was also a history of debate between those who preached non-violent protest and those, such as the Black Panther movement, who argued for more direct action. But, it was also a history, as I pointed out in chapter 1, that, as realised in a black nationalist aesthetic, was essentially male, as well as black, and which occluded women and the physical and sexual abuse they suffered from black men.

In particular, Morrison is interested in *Paradise* in the way the existence of separatist communities redraws the geographical and psychological landscape of the regions in which they are situated: 'Who could have imagined that twenty-five years later [after leaving Haven] in a brand-new town a Convent would beat out the snakes, the Depression, the tax man and the railroad for sheer destructive power?' (p. 17). In the course of the novel, she develops the suspicion of cults and the fear of what lies outside the social norms that are an integral part of the history in many utopian/dystopian narratives of the 1960s/1970s. This is exemplified, ironically as things turn out, in Steward Morgan's explanation to the child Anna Flood of the Scorpion – which only raised its tail because it was as scared of her as she was of it (p. 116):

> Strange neighbors, most folks said, but harmless. More than harmless, helpful even on occasion. They took people in – lost folk or folks who needed a rest. Early reports were of kindness and very good food. But now everybody knew it was all a lie, a front, a carefully planned disguise for what was really going on. (p. 11)

In *Beloved*, the way in which white America configures African-Americans, as I argued in the previous chapter, says more about white fears and what white people are capable of than it does about black peoples. In *Paradise*, the response of the black community to the Convent is similarly de-facing, so that the oppression, self-interestedness and cruelty within Ruby, and within individuals themselves, stand more fully revealed. As Connie says to Mavis: 'Scary things not always outside. Most scary things is inside' (p. 39). The way in which a whole range of characters in the novel stand more fully revealed to us in their response to the Convent may have been a narrative strategy that Morrison learned from William Faulkner, since *The Sound and the Fury* and *As I Lay Dying*, for example, are both structured around a central character to whom others respond in self-revealing ways. In these novels, as in *Paradise*, the responses suggest that the centre of the community is located more at its outer limits than we expected. In *Paradise*, Gigi's discovery that the centre of Ruby is also its edge is both a literal and a figurative truth. One of the key histories that is developed in the novel lies in the reaction of the men of Ruby to the Convent – a history of misogynism, which includes fear of the female body and of female sexuality, and a deep-rooted desire to control women.

The men's boast that there isn't 'a slack or sloven woman anywhere in town' (p. 8) betrays how much real freedom women lack in Ruby. Indeed, the narrator points out that if the Old Father Zechariah's name is taken as an allusion to the Old Testament prophet rather than the father of John the Baptist, then it is associated with a curse, in which a woman perceived as 'wickedness' is, according to Patricia's version, sealed in a basket with a lid of lead and hidden away in a house (p. 192). Steward Morgan's view of domesticity, later in the novel but earlier in the chronology, reinforces this oppression of women:

> Quiet white and yellow houses full of industry; and in them were elegant black women at useful tasks; orderly cupboards minus surfeit or miserliness; linen laundered and ironed to perfection; good meat seasoned and ready for roasting. It was a view he would be damned if K. D. or the idleness of the young would disturb. (p. 111)

The narrative, in presenting us here with Steward's perspective, allows us to hear his language. 'Damned' is a word with which he is associated at several points in the novel; ironically because in leading the massacre on the Convent, ostensibly to protect what he takes pride in in Ruby, he does indeed damn himself and the town, although in the miraculous disappearance of the bodies, the men would appear to have been 'given' a second chance. But this novel interlocks with a further aspect of Faulkner's fiction – along with Virginia Woolf's work the subject of the dissertation for Morrison's Master's degree – its depiction of the old South as ruined by its suicidal social order and by antebellum planters who could not cope with the modern world. It is particularly ironic that Ruby is in part destroyed by its social order which is based on skin colour and by men who refuse to recognise that in the wider world the old antagonistic binarisms are being eroded in more complex interracial relationships. At one level, the Convent becomes a scapegoat for the decline of the town, itself a familiar motif in small-town writing from many different parts of the world. But Morrison stresses that individual towns and regions, now subject to global economic and social forces, are no longer the sole determinants of their prosperity or decline. The population of Haven, for example, declined as cotton collapsed; railroad companies laid their tracks elsewhere, the young people left and more inhabitants became involved in mixed-race relationships.

In the way in which the men of Ruby, having scapegoated the Convent, seek justification for the massacre by trying to find evidence of a neglect of domestic duties, there is a long history of the oppression of women. But this history is conflated with another that is based on the Bible. Their belief that the Convent is really 'the devil's bedroom, bathroom, and his nasty playpen' (p. 17) – bedroom and bathroom are pointedly elided here – is based not only on evidence of a lack of attention to household duties, for example that the women have not washed the mason jars ready for storing food, but on evidence of satanic practices. The implication is that the two are interconnected. While in the former there is a history of the oppression of women within the house, in the latter there is a history which 'others' opponents of Judaeo-Christianity as idolaters, evident in the allegation that 'graven idols were worshipped' (p. 9) in the Convent. Invoking this history, the men of Ruby seek to justify the massacre by associating it with the killing of the idolaters at Moses's command in the Old Testament (Exodus 32). Again this is ironic, for in making a shrine out of a utility, the Oven, the men of Ruby have committed an analogous kind of blasphemy according to the Bible (p. 103).

When the men enter the Convent and massacre its inhabitants, the innermost reaches of the mansion are associated with the female body and with an unbridled sexuality. Their conviction that there is a 'female malice that hides here' transforms what would otherwise be regarded as wholesome domestic smells such as 'the yeast-and-butter smell of rising dough' (p. 4). Indeed, the youngest man sees, or thinks he sees, colours that reinforce the presence of unlicensed sexual activity: 'imperial black sporting a wild swipe of red, then, thick, feverish yellow. Like the clothes of an easily had woman' (p. 4). In this last phrase, there is not only hypocrisy, of course, but a deep-rooted ambivalence toward the sexualised, female body itself. The first woman to be shot appears to wave her fingers at them, a reminder of a further history in the representation of women, based on the association in the Bible of Eve with the serpent, of wayward women as the guilty seducers of God-fearing men. Not coincidentally, the room that worries the men most is the bathroom, so closely associated, as Morrison says, with female 'liquid', with the real biological female body at which the men balk – 'With relief he backs out and closes the door. With relief he lets his handgun point down' (p. 9) – rather than with the iconicised, sanitised woman.

Thus, fear of female sexuality is a recurring motif in *Paradise*. Mikey's tale of the reaction of a Methodist community to a rock formation of a couple making love suggests an uncomfortableness on their part not only with sexuality but with lesbianism: 'The committee members said their objections were not antisex at all but antiperversion, since it was believed by some, who had looked very carefully, that the couple was two women making love in the dirt' (p. 63). But another history is invoked here; a history in which sexual relationships between women have been occluded, rendered as an evil 'other' or eroticised within a male gaze. Mikey's story demonstrates, as does the Convent near Ruby and the arrival in the town of Gigi, how the presence of any suggestion of overt, and especially different, sexuality can change the social, psychological and geographical map of an area and produce extreme reactions – Mikey reports that the Methodists consider blowing up the rock formation or disguising it with cement. The subject of lesbian relationships was not fully explored in African-American writing until the 1970s, by which time it was beginning, at least in metropolitan America, to lose some of its taboo status. But even in Ann Allen Shockley's *Loving Her* (1974), the first black novel to deal candidly with interracial lesbian love, the least tolerance toward the novel's central relationship is shown by the black community not because it is mixed race but because it is lesbian.

Appearing, when the bus departs, between the schoolhouse and the Holy Redeemer, Gigi literally and metaphorically disrupts the continuum between these two poles of Ruby. In a rather unsubtle rendering of how the men of Ruby see Gigi, she is initially presented to us as the girl with the 'screaming tits'. She becomes the new 'centre' for all the men lounging at the Oven and for K.D.'s pregnant girlfriend, Arnette, who, recognising the competition, immediately denounces her as a 'tramp'. But, like the Convent itself, Gigi de-faces Ruby. In their reactions to her, as to the relationship between K. D. and Arnette, the men reveal themselves for what they really are. However, it is not just the way in which women are regarded as sex objects that is disturbing but the devious way in which they are surveyed. When he gives her a lift on his way to collect Mother's body from the Convent, Roger Best, for example, pretends to be looking at the scenery while all the time staring at Gigi's navel, undressing her with his eyes and almost committing a visual rape. But the other side of the coin is how far Ruby de-faces Gigi. De-faced by the town and by her behaviour at the Convent, Gigi is rendered an ambivalent and confusing character. It is appropriate that the chapter 'Grace' ends with her naked for it encourages us to reflect upon how far she stands revealed in the narrative. In other words, the novel questions the extent to which Gigi can be said to be – or indeed is aware of herself as – a black Woman, that is a woman acting out male expectations of a woman as opposed to a black woman who is actually in control and only masquerading as a Woman.

It is no coincidence that in the discussion prior to the raid on the Convent, the mind-reading midwife, Lone DuPres, allegedly 'overhears' the women described as 'Bitches. More like witches' (p. 276). Convent and coven, it would appear, are easily elided. In fact, witchcraft had a strong presence in women's separatist writing and activities in the 1960s and 1970s even though some feminists saw it as a diversion from political goals. For example, in 1971, a number of Californian covens joined together in a ritual to try to end the Vietnam War. But witchcraft is often approached in one of two ways, either as satanic practice, which is how the men of Ruby see the activities at the Convent, or as neo-paganism, the perspective from which at times the novel itself elides the Convent and the coven as well as blurring the boundaries between the Convent and the town. Connie and several women from the town share a common language of magic and miracle, to which I will return later. But within the Convent, where, as in the neo-pagan model of witchcraft the body/soul dualism is rejected, the paganism is taken further than in Ruby. There is an overt emphasis upon the worship of life rather than an abstract male god of death and upon women's autonomy and their potential divinity – Pallas is renamed 'Divine'. These neo-pagan beliefs are highlighted at the end of the novel when the rains for which the Convent women have longed finally arrive – analogous to amniotic fluids breaking. The experience is not only cleansing but sensual and sexual: 'It was like lotion on their fingers so they entered it and let it pour like balm on their shaved heads and upturned faces' (p. 283). Indeed, the indictment Lone allegedly overhears, that women 'don't need men and they don't need God' (p. 276), reinforces the elision of the Convent and coven because witchcraft is a goddess-centred religion. From a feminist perspective, witchcraft runs counter to Judaeo-Christian tradition which in its iconicising of a passive, asexual virgin and a virgin birth can be seen as denying the female body, denying women their sexuality, and disallowing women their divinity. Connie, as Consolata Sosa, urging the women not to accept the body/spirit dualism that inevitably privileges one over the other, recommends a female rather than a male Biblical narrative: 'Never put one over the other. Eve is Mary's mother. Mary is the daughter of Eve' (p. 263). Indeed, one must remember that Zechariah Morgan's name may be taken to allude to the father of John the Baptist who was temporarily struck dumb – an inversion of the way in which women are generally silenced – until his wife, Elizabeth, gave birth to John. Elizabeth herself belongs with Sarah, Rebekah and Hannah in the Old Testament, women who suffered because they were unable to bear children or were unable to do so for a long period of time. These women, who knew suffering at the hands of men, constitute a female presence which challenges the dominant male narratives in the Bible, providing in effect a different means of accessing the Bible from the conventional father/son narrative.

Lone apparently 'overhears' that the women at the Convent need neither God nor men and the latter reinforces the awe and the fear with which women, and their independence, are viewed by the men of Ruby. This is reflected in the way women start to go to the hospital in Demby rather than to Lone to have their babies. While one explanation for this is that she is blamed for the deformed Flood children, another is that the men are afraid of her skills and would rather attend the hospital where men are in charge and they can wait with other men.

Thus, in *Paradise* Morrison explores an aspect of writing about separatist women's cults that has been overlooked, the history of how female sexual independence has been set up as something to be feared. The chapter entitled 'Consolata', which fleshes out Connie's history, through allusions to Bram Stoker's *Dracula* and the numerous vampire narratives from which it was derived – the first literary vampire in an English narrative was created by Byron in the same session where Mary Godwin was prompted to write *Frankenstein* – places this dimension of the separatist narrative in a wider literary-historical context. Connie sleeps in a cellar and is said to have only 'rose aboveground' (p. 221) at night or in the shadowy part of the day – the use of the word 'rose' here is an especially pointed allusion to the vampire narrative as is her depiction as a creature of the night. She can hardly bear light, a salient characteristic of vampires, and as a result of a sunshot searing her right eye, she has bat vision – bats, of course, are creatures into which vampires traditionally transform themselves. She is said to be in love with the cemetery and to long for death, the release that vampires traditionally desire. In this particular chapter, the mansion is described as a castle, a frequently depicted haunt of vampires, and when the other women visit her, they are said to 'float down the stairs [...] like maidens entering a temple or a crypt' (p. 222). If all this were not enough, she bites Deacon's lip and is described as having 'hummed over the blood she licked from it' (p. 239), a relationship that releases her from a death-in-life trance – a 'stone cold womb' (p. 229) and 30 years of celibacy.

Morrison is not suggesting, of course, that Connie is a vampire. Bloodsucking in the conventional vampire narrative signifies sexual intercourse or, indeed, rape, usually of a female by a male. But here the convention is inverted: it is Connie who, symbolically, 'rapes' Deacon. In the vampire story, usually the female victim, guiltily, desires sexual intercourse and is secretly grateful for the vampire's attentions. But Deacon, in the inverted scenario, is outraged and frightened: 'Don't ever do that again' (p. 339). Morrison also inverts the conventional scenario whereby it is the male who regains his strength and power through a beautiful female. Here the power is situated not in a male but in a female body; in other words, in her difference from men. While women, we are reminded, are defined by men in terms of their biology, they are denied subjectivity because of their 'otherness' and because of the uncontrollable, and, from a male perspective, frightening power that it engenders.

Vampirism reflected nineteenth-century, and especially Victorian, anxiety about sexual disease and prostitution for, like sexual disease, it is spread through blood. But vampirism, as displaced sexual activity, also betrayed the need in Victorian society to control women and the spaces that they occupied. Indeed, as far as the latter is concerned, the history that Morrison discovered in the vampire narrative, and which informs the numerous allusions to the Dracula story in *Paradise*, is not dissimilar from that which she found in the Clarence Thomas/Anita Hill case – 'the problematics of governing and controlling women's bodies'. In other words, the vampire story contains a history of sexuality informed by an ideology of gender that mirrors the conservative gender relations that the men, at least publicly, try to preserve in Ruby. While vampire narratives are usually read with an emphasis upon hunting the male vampire, often the most graphic scenes are those in which female vampires are destroyed, traditionally by a male hunter or under his supervision. The destruction of the vampire that was once Lucy in Bram Stoker's *Dracula*, for example, is so graphic and melodramatic that, I would argue, it is an exposure rather than merely an expression of misogynism. In this scene, she is transformed in a displacement of rape from what is symbolically an overt sexualised woman to the Victorian, patriarchal ideal of the pure, acquiescent maiden: 'There in the coffin lay no longer the foul Thing that we had so dreaded ... but Lucy as we had seen her in her life, with her face of unequalled sweetness and purity' (*Dracula*, ch. 16). Thus, what is also involved in the vampire story is a return to conventional power relationships.

When Connie bites Deacon's lip, she inverts the cultural conventions controlling gender and sexual relationships. But when she hums over the blood that she has drawn from his lips, she hums over not only the inverted power relationship it signifies but the power within her own body. The force of his reaction reveals his anxiety over his loss of (male) control. But it also reminds us of the far more violent and ruthless 'bloodsucking' of many of the men in this novel which, in turn, epitomises gender relationships under patriarchy. Indeed, one could easily see Bram Stoker's imagined

Transylvania and the Transylvania that has developed from it – with its terrifying forests and villages where the inhabitants cross themselves and hang garlic from doors – as an analogue of the 'Out There' endured in *Paradise* by African-American women.

VII

While *Paradise* is overtly engaged by the history embodied in separatist narratives, throughout the novel, reflected in its unusually wide range of characters, a number of disparate genres are invoked, including the open-road genre, the small-town and migrant novel, and the family or dynasty based, historical chronicle.

The development of the history in the open-road narrative in *Paradise* provides a means by which Morrison explores, as in *Sula*, the boundaries between self-interestedness and independence. It is no coincidence that at times Gigi is redolent of Sula – enjoying very often the way in which she arouses the men as does Sula in her black community. Indeed, the way in which she exaggerates the switch of her bare buttocks to Mavis, when Mavis discovers her nude sunbathing, is redolent of the way in which Sula turns her bare bottom insultingly to her mother. In some respects, Gigi is a stock character from the feminist revisions of the open-road genre, invoked in the chapter 'Mavis', that had its origins in the 1950s and 1960s. While the open road has long been a key motif in American literature, it was Jack Kerouac's *On the Road* (1957) that most popularised it as a young, male fantasy. The account of Mavis's escape from her partner whom she believes is encouraging her children to kill her is a development of, and engagement with, the history that underpins the open-road narrative. It is a history that, like the history that Morrison develops and revisions in the city novel in *Jazz*, raises questions about the gendered nature of space, access to public places and the control of movement; in *Paradise*, it is mostly the men who drive along the roads and the women who walk.

In this respect, Mavis's experiences, like the character of Gigi, can be seen in relation not only to the open-road genre as a masculinist fantasy but to the numerous post-1970 feminist revisions of it – the most famous being the road film, *Thelma and Louise*. *Thelma and Lousie*, a movie with which I suspect most readers of this book will be familiar, is not simply a celebration of the open road from a feminist perspective but an exploration of the boundaries between freedom and the illusion of freedom. It raises questions – as do some of the incidents Mavis encounters on the road – as to whether there are behaviours that might be categorised as 'masculine', and as such should be avoided by women, or whether we should recognise that there are behaviours that have not only been labelled 'masculine' or 'feminine' but have been colonised, either by design or default, by a particular gender to its advantage or detriment. *Thelma and Louise* has been criticised as a feminist movie for its virtual celebration of behaviours associated with men. Much the same might be said of the two soldiers Mavis picks up or Bennie, whose androgynous name anticipates the fact that, in stealing Mavis's raincoat and her daughter's boots, she behaves as the anarchic males in the conventional, masculinist, open-road narrative. But *Paradise,* like *Thelma and Louise,* suggests that women who take to the road are more likely to be outlawed than men. Significantly, Mavis, like Thelma and Louise, is declared a fugitive on charges – grand larceny, abandonment and suspicion of murdering her children – that say much about the status and the role of women in relation to men and to an essentially male-dominated society.

The binarism of the antagonism between the cult and the community in fiction about cults is complicated, as it is in the most insightful writing on the subject, by the exploration of intrarivalries and the presence of complex conflicts and affiliations. The history that Morrison evidently finds in separatist fiction and in black nationalist aesthetics consists of an uneasy tension between the public avowal of separatism and the lived experiences in which it is constantly contradicted and undermined. Apart from the fact that there is a female collectivity within Ruby itself as well as in the neighbouring Convent, the boundaries between these two 'collectives' are blurred, as I suggested earlier. The rebellious young women of the town, for example, Arnette and Billie Delia, go out to the Convent, as do Soane, Dovey and Anna in response to Connie's fire in the fields after Mary Magna's death. There is an even profounder affiliation between Connie, who is transformed shortly before the raid into a much stronger presence as Consolata Sosa and is able to reclaim the dying from death, Lone DuPres, the mind-reading town midwife who first recognised that Connie was 'gifted', and Soane Morgan, based upon the shared language of magic, miracle and faith to which I referred in the discussion of witchcraft. At a different level, despite public discourse to the contrary, some of the men of the town have their own affiliations with the Covent: for example, Menus, who went to the Convent on one of the occasions when he was drunk, was cleaned up and looked after by the women; Deacon Morgan who has a relationship with Connie; and K. D. who has a two-year affair with Gigi. Indeed, Arnette, who first had sexual intercourse with K. D. when she was 14 and is pregnant by him, has her baby delivered, ostensibly in secret, at the Convent. Moreover, neither the Convent nor the town are the homogeneous entities that they initially appear to be. This is a recurring feature of separatist writing that, again, has a long literary history. Adela Orpen's *Perfection City* (1897) includes a critique of ideas of sharing and co-operation, and most members within the community are hypocritical, selfish and lazy. Within the Convent in *Paradise*, Mavis and Gigi cannot stand each other; Connie herself despairs for a time of the people under her roof; and Gigi, on finding a concealed box hidden in the bathroom wall, plans to keep any valuables it may contain for herself.

In order to present the complex nature of the Ruby community, Morrison draws on the small-town novel and the genealogical framework that informs the family or dynasty chronicle. Both these genres have a long history in America. Edgar Watson Howe's *The Story of a Country Town* (1883) and Harold Frederic's *The Damnation of Theron Ware* (1896) were seen at the time as pioneering in their revelation of American rural and small-town life, but they initiated what were to become generic features of the small-town novel – the exposure of bigotry, narrow mindedness and hostility to the new or unfamiliar. Further developed in the post-war American fiction – for example, Sherwood Anderson's *Winesburg, Ohio* (1919) and Sinclair Lewis's *Main Street* (1920) – these are features that emerge from the scrutiny of Ruby in *Paradise*. Indeed, there are some quite specific parallels between *Paradise* and *The Damnation of Theron Ware*. For, like Morrison's Reverend Misner, Reverend Ware arrives in a small town to find himself not only confronted by a community that is uncharitable, hypocritical and corrupt but to discover that his own liberal views bring him into conflict with the flinty fundamentalism of a splinter group.

It is also important to remember that the small-town novel furnished the staple diet of American cinema in the 1940s and 1950s, ranging from those films that idealised the small town for white middle-American audiences to those that charted young people growing up into cruelty and madness, as in *Kings Row* (1941), to those such as *Peyton Place* (1957) – based upon what was at the time a scandalous bestseller – and *The Chase* (1960) that exposed the infidelities, the frustrations and the violence fermenting under an often placid surface. A significant difference, however, between white American and African-American small-town or community fiction is that the latter is often employed, as by Alice Walker in *The Third Life of Grange Copeland* (1970), to explore the external circumstances – social injustice, segregation, unemployment – that are partly responsible for cruelty within black families without alleviating individuals of their responsibility for their actions. Indeed, there is a strong legacy of African-American writers drawing on the white, small-town or community novel in order to delineate and explore the struggles that black people have had to endure. Mary Elizabeth Vroman's *Esther* (1963), set in a small, rural Southern town, can clearly be seen to have been written at a point of intersection between traditional African-American narrative and the small-town novel in the figure of the black midwife – a conventionally independent African-American grandmother – who saves enough money to finance her granddaughter's education and career as a nurse within a segregated community.

Despite its mixed critical reception, one of the most innovative African-American works to invoke the small-town novel is Gloria Naylor's *Linden Hills* (1985) which incorporates many of the themes of *Paradise*: the racialism attached to skin colour within the African-American community; the oppression of black women; and discrepancies between the public face of 'separatist' black communities and the private, lived experiences of its inhabitants. It is set in a community for prosperous and successful African-Americans founded by Luther Nedeed I in the 1820s. Willa, the wife of the present day Luther Nedeed, confined to a cellar after she has given birth to a mixed-race child which her husband takes as evidence of her adultery, charts how the community, through successive generations, has become increasingly morally and spiritually bankrupt and discovers the abuse suffered by three generations of Nedeed wives.

Further important themes in *Paradise* – the loss of an African-American identity informed by an Africanist presence and the advantages and disadvantages of a sense of collective identity – are explored in Naylor's *Mama Day* (1988). The novel is focused on the 'separatist' community of Willow Springs – a subtropical island on the border between South Carolina and Georgia owned by descendants of former slaves who were given it by their slave master. The community which has retained a great deal of African culture – traditions and religious customs – is a matriarchy 'governed' by Miranda, known as 'Mama Day'. She is a traditional African medicine woman who relies on traditional remedies and plants grown on the island but also practises modern medicine when the traditional medicine is ineffective. 'Miranda', reminding us immediately of *The Tempest*, signals the novel's concern with how much of life on the island that appears uncontaminated by modern white America is viable. Like most 'separatist' writing, the novel is concerned with a clash of cultures, in this case between the islanders, especially Mama Day, and two newcomers from New York, Cocoa and her husband.

While *Paradise* may invoke novels chronicling the history of a specific family or dynasty in general terms, it is more specifically indebted to William Faulkner's Yoknapatawpha novels, set around the fictional town of Jefferson. Like *Paradise*, they are historical chronicles concerned not simply with the facts of history but with historical forces and the significance of key events. The irony is that while the depiction of Ruby, like Faulkner's Jefferson, stands counter to abstraction, its people revert to abstraction in seeing African-Americans as types. Nevertheless, the historical chronicle enables Morrison, as it did Faulkner, to pursue notions of historiography as well as history. One of the most obvious consequences for *Paradise*, as for Faulkner's novels, of its indebtedness to the family chronicle genre is that it has more characters than Morrison's previous novels and more space devoted to charting, embellishing and revisiting various genealogical histories. But, more importantly, the novel employs a number of stock motifs from these genres: rivalry between a powerful, influential family and another of lower status; an errant son who is the heir apparent; a young woman who becomes pregnant by him and is regarded as responsible by his family; the families forced to find a face-saving solution; and the daughter who disappears. Generally speaking, the history in these novels – as the chapter featuring Patricia, the amateur local historian, and her supplementary family histories makes clear – is one in which the public face of family histories stands in contradistinction to occluded histories, and to interests and motives that not only lie behind these facades but are closer to the 'truth' of lived experience.

Again, *Paradise* may be said, like *Jazz*, to revisit familiar African-American narratives. For the public history that is subjected to scrutiny in *Paradise* is based on a black nationalist model. The critique of the public history of Ruby is at times a critique of the black nationalist approach to African-American history. Behind the black 'nationalism' of Ruby lies feuding, as indeed there was in black nationalism, between different 'political' factions. While K. D. and Arnette's wedding is meant to bring the Morgans and the Floods together it fails to do so because of ideological rivalry between the Reverend Pulliam and the Reverend Misner. But not all the feuding in Ruby is a product of ideological conflict. Indeed, the clash of vested interests and individual ambitions is more important. Steward Morgan, it is revealed, 'didn't give a damn' (p. 94) as to whether the motto at the Oven read 'Beware the Furrow of His Brow' or 'Be the Furrow of His Brow', he is only concerned with what Reverend Misner might have gained in terms of the town's 'politics' by instigating the alternative version. The self-interestedness of the Morgans is further evident in their attitude toward their son's affair with Arnette. Disgusted not so much by their son's behaviour as by his lack of judgement in becoming involved with a Fleetwood girl, they are anxious that what their family has achieved, which he sees in materialist terms – ranches, houses, a bank with mortgages on a feed store, a drug store and a furniture store – does not pass through marriage into the Fleetwood family. But, as in the employment of stock motifs and themes from the Southern romance narrative in the central sections of *Jazz*, Morrison in this instance, too, rescues history from stereotype. Admittedly, the stock motifs and characters are rendered less conventionally than are some of those in *Jazz*. But the two novels are comparable in the way in which stock motifs are employed to suggest how what may be valuable in the past is occluded by generic historical narratives. And how these formulaic, historical fictions are undermined by narratives that are closer to lived experience – in this case, the militancy and disobedience of the young.

While *Jazz* is focused on the importance of recognising and retaining the 'traces' of the past, *Paradise* is concerned with the kind of reactions a fear of 'tracery' can provoke in a community committed to preserving the past, or rather a particular version of it. The achievements of the men of Haven/Ruby are all the more important because they were once slaves and, as Deacon Morgan points out to Destry, the families do not want to be thought of as simply ex-slaves. But, as I indicated earlier, in establishing a community in which African-Americans with black skin are ranked higher than

African-Americans with light skin they have supplanted one form
of racial tyranny by another. Their ideology is not simply a product
of blind prejudice; their fear is that Ruby will end up like the other
black communities that they have heard of that have merged with
white towns and 'shriveled into tracery' (p. 6). But what was once
an inspirational and liberating dream, in a later, less racialised
period, more tolerant of interracial relationships, is oppressive. In
developing the history in the family or dynasty and small-town
narratives from an African-American perspective, Morrison
employs some of the stock motifs and characters to explore the
boundaries between the past as an inspirational fantasy and as a
site of oppression, denying change, preventing the realisation of
new opportunities and possibilities, and inhibiting growth.

Further African-American perspectives are brought to bear on
the history in migrant literature in the way in which Oklahoma is
seen by the Ruby inhabitants. What is the 'frontier' in white
American mythology becomes 'Out There' in African-American
mythology:

> Ten generations had known what lay Out There: space, once
> beckoning and free, became unmonitored and seething; became a
> void where random and organized evil erupted when and where
> it chose – behind any standing tree, behind the door of any
> house, humble or grand. Out There where your children were
> sport, your women quarry, and where your very person could be
> annulled; where congregations carried arms to church and ropes
> coiled in every saddle. Out There where every cluster of white-
> men looked like a posse, being alone was being dead. (p. 16)

The 'Out There' in African-American mythology is not simply the
Old West or the scarcely populated rural territories. As the experience of Scout and Easter, who feel safer going to war than living in
other towns or cities, makes clear, 'Out There' in African-American
mythology is very much an urban experience. However, 'Out
There' is not based solely on the antagonism of black and white.
What has happened to the previous generations does not justify but
helps explain the solipsism and the behaviour of the men of Haven:

> It stung them into confusion to learn they did not have enough
> money to satisfy the restrictions the 'self-supporting' Negroes re-
> quired. In short, they were too poor, too bedraggled-looking to

enter, let alone reside in, the communities that were soliciting Negro homesteaders. This contemptuous dismissal by the lucky changed the temperature of their blood twice. First they boiled at being written up as 'people who preferred saloons and crap games to homes, churches and schools'. Then, remembering their spectacular history, they cooled. What began as overheated determination became cold-blooded obsession. 'They don't know we or about we,' said one man. 'Us free like them; was slave like them. What for is this difference?' (p. 14)

Of course, a key irony in the book is that for all the talk of Oklahoma being 'Out There', it is the Convent that finds itself in that position, underscoring how there is another 'Out There' for women. Here, the threat comes not only from white but black men and in some cases from females – exemplified in Arnette's behaviour, the way in which Mavis believes that her daughter, at her husband's instigation, is going to kill her, or the way Seneca is picked up and used by Mrs Norma Keene Fox, who has an unsubtly appropriate name. Nearly all the women who come to the Convent have suffered physical, sexual and mental abuse, usually from men. And here, once again, *Paradise* invokes a tradition of women's utopian writing that can be traced back to Caroline Atwater Mason's *A Woman of Yesterday* (1900) in which a young wife who finds refuge from her marriage discovers sufficient independence and self-esteem in a Christian socialist community to return eventually to the outside world. In *Paradise*, Connie is abused at nine years of age, an experience followed by 30 years of celibacy; Mavis is regularly abused by her husband and lives in fear of being killed by her own children; Seneca is harassed by a truck driver who finds her hiding in his vehicle; and it is eventually revealed that Mavis's daughter lived in perpetual fear of her father who abused her when he was drunk. It is ironic that when Connie asks Pallas who hurt her, she describes those who helped her, as if to suggest the blurred nature of the two and the way one leads so often to the other. The various details gradually build up a picture of the 'Out There' for women. And because they are released piecemeal and often out of chronological sequence, they not only reflect the chaotic, arbitrary nature of the violence and the harassment but provide us with the kind of raw, unnarrativised black woman's history that interests Morrison in *Beloved* and *Jazz*. Presented in this way, the violence and the abuse which women have suffered

'Out There' is contextualised within a larger pattern of institution-alised or arbitrary abuse – the way in which people in Ruby are ranked according to their skin colour and the way in which Eddie Turtle runs his car over a child and leaves her there. Not surprisingly, the Convent offers women, from Pallas's point of view, 'a blessed malelessness, like a protected domain, free of hunters'. But it is a place, too, where she, and other women, 'might meet herself here – an unbridled, authentic self [...] in one of this house's many rooms' (p. 177). This in itself suggests that there are a number of identities that women may assume and may negotiate for themselves in contradistinction to the monolithic identity imposed on women in Ruby. There is, of course, a flipside to all of this and the novel also complicates its rendering of 'Out There' by including women who are complicit in its lack of morality, as is Gigi who has a two-year affair with K. D. in order to get enough money to get out of the state.

The way in which 'Out There' is rendered complex in *Paradise* reflects the increasingly complicated and contradictory nature of identity in Morrison's work. This is, in itself, at least partly responsible for the increase in the cast of characters in this final novel of the '*Beloved* trilogy'. There are similarities in all three novels such as the preoccupation with obsession and the concern with a specific event linked to a clearly identifiable episode in African-American history. But the range of verbal narratives invoked in *Paradise* is wider than in the other novels and the way in which they do not simply reflect but act as agents in the construction of historical narratives even more pronounced.

6

Postscript

> The original definitions of me as a Black writer were an attempt to reduce the area in which I wrote, to ghettoise me – I'm forceful so I turned that around as those are the sensibilities out of which I write. (Morrison, in interview with Olga Kenyon, 1993, p. 12)

In the 1990s, critics stressed the interconnection in Morrison's work of history, memory and trauma. There have been three principal approaches to this topic: Morrison has been seen as bearing 'witness' to unarticulated or obscured histories; as employing trauma to explore how history comes back as an eruption into the present that is enabled by the past; or as offering the reader different ways of imagining the individual as subject in history. Of course, Morrison's novels are not unique in challenging American collective memory in the way that they do or for the reasons that they do. However, as I have tried to show throughout the course of this study, Morrison's fiction frequently invokes, usually subversively, familiar or well-established verbal genres. But her work is not simply engaged by the generic conventions of, for example, the slave narrative, the ghost story, the black folk tale, the trickster narrative, the city novel, or the utopian narrative. Her novels are engaged by the history and the cultural assumptions that underpin them; by preconceptions and narratives in which the African-Americanist presence has often been obscured, distorted or, even in some black verbal narratives, silenced altogether.

Deborah McDowell, revising her earlier paper (in McKay, 1988), suggests that two seminal articles helped shape critical attitudes to black women's writing in the late 1980s (in Baker and Redmond, 1989, p. 56). In the first of these, Hazel Carby (1985) has demonstrated that black women's writing can generate its own distinctive, critical discourses, while in the second, Joanne Braxton (1986) has shown that the customary critical frameworks and paradigms need not be reflexively and habitually employed. The conventional approaches, to which Braxton refers, have tended to include an image-conscious criticism, in which race is the sole determinant of identity, subsuming sexual difference, and have tended to presume that identity is pre-existent, coherent and knowable. Reclaiming female voices and narratives has always been one of Morrison's objectives in writing as she explains in the interview with Olga Kenyon:

> Well, in the sixties our principal interpreters were Black men. Of course their position is unassailable; but I have little in common with Wright and Ellison because there was a void at the centre, no female voice. I had the feeling they were not talking to me, their editorial address was explanatory, to other men, possibly to white men. I realise now I wanted an interior life, experienced by a woman, at a particular time. I was longing for something that didn't exist in their work. (Kenyon, 1993, p. 14)

In Morrison's novels the communal 'we' is the site of internecine, internal struggles mediated, as we have seen in so many individuals, such as Claudia, Sula, Jadine, Sethe, Violet, Gigi and Connie, and in so many locations, such as the 'Bottom', Sweet Home, Harlem, Ruby, and the Convent, by multiple subjectivities. Categorisation and self-labelling, which are acknowledged as part of the process by which identities are developed, are seen primarily as agents of control, restriction or inhibition. Identities are not perceived as pregiven, automatic or fixed, but as socially organised, contingent, changeable and relational.

Morrison's fiction is concerned, of course, with people who in terms of their ancestry are displaced, dispossessed and separated from their identity and history. But there is a strong appreciation throughout her work that this identity and history should not be seen as stable or essentialist. Boundaries and limits are perceived as signifying spaces in which cultural, political and economic power are contested, negotiated or reaffirmed. This is not to say there is no sympathy for how the past, in the context of the instability and unpredictability of the present, becomes a locus for an imagined community, a fantasy of identity and belonging that turns on notions of origins, roots, unarticulated histories and shared heritage. But in her novels this always stands in contradistinction to suspicions about mythologising, as in *Song of Solomon* or *Paradise*, for example. There is no easy retreat, as Son discovers in *Tar Baby* or the Old Fathers of Ruby would have the town's inhabitants believe, into ethnic absolutism or illusory notions of classless, organic community. *Tar Baby* particularly refocuses attention on the displaced person, the migrant and the stranger, as separated from their history and identity. Resisting fixed or essentialist interpretations of these categories, the novel predicates the identity of the displaced person – Son, Jadine, Valerian, Margaret, Sydney, Ondine – on a new social space, the product of a complex global economy, new forms of economic imperialism and transnational communication.

It is this new world of which the Old Fathers in *Paradise* are afraid but which some of the younger inhabitants are keen to embrace. From *The Bluest Eye* to *Paradise*, it is possible to chart in Morrison's fiction a growing realisation that geopolitical boundaries at the local, national and international level are fluid. They become, increasingly, sites of contested authority and power that are, in turn, embroiled with internal crises of coherence and stability in African-American identity. Throughout Morrison's work identity is the product of psychic struggle. The self is perceived as perpetually in process and her novels frequently employ strategies, as Baruch Hoffman (1985) points out, for 'rupturing' coherence of character. Often it is the unconscious, a sphere of conflict between ideas, longings and desires that disrupts consciousness through dreams, memories, neurotic symptoms or unpredictable, even perverse, behaviours, as in the different cases of Pecola and Pauline in *The Bluest Eye*, Jadine in *Tar Baby*, Sethe and Paul D in *Beloved*, Violet and Joe in *Jazz*, or Connie in *Paradise*.

Often the innovatory nature of Morrison's work at the level of what Gérard Genette called 'récit' is a product of its 'relational perspective', that is, a perspective which tries to understand events and practices as aspects of wider, social relations in order to unravel the contexts in which they become meaningful. As I suggested in the discussions of Cholly's rape of his daughter in *The Bluest Eye*, Sethe's murder of her child in *Beloved*, and the raid on the Convent in *Paradise*, this involves understanding the power relations at play and the cohesive limits that are placed on choice for black people. It also necessitates reclaiming Morrison from what Michelle Wallace describes as 'a newly depoliticised, mainstreamed, and commodified black feminist literary criticism' (1992, p. 661). She argues that critics, such as Henry Louis Gates, Jr, have failed to portray African-American writing 'as a "minority" literature hotly engaged in an antagonistic dialogue with a majority "white culture" in order to transcend and/or transform it' (p. 660). New politics of sexuality and race creates new spaces but also opens up new fissures, creating new hostilities. The critique of black essentialism which to some extent underpins all of Morrison's work casts light in the novels on hidden but controlling assumptions and opens up new questions about history, power, meaning, diversity and choice. Ultimately all Morrison's novels are anchored in an ever growing social complexity; the new pluralism of racial, ethnic, class and cultural forms. Many of the novels search for a collective way of dealing with differentiated identities, themselves the products of racial, gender and geographical differences.

In the early novels there is clear evidence of the influence of 1960s feminism with its stress on masculinised sexual codes perpetuating female oppression. But this perspective is developed by more emphasis being placed on the politics of female desire. Without eschewing issues around power, violence, victimisation and exploitation, the possibilities of sexual freedom and questions of pleasure and personal autonomy are pursued, for instance, in the cases of Sula and First Corinthians in *Song of Solomon*, Jadine in *Tar Baby*, Dorcas in *Jazz*, and the women in the Convent in *Paradise*. But, as the experience of many of these women indicates, sexual expression can only become an act of self-exploration where an individual is not 'fixed' on one locatable ego (McDowell, in Redmond and Baker, 989, pp. 64–5).

In order to be fully resistant to approaching African-American women's writing through a depoliticised, mainstreamed, and commodified literary criticism, it would be necessary to pursue some difficult questions. The publication of black writers to academic acclaim and their critical success in conferences, in journals and in colleges dominated by white Europeans must contribute to ongoing debates. These should include: ways in which their work calls into question academic notions of canonical literary traditions; the elitist nature of the avant-garde; and the consistency of their work with the tastes of the majority of black people. Issues such as these would require a book three times as long as this study to even begin to do them justice.

Within the limitations of the space available, this study has tried to bear in mind the potential impact of Morrison's work on how racism and sexism are perceived in contemporary culture. It has tried to show that Morrison's novels cannot be fully understood within the parameters of Euro-American or African-American literary criticism alone. Whilst bearing in mind the overall development of Morrison's work, the discussions of the individual novels have sought to demonstrate how each generates its own critical discourse. The experiment with form in her novels derives from their perception of boundaries and limits as spaces in which cultural, political and economic power are contested; from their resistance to illusory notions of community or ethnic absolutism; from their concern with internecine struggles mediated by multiple subjectivities.

Select Bibliography

WORKS BY TONI MORRISON

Fiction

The Bluest Eye (New York: Holt, Rinehart, and Winston, 1970).
Sula (New York: Knopf, 1973).
Song of Solomon (New York: Knopf, 1977).
Tar Baby (New York: Knopf, 1981).
Beloved (New York, Knopf, 1987).
Jazz (New York: Knopf, 1992).
Paradise (New York: Knopf, 1998).

Criticism

Playing in the Dark: Whiteness and the Literary Imagination (Cambridge, MA, and London: Harvard University Press, 1992).

Edited works

The Black Book, comp. Middleton Harris (New York: Random House, 1974).
Race-ing Justice, En-gendering Power: Essays on Anita Hill, Clarence Thomas and the Construction of Social Reality (New York: Pantheon, 1992).
(with Claudia Brodsky Lacour) *Birth of a Nation'hood: Gaze, Script, and Spectacle in the O. J. Simpson Case* (New York: Pantheon, 1997).

Non-fiction

'Rediscovering Black History', *New York Times Magazine*, 11 August 1974.
Foreword, Camille Billops, James Van Der Zee and Owen Dodson, *The Harlem Book of the Dead* (New York: Morgan and Morgan, 1978).
'City Limits, Village Values: Concepts of the Neighbourhood in Black Fiction', in Michael C. Jaye and Ann C. Watts, *Literature and the American Urban Experience: Essays on the City and Literature* (Manchester: Manchester University Press, 1981).
'Rootedness: The Ancestor as Foundation', in *Black Women Writers (1950–1980): a Critical Evaluation*, ed. Mari Evans (New York: Anchor Books, 1984). Also in *Literature in the Modern World: Critical Essays and Documents*, ed. Denis Walder (London: Oxford University Press, 1990).
'Memory, Creation, and Writing', *Thought: A Review of Culture and Idea*, 59 (1984), 385–90.
'The Site of Memory', in *Inventing the Truth: The Art and Craft of the Memoir*, ed. William Zinsser (Boston: Houghton Mifflin, 1987), pp. 103–24.

'Unspeakable Things Unspoken: The Afro-American Presence in American Literature', *Michigan Quarterly Review*, 28 (1989), 1–34.
'A Bench by the Road', *The World*, 3:1 (1989), 4–5, 37–41.
'On the Backs of Blacks', in *Arguing Immigration: The Debate Over the Changing Face of America*, ed. Nicolaus Mills (New York: Touchstone Books, 1994).

Lectures

Lecture and Speech of Acceptance, Upon the Award of the Nobel Prize for Literature, *The Nobel Lecture in Literature* (New York: Knopf, 1994).

Interviews

Bakerman, Jane, '"The Seams Can't Show": An Interview with Toni Morrison', *Black American Literature Forum*, 12 (1978), 556–60.
Bigsby, Christopher, 'Jazz Queen', *The Independent*, 26 April 1992, 28–9.
Darling, Marsha, 'In the Realm of Responsibility: A Conversation with Toni Morrison', *Women's Review of Books* (March, 1988), 5–6.
Gilroy, Paul, 'Living Memory: A Meeting with Toni Morrison', *Small Acts: Thoughts on the Politics of Black Cultures* (London: Serpent's Tail, 1993), pp. 175–82.
Guthrie-Taylor, Danielle (ed.), *Conversations with Toni Morrison* (Jackson: University of Mississippi Press, 1994).
Kenyon, Olga, 'Interview with Toni Morrison', *Baetyl*, 2 (1993), 11–23.
LeClair, Thomas, 'The Language Must Not Sweat', *New Republic*, 21 (March, 1981), 25–9.
Lester, Rosemarie K., 'An interview with Toni Morrison', in *Critical Essays on Toni Morrison*, ed. Nellie McKay (Boston: G. K. Hall, 1988), pp. 47–54.
McKay, Nellie, 'An Interview with Toni Morrison', *Contemporary Literature*, 24 (1983), 418–22.
Naylor, Gloria, 'A Conversation, Gloria Naylor and Toni Morrison', *The Southern Review*, 21 (1985), 567–93.
Rushdie, Salman, Interview with Toni Morrison, *The Late Show*, BBC 2, 21 October 1992.
Tate, Claudia, 'A Conversation with Toni Morrison', *Black Women Writers at Work*, ed. Claudia Tate (New York: Continuum, 1983), pp. 117–31.
Wilson, Judith, 'A Conversation with Toni Morrison', *Essence*, 12 (July, 1981), 84, 86, 128, 130, 133, 134.

CRITICISM

Bibliography

Middleton, David, L., *Toni Morrison: An Annotated Bibliography* (New York: Garland, 1987).

Mix, Debbie, 'Toni Morrison: A Selected Bibliography', *Modern Fiction Studies*, 39: 3–4 (1993), 795–817.

Book-length studies of Toni Morrison

Bjork, Patrick Bryce, *The Novels of Toni Morrison* (New York: Peter Lang, 1992).
Carmean, Karen, *Toni Morrison's World of Fiction* (Troy, New York: Whitson, 1993).
Furman, Jan, *Toni Morrison's Fiction* (Columbia, SC: University of South Carolina Press, 1996).
Harris, Trudier, *Fiction and Folklore: The Novels of Toni Morrison* (Knoxville: University of Tennessee Press, 1991).
Heinze, Denise, *The Dilemma of 'Double-Consciousness': Toni Morrison's Novels* (Athens, GA: University of Georgia Press, 1993).
Matus, Jill, *Toni Morrison* (Manchester: Manchester University Press, 1998).
Mbalia, Doreatha Drummond, *Toni Morrison's Developing Class Consciousnes* (Selingsgrove: Susquehanna University Press, 1991).
Otten, Terry, *The Crime of Innocence in Toni Morrison's Fiction* (Columbia: University of Missouri Press, 1989).
Page, Philip, *Dangerous Freedom: Fusion and Fragmentation in Toni Morrison's Novels* (Jackson: University of Mississippi Press, 1995).
Plasa, Carl, *Beloved* (Cambridge: Icon Books, Icon Critical Guides, 1998).
Rigney, Barbara, *The Voices of Toni Morrison* (Columbus: Ohio State University Press, 1991).
Samuels, Wilfred D. and Clenora Hudson-Weems, *Toni Morrison* (Boston: Twayne, 1990).

Collections of critical essays

Bloom, Harold (ed.), *Toni Morrison: Modern Critical Views* (New York: Chelsea House Publishers, 1990).
Gates, Henry Louis, Jr and K. Anthony Appiah (eds), *Toni Morrison: Critical Perspectives Past and Present* (New York: Amistad, 1993).
McKay, Nellie (ed.), *Critical Essays on Toni Morrison* (Boston: G. K. Hall, 1988).
Middleton, David, L. (ed.), *Toni Morrison's Fiction: Contemporary Criticism* (New York: Garland, 1997).
Peach, Linden (ed.), *Toni Morrison: Contemporary Critical Essays* (London: Macmillan, New Casebooks, 1998).
Peterson, Nancy J. (ed.), 'Toni Morrison', *Modern Fiction Studies*, double issue, 39: 3–4 (1993).
Smith, Valerie (ed.), *New Essays on Song of Solomon* (Cambridge: Cambridge University Press, 1995).

Articles and essays on Toni Morrison

Awkward, Michael, 'Roadblocks and Relatives: Critical Revision in Toni Morrison's *The Bluest Eye*', *Critical Essays on Toni Morrison* ed. Nellie McKay (Boston: G. K. Hall, 1988), pp. 57–68.

Bakerman, Jane S., 'Failures of Love: Female Initiation in the novels of Toni Morrison', *American Literature*, 52, (1981), 541–63.

Barnett, Pamela E., 'Figurations of Rape and the Supernatural in *Beloved*', *PMLA*, 112 (1997), 418–27.

Bell, Bernard W., '*Beloved*: A Womanist Neo-Slave Narrative; or, Multivocal Remembrances of Things Past', *African-American Review*, 26 (1992), 7–16.

Boudreau, Kristin, 'Pain and the Unmaking of Self in Toni Morrison's *Beloved*', *Contemporary Literature*, 36: 3 (1995), 447–65.

Burton, Angela, 'Signifyin(g) Abjection: Narrative Strategies in Toni Morrison's *Jazz*', in *Toni Morrison: Contemporary Critical Essays*, ed. Linden Peach (London: Macmillan, New Casebooks, 1998), pp. 170–93.

Bowers, Susan, '*Beloved* and the new Apocalypse', *Journal of Ethnic Studies*, 18: 21 (1990), 59–77.

Christian, Barbara, 'Community and Nature in the Novels of Toni Morrison', *Journal of Ethnic Studies*, 7 (Winter 1980), 64–78.

Christian, Barbara, 'Fixing Methodologies: *Beloved*', *Cultural Critique*, 24 (Spring, 1993), 5–15.

Coleman, Alisha R., 'One and One Makes One: A Metacritical and Psychoanalytic Reading of Friendship in Toni Morrison's *Sula*', *CLA Journal*, 37: 2 (1993), 145–55.

Comfort, Susan, 'Counter-Memory, Mourning and History in Toni Morrison's *Beloved*', *Literature, Interpretation, Theory*, 6: 1–2 (1995), 121–32.

Davies, Cynthia A., 'Self, Society, and Myth in Toni Morrison's Fiction', *Contemporary Literature*, 23: 3 (1982), 323–42.

Dickerson, Vanessa D., 'The Naked Father in Toni Morrison's *The Bluest Eye*', in *Refiguring the Father: New Feminist Readings of Patriarchy*, ed. PatriciaYeagar and Beth Kowaleski-Wallace (Carbondale: Southern Illinois University Press, 1989), pp. 108–27.

Erickson, Peter B., 'Images of Nurturance in Toni Morrison's *Tar Baby*', *CLA Journal*, 28: 1 (1984), 11–32.

Fabre, Genevieve, 'Genealogical Archaeology or the Quest for Legacy in Toni Morrison's *Song of Solomon*', in *Critical Essays on Toni Morrison*, ed. Nellie McKay (Boston: G. K. Hall, 1988), pp. 105–14.

Ferguson, Rebecca, 'History, Memory and Language in Toni Morrison's *Beloved*', in *Feminist Criticism: Theory and Practice*, ed. Susan Sellers and Linda Hutcheon (Toronto: University of Toronto Press, 1991), pp. 109–27.

FitzGerald, Jennifer, 'Selfhood and Community: Psychoanalysis and Discourse in *Beloved*', 39: 3–4(1993), 669–87.

Fultz, Lilian, 'Images of Motherhood in Toni Morrison's *Beloved*', in *Double Stitch: Black Women Write About Mothers and Daughters*, ed. Patricia Bell-Scott (Boston, MA: Beacon Press, 1991), pp. 32–41.

Grant, Robert, 'Absence into Presence: The Thematics of Memory and "Missing" Subjects in Toni Morrison's *Sula*', in *Critical Essays on Toni Morrison*, ed. Nellie McKay (Boston: G. K. Hall, 1988), pp. 90–103.

Hamilton, Cynthia S., 'Revisions, Rememories and Exorcisms: Toni Morrison and the Slave Narrative', *Journal of American Studies*, 30:3 (1996), 429–45.

Handley, William, 'The House a Ghost Built: *Nommo*, Allegory and the Ethics of Reading in Toni Morrison's *Beloved*', *Contemporary Literature*, 36: 4 (1995), 676–701.

Henderson, Mae G., 'Toni Morrison's *Beloved*: Re-Membering the Body as Historical Text', in *Comparative American Identities: Race, Sex and Nationality in the Modern Text*, ed. Hortense J. Spillers (New York: Routledge, 1991), pp. 62–86.

Hirsch, Marianne, 'Maternity and Rememory: Toni Morrison's *Beloved*', in *Representations of Motherhood*, ed. Donna Bassin, Margaret Honey and Meryle Mahrer Kaplan (New Haven: Yale University Press, 1994), pp. 92–110.

Harris, Trudier, 'Reconnecting Fragments: Afro-American Folk Tradition in *The Bluest Eye*', in *Critical Essays on Toni Morrison* ed. Nellie McKay (Boston: G. K. Hall, 1988), pp. 68–76.

House, Elizabeth B., 'Artists and the Art of Living: Order and Disorder in Toni Morrison's Fiction', *Modern Fiction Studies*, 34 (1988), 27–44.

Horvitz, Deborah, 'Nameless Ghosts: Possession and Dispossession in *Beloved*', *Studies in American Fiction*, 17 (1989), 157–67.

Johnson, Barbara, '"Aesthetic" and "Rapport" in Toni Morrison's *Sula*', *Textual Practice*, 7:2 (1993), 165–72.

Keenan, Sally, '"Four Hundred Years of Silence": Myth, History, and Motherhood in Toni Morrison's *Beloved*', in *Recasting the World: Writing After Colonialism*, ed. Jonathan White (Baltimore: Johns Hopkins University Press, 1993), pp. 45–81.

Kenyon, Olga, '"Writing as a Black Woman Makes My World Larger": the Writings of Toni Morrison', *Baetyl*, 2 (1993), 24–46.

Krumholz, Linda, 'The Ghosts of Slavery: Historical Recovery in Toni Morrison's *Beloved*', *African American Review*, 26:3 (1992), 395–408.

Krumholz, Linda, 'Dead Teachers: Rituals of Manhood and Rituals of Reading in *Song of Solomon*', *Modern Fiction Studies*, 39: 3–4 (1993), 551–74.

Kuenz, Jane, 'The *Bluest Eye*: Notes on History, Community, and Black Female Subjectivity', *African American Review*, 27: 3 (1993), 421–31.

Lee, Dorothy H., 'Song of Solomon: to Ride the Air', *Black American Literature Forum*, 16 (1982), 64–70.

Lewis, Barbara, 'The Function of Jazz in Toni Morrison's *Jazz*', in *Toni Morrison's Fiction: Contemporary Criticism*, ed. David L. Middleton (New York: Garland, 1997), pp. 271–81.

Marshall, Brenda K., *Teaching the Postmodern: Fiction and Theory* (London and New York: Routledge, 1992), pp. 179–93.

Mayberry, Katherine, 'The Problem of Narrative in Toni Morrison's *Jazz*', in *Toni Morrison's Fiction: Contemporary Criticism*, ed. David L. Middleton (New York: Garland, 1997), pp. 297–309.

Mbalia, Doreatha Drummond, 'Women Who Run With Wild': the Need for Sisterhoods in *Jazz*', *Modern Fiction Studies*, 39: 3–4 (1993), 623–46.

McDowell, Deborah, '"The Self and Other": Reading Toni Morrison's *Sula* and the Black Female Text', in *Critical Essays on Toni Morrison*, ed. Nellie McKay (Boston: G. K. Hall, 1988), pp. 77–90.

Mobley, Marilyn Saunders, 'A Different Remembering: Memory, History and Meaning in Toni Morrison's *Beloved*', in *Toni Morrison: Modern Critical Views*, ed. Harold Bloom (New York: Chelsea House, 1990), pp. 189–99.

Nicholls, Peter, 'The Belated Postmodern: History, Phantoms, and Toni Morrison', in *Psychoanalytic Criticism: A Reader*, ed. Sue Vice (Oxford and Cambridge, MA: Polity Press, 1996), pp. 50–67.

Pérez-Torres, Rafael, 'Knitting and Knotting the Narrative Thread – *Beloved* as a Postmodern Novel', *Modern Fiction Studies*, 39: 3–4 (1993), 689–707.

Rice, Alan, 'Jazzing it up a Storm: The Execution and Meaning of Toni Morrison's Jazzy Prose Style', *Journal of American Studies*, 18:3 (1994), 421–32.

Rigney, Barbara Hill, '"A Story to Pass On": Ghosts and the Significance of History in Toni Morrison's *Beloved*', in *Haunting the House of Fiction: Feminist Perspectives on Ghost Stories by American Women*, ed. Lynette Carpenter and Wendy K. Kolmer (Knoxville: University of Tennessee Press, 1991), pp. 229–35.

Rodrigues, Eusebio L., 'Experiencing *Jazz*', *Modern Fiction Studies*, 39: 3–4 (1993), 733–54.

Rushdy, Ashraf H. A., '"Rememory": Primal Scenes and Constructions in Toni Morrison's Novels', *Contemporary Literature*, 31: 3 (1990), 300–23.

Rushdy, Ashraf H. A., 'Daughters Signifyin(g) History: The Example of Toni Morrison's *Beloved*', *American Literature*, 64:3 (September, 1992), 566–97.

Schapiro, Barbara, 'The Bonds of Love and the Boundaries of Self in Toni Morrison's *Beloved*', *Contemporary Literature*, 32: 2 (1991), 194–210.

Tate, Claudia, 'On Black Literary Women and the Evolution of Critical Discourse', *Tulsa Studies in Women's Literature*, 5 (1986), 111–23.

Traylor, Eleanor W., 'The Fabulous World of Toni Morrison: *Tar Baby*', in *Critical Essays on Toni Morrison*, ed. Nellie McKay (Boston: G. K. Hall, 1988), pp. 135–50.

Werner, Craig H., 'The Briar Patch as Modernist Myth: Morrison, Barthes and *Tar Baby* As-Is', in *Critical Essays on Toni Morrison*, ed. Nellie McKay (G. K. Hall, 1988), pp. 150–67.

Wilkerson, Margaret B., 'The Dramatic Voice in Toni Morrison's Novels', in *Critical Essays on Toni Morrison*, ed. Nellie McKay (Boston: G. K. Hall, 1988), pp. 179–90.

Wolff, Cynthia Griffin, '"Margaret Garner": A Cincinnati Story', *Massachusetts Review*, 32 (1991), 417–40. Also in *Discovering Difference: Contemporary Essays in American Culture*, ed. Christopher K. Lohmann (Bloomington, Indiana University Press, 1993), pp. 105–22.

General works

Albinski, Nan Bowman, *Women's Utopias in British and American Fiction* (London and New York: Routledge, 1988).

Andrews, William L., 'The 1850s: The First Afro-American Literary Renaissance', in *Literary Romanticism in America*, ed. William L. Andrews (London and Baton Rouge: Louisiana State University Press, 1981).

Awkward, Michael, *Inspiring Influences: Tradition, Revision and Afro-American Women's Novels* (New York: Columbia University Press, 1989).

Baker, Houston A., Jr, *Blues, Ideology and Afro-American Literature: A Theory of Literature* (Chicago: Chicago University Press, 1984).

Baker, Houston A., Jr and Patricia A. Redmond (eds), *Afro-American Literary Study in the 1990s* (Chicago: Chicago University Press, 1988).

Bakhtin, M. M., *The Dialogic Imagination*, ed. Michael Holquist, trs. Caryl Emerson and Michael Holquist (Austin: University of Texas Press, 1981).

Barthes, Roland, 'Theory of the Text', in *Untying the Text: a Post-structuralist Reader*, ed. Robert Young, trs. Ian McLeod (London: Routledge, 1981).

Barthold, Bonnie, *Black Time: Fiction of Africa, the Caribbean, and the United States* (New Haven, CT: Yale University Press, 1981).

Bhabha, Homi K., *The Location of Culture* (London: Routledge, 1994).

Bigsby, Christopher, *The Second Black Renaissance: Essays in Black Literature* (London: Greenwood Press, 1980).

Billops, Camille, James Van Der Zee and Owen Dodson, *The Harlem Book of the Dead* (New York, Morgan and Morgan, 1978).

Birch, Eva Lennox, *Black American Women's Writing* (Brighton: Harvester Wheatsheaf, 1994).

Bradbury, Malcolm and David Palmer (eds), *The American Novel in the Nineteen Twenties* (London: Edward Arnold, 1971).

Braxton, Joanne M., '"Harriet Jacobs" Incidents in the Life of a Slave Girl', *Massachusetts Review*, 27 (1986), 380–1.

Braxton, Joanne M. and Andrée Nicola McLaughlin (eds), *Wild Women in the Whirlwind: Afra-American Culture and the Contemporary Literary Renaissance* (London: Serpent's Tail, 1990).

Butler-Evans, Elliott, *Race, Gender and Desire: Narrative Strategies in the Fiction of Toni Cade Bambara, Toni Morrison and Alice Walker* (Philadelphia: Temple University Press, 1989).

Carby, Hazel, '"On the Threshold of Woman's Era": Lynchings, Empire and Sexuality in Black Feminist Theory', *Critical Inquiry*, 12 (1985).

Carby, Hazel, *Reconstructing Womanhood: The Emergence of the Afro-American Woman Novelist* (Oxford: Oxford University Press, 1987).

Christian, Barbara, *Black Feminist Criticism: Perspectives on Black Women Writers* (New York: Pergamon Press, 1985).

Clarke, Graham (ed.), *The New American Writing: Essays on American Literature since 1970* (London: Vision Press, 1990).

Collins, Patricia Hill, *Black Feminist Thought: Knowledge, Consciousness, and the Politics of Empowerment* (London and New York: Routledge, 1991).

Connor, Steven, *The English Novel in History 1950–1995* (London and New York: Routledge, 1996).

Coward, Rosalind, *Female Desire* (1984; rpt. London: Paladin Books, 1985).

Davies, Carol Boyce, *Black Women, Writing and Identity: Migrations of the Subject* (London and New York: Routledge, 1994).

de Weever, Jacqueline, *Mythmaking and Metaphor in Black Women's Fiction* (New York: St. Martin's Press, 1991).

Derrida, Jacques, *Marges de la Philosophie,* trs. Alan Bass (Chicago: Chicago University Press, 1982).

Derrida, Jacques, *La Carte Postale,* trs. Alan Bass (Chicago: Chicago University Press, 1987).

Dubey, Madhu, *Black Women Novelists and the Black Aesthetic* (Bloomington: Indiana University Press, 1994).

During, Simon, 'Postmodernism or Post-Colonialism Today', *Textual Practice,* 1:1 (1987), 32–47.

Ekpo, Denis, 'Towards a Post-Africanism: Contemporary African Thought and Postmodernism', *Textual Practice,* 9:1 (1995), 121–35.

Fabre, Genevieve, and Robert O'Meally (eds), *History and Memory in African-American Culture* (Oxford: Oxford University Press, 1994).

Foster, Frances Smith, *Written By Herself: Literary Production by African American Women, 1746–1992* (Bloomington: Indiana University Press, 1993).

Fry, Gladys-Marie, *Night Riders in Black Folk History* (Knoxville: University of Tennessee Press, 1975).

Gates, Henry Louis, Jr (ed.), *'Race', Writing, and Difference* (Chicago: University of Chicago Press, 1985).

Gates, Henry Louis, Jr (ed.), *Black Literature and Literary Theory* (London: Routledge, 1984).

Gates, Henry Louis, Jr, *Loose Canons: Notes on the Culture Wars* (London: Oxford University Press, 1992).

Genette, Gérard, *Narrative Discourse: An Essay in Method,* trs. Jane E. Lewin (Ithaca, NY: Cornell University Press, 1980).

Gikandi, Simon, *Reading the African Novel* (London: Curry, 1987).

Gilroy, Paul, *Small Acts: Thoughts on the Politics of Black Cultures* (London: Serpent's Tail, 1993).

Greenblatt, Stephen, 'Introduction: The Forms of Power', *Genre,* 7 (1982), 3–6.

Grossberg, Lawrence, Cary Nelson, and Paula Treichler, *Cultural Studies* (London: Routledge, 1992).

Harper, Michael S., and Robert B. Stepto, *Chant of Saints* (Urbana: University of Illinois Press, 1979).

Hernton, Calvin, 'The Sexual Mountain and Black Women Writers', in *Wild Women in the Whirlwind: Afro-American Culture and the Contemporary Literary Renaissance,* ed. Joanne M. Braxton and Andrée Nicola McLaughlin (London: Serpent's Tail, 1990), pp. 195–212.

Hoffman, Baruch, *Character in Literature* (Ithaca, NY: Cornell University Press, 1985).

hooks, bell, *Thinking Feminist – Thinking Black* (London: Sheba Feminist Publishers, 1989).

hooks, bell, *Yearning: Race, Gender and Cultural Politics* (Boston, MA: South End Press, 1990).

hooks, bell, 'Representing Whiteness in the Black Imagination', in *Cultural Studies,* ed. Lawrence Grossberg, Cary Nelson and Paula Treichler (London and New York: Routledge, 1992).

hooks, bell, *Wounds of Passion: A Writing Life* (London: The Women's Press, 1998).

Hughes, Langston, *The Big Sea* (New York: Thunder's Mouth Press, 1986).

Hull, Gloria T., Patricia Bell-Scott and Barbara Smith (eds), *All the Women Are White, All the Blacks Are Men, But Some of Us Are Brave: Black Women's Studies* (Old Westbury, New York: Feminist Press, 1982).

Jarvis, Brian, *Postmodern Cartographies: The Geographical Imagination in Contemporary American Culture* (London: Pluto Press, 1998), pp. 113–35.

Jaye, Michael C. and Ann C. Watts (eds), *Literature and the American Urban Experience: Essays on the City and Literature* (Manchester: Manchester University Press, 1981).

Jones, Gayl, *Liberating Voices: Oral Tradition in African American Literature* (Cambridge, MA, and London: Harvard University Press, 1991).

Keith, Michael and Steve Pile, *Place and the Politics of Identity* (London: Routledge, 1993).

Kenyon, Olga, *Writing Women: Contemporary Women Novelists* (London: Pluto Press, 1991).

Lewis, Peter, 'Making Magic', *The Independent*, 3 April 1993, 24–6.

Lomax, L. E., *The Negro Revolt* (London: Hamish Hamilton, 1962).

McDowell, Deborah, *The Changing Same: Black Women's Literature, Criticism and Theory* (Bloomington: Indiana University Press, 1995).

Nasta, Susheila (ed.), *Motherlands: Black Women's Writing from Africa, the Caribbean and South Asia* (London: The Women's Press, 1991).

Oakley, Giles, *The Devil's Music: A History of the Blues* (London: British Broadcasting Corporation, 1976).

Palmer, Pauline, 'The City in Contemporary Women's Fiction', in *Forked Tongues? Comparing Twentieth-Century British and American Literature* (London and New York: Longman, 1994).

Phobee, John, 'Aspects of African Traditional Religion', *Sociological Analysis*, 37 (1976), 1–18.

Piersen, William D., *Black Legacy: America's Hidden Heritage* (Boston: University of Massachusetts Press, 1994).

Radin, Paul, *The Trickster* (London: Routledge, 1956).

Rice, Alan, 'Take It From The Top', *The Times Higher Education Supplement*, 19 June 1992, 16.

Rody, Caroline, 'Toni Morrison's *Beloved*: History, "Rememory", and a "Clamor for a Kiss"', *American History*, 7 (1995), 92–119.

Segy, Ladistas, *Masks of Black Africa* (New York: Dover Publications, 1976).

Shaw, Arnold, *The Jazz Age* (London: Oxford University Press, 1987).

Showalter, Elaine (ed.), *The New Feminist Criticism: Essays on Women, Literature and Theory* (London: Virago, 1986).

Singh, Amritjit, Joseph Skerrett, Jr, and Robert Hogan (eds), *Memory and Cultural Politics: New Approaches to American Ethnic Literatures* (Boston: Northeastern University Press, 1996).

Slemon, Stephen, 'Magic Realism as Post-Colonial Discourse', *Canadian Literature*, 116 (1989), 9–24.

Smith, Valerie, *Self-Discovery and Authority in Afro-American Narrative* (Cambridge, MA: Harvard University Press, 1987).

Soja, Edward W., *Postmodern Geographies: the Reassertion of Space in Critical Social Theory* (London: Verso, 1989).

Walker, Melissa, *Down From the Mountaintop: Black Women's Novels in the Wake of the Civil Rights Movement, 1966–1989* (New Haven, CT, and London: Yale University Press, 1991).

Walker, Nancy, 'Reformers and Young Maidens: Women and Virtue', in *Mark Twain's Adventures of Huckleberry Finn: Modern Critical Interpretations*, ed. Harold Bloom (New York: Chelsea House, 1986).

Wall, Cheryl A. (ed.), *Changing Our Own Words: Essays on Criticism, Theory and Writing by Black Women* (London and New York: Routledge, 1990).

Wallace, Michelle, 'Towards A Black Feminist Cultural Criticism', in *Cultural Studies*, ed. Lawrence Grossberg, Cary Nelson and Paula Treichler (London and New York: Routledge, 1992).

Werner, Craig H., *Playing the Changes: From Afro-Modernism to the Jazz Impulse* (Urbana: University of Illinois Press, 1994).

Wilentz, Gay, *Binding Cultures: Black Women Writers in Africa and the Diaspora* (Bloomington: Indiana University Press, 1992).

Willis, Susan, *Specifying: Black Women Writing the American Experience* (Madison: University of Wisconsin Press, 1986).

Wintz, Cary D., *Black Culture and the Harlem Renaissance* (Houston: Rice University Press, 1988).

Wisker, Gina (ed.), *Black Women's Writing* (London: Macmillan, 1993).

Index